ADVANCE PRAISE FOR
"From Animal House to Our House: A Love Story"

"When I was a few pages into *From Animal House to Our House*, I wanted to shout, "Go back! Go back!" But Tanner and his girlfriend persisted with their daunting home-renovation project, and ended up with (spoiler alert) a beautiful house, a marriage that survived beyond the last page, and an excellent book. And the man is a talented illustrator as well: he draws a mean perforated PVC drainpipe. This is the perfect read for anyone who has ever wandered the aisles at Home Depot in a blissful daze."

—David Owen, staff writer for the *New Yorker*, author of
Green Metropolis

"In addition to being a love story, a how-to guide, an urban adventure, and even a coming-of-age memoir, *From Animal House to Our House* is a classic American tale, a portrait of an artist compelled to replace destruction with dignity, to consecrate the past, and to create—via hope and sweat—a life of beauty and meaning. It's rare for a book to appeal to poets and plumbers, but Ron Tanner's experiences are intensely human; this book is for anyone who's ever been seduced by a dream and yearned for the deepest sort of restoration."

—Lia Purpura, author of *On Looking* and *Rough Likeness*

"I might seem the worst possible person to comment on Ron Tanner's memoir as I am totally uninterested in old houses and home renovation. Actually, this makes me the perfect person. Can you imagine how good a book it would have to be for me to like it? For me, the introspection, the humor, the incredible wisdom about bugs, the love story and the charming illustrations had to carry the book. They certainly do. Tanner is a master of small, sharp, hilarious insights, such as 'There was no middle ground for mom. Either our lives were pitiful or miraculous.' I love that."

—Marion Winik, author of *Glen Rock Book of the Dead*

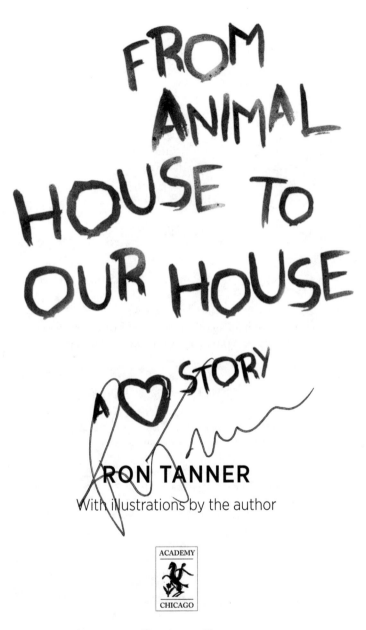

FROM ANIMAL HOUSE TO OUR HOUSE

A ♥ STORY

RON TANNER

With illustrations by the author

ACADEMY CHICAGO PUBLISHERS

Published in 2012 by
Academy Chicago Publishers
363 West Erie Street
Chicago, Illinois 60654

© 2011 by Ron Tanner

First edition.

Printed and bound in the U.S.A.

Library of Congress Cataloging-in-Publication Data

Tanner, Ron, 1963–
From animal house to our house : a love story / Ron Tanner ;
with illustrations by the author.—1st ed.
p. cm.
ISBN 978-0-89733-624-6 (hardcover)
1. Dwellings—Remodeling—Maryland—Baltimore—Anecdotes.
2. Tanner, Ron, 1963——Homes and haunts—Anecdotes.
3. Home ownership—Anecdotes.
I. Title.
TH4816.T36 2012
643'.7—dc23
2011052617

To Jill

ACKNOWLEDGEMENTS

MY DEEP GRATITUDE to the following readers who gave me the benefit of their keen insight: Lia Purpura, Ned Balbo, Mark Osteen, Jessica Anya Blau, Geoffrey Becker, Glen Scott Allen, Michael Kimball, and Jill Eicher; also to Norton Island Residency (Eastern Frontier Foundation) and the Ledig House for giving me time and a quiet place to make sense of this story; and to Loyola University for its continued support of my work.

An excerpt of this book, titled "From Animal House to Our House," appeared in *This Old House* magazine, January/February 2008. Another excerpt appeared in the spring 2010 *Southern Humanities Review*, in the essay "Nana Gragg."

Our buildings are not ours. They belong partly to those who built them and partly to the generations of mankind who are to follow us. The dead still have their right to them. That which they labored for... we have no right to obliterate.

— JOHN RUSKIN

Belief in the significance of architecture is premised on the notion that we are, for better or for worse, different people in different places—and on the conviction that it is architecture's task to render vivid to us who we might ideally be.

— ALAIN DE BOTTOM

Love must be as much a light as it is a flame.

— THOREAU

1

THE MYSTERY HOUSE

MY GIRLFRIEND JILL AND I first saw the big brick Victorian brownstone in December 1999. It was in an old Baltimore neighborhood and had sat abandoned for nearly a year. It was such a wreck that most prospective buyers walked in, took one look, then promptly walked out. The place had been owned by a notorious fraternity for one riotous decade. We didn't know this at the time. You couldn't tell from the outside how bad the inside was. Three stories tall, made of pumpkin-colored brick, with three bays on every floor and a witch's cap tower at its foremost corner, the house was the jewel of the block—or had been. It seemed the kind of place that might have grand rooms, secret passageways, and ghosts.

Jill and I love old houses and had started looking for one just a month after we began dating. This is not to say that Jill had agreed to live with me. She wasn't nearly as impulsive as I. She had agreed to nothing more than helping me look for a place and, if need be, fix it up. But it sounded like, it *felt to me* like, she had agreed to move in with me. This kind of wishful thinking has made me a disaster in matters of the heart. A few years before I met Jill, my second marriage had crashed and burned after a bumpy flight of only four years. I then promised myself I'd never again rush head-long into love.

But, before the divorce papers were signed, I had already moved in with a woman who was, apparently, as crazy as I.

We lasted two volatile years and then she kicked me out. I congratulated myself on not having asked her to marry me. By the time I met Jill, I thought I had grown fairly cautious. But the facts don't lie: I knew I'd buy a house—any house—if Jill would agree to move in with me.

I was certain I loved her. In fact, I had already taken her to meet my mother—a critically important step for Southern families. Jill was gracious and charming and my mother was relieved that this time, maybe, I had gotten it right. Although Jill had never been married, she did not judge me for my two previous failures. At thirty-five, she was old enough to understand how things go wrong. She herself had recently ended a thirteen-year relationship with a man who had commitment issues. I joked with Jill that she would have no commitment problems with me. Jill likes a good joke. She is a smart-aleck, a wise-cracker.

Another trait that attracted me to Jill was her sense of adventure. She seemed game for just about anything. One afternoon, as we drove past a Dumpster brimming with junk, she said, "Turn around! Did you see the cool stuff in that Dumpster?" We spent nearly an hour digging around in the trash and came away with some huge old windows. Never mind that we had no house to put them in. Both of us were avid junk collectors, stockpiling lights and corbels and hinges and all kinds of things we hoped to install in a grand old manse someday. Already we were sharing a dream. I was crazy about her.

It was late afternoon when I took her to see the house I had found. Unlike other historic neighborhoods we had visited, this one seemed fairly safe. Anyone from Baltimore will tell you, ours is a city of neighborhoods—meaning a two-block walk can take you into a very different place. I had driven through this neighborhood plenty of times. Saint Paul Street was the nicest it had to offer, a canyon of once-grand and still impressive three-story row houses. I feared it'd be too pricey for me.

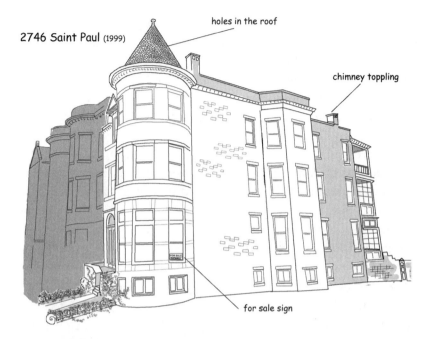

2746 Saint Paul (1999)

holes in the roof

chimney toppling

for sale sign

I made a modest income as a college writing instructor, I had no savings; in fact, my last divorce had nearly bankrupted me, and I was leasing a car. If I could get a loan for a house, it wouldn't be much of a loan. This house—the mystery house, we called it—looked bigger than anything I could ever afford. This only made me want it more. This could be a peculiarly American inclination, to go for the thing that will certainly ruin you. I'd done it in romance, why not do it in real estate too?

It was early December and very cold, the sidewalks deserted. The snow hadn't arrived yet but was due any day now, the sky muddied with clouds. "Holy cow!" Jill said when we pulled up to the house. "Why is this thing still on the market?"

Who could say? It was winter; it was an old house in an old neighborhood. Maybe nobody had noticed the small *for sale* sign in the window of the front bay. "A tower—the house has a tower!"

Jill gaped in wonder. I was thrilled that she was thrilled. It was as if I had hunted down a mastodon and brought it back to the cave for my mate. The old Queen Anne might as well have been a mastodon, it was so unusual, so antique, and so frigging big.

Up to this point, nothing much in my life had gone according to plan. I had made so many wrong turns, I couldn't say where I'd end up next. I'm the youngest of my mother's three sons, the one who never quite fit in. "You always pick the hard way," she would tell me. For the past ten years she'd been saying, "Why don't you just do something in *business*?" I heard this always as an insult, so much so that I never asked what *kind* of business. My mother's advice was another way of saying, "Just stop doing what you're doing because it's not working." Privately I said to myself, "I'm a late bloomer, what's wrong with that?" But I couldn't deny that now was the time to make something *stick*. Buying a house would anchor me. And it would keep Jill in town. A few years earlier, she had followed her boyfriend to Baltimore from Detroit. When she ended their long-troubled relationship, she seriously considered returning to the Midwest. Then she met me.

"This place is huge!" she exclaimed. She yanked at the padlocked bicycle chain wrapped around the big brass pulls of the double doors. "I guess nobody's home?"

"Probably belonged to an old lady who died," I said.

Jill peered through the beveled glass of the double front doors. Just inside the locked doors was the vestibule, then another door: a big generic slab that blocked our view of the interior.

Unlike the brownstones farther downtown, this one had a small front yard of weeds and a perimeter of ivy strangling the rusty remnants of the original knee-high iron fence. The massive front steps were red sandstone. The windows of the tower bay were as tall and wide as doors. Standing on tip-toes and cupping our faces to one huge window, we peeked through a gap of the papered-over windows; we could see cheap furniture and high ceilings and one room that opened into another and then another. We saw on the most distant wall—surprisingly far away—a bold blue and gold fraternity insignia painted above the hole of a ruined fireplace. A stop sign tacked to a nearer wall caught the waning light from the bay's transom windows and glowed like a warning: *STOP.* Strewn across the dirty wood floor were shards and lengths of wood, disgorged plastic bags of fast food, tangles of dirty clothing, gutted sofa cushions, a few shutter panels from the windows, overturned office chairs, orange traffic cones. . . What had happened here?

As we walked around to the rear, in the cold shadow of the building's brick expanse, the house seemed to go back a long way. The place was so big, I could hardly imagine handling it, much less owning it. It'd be like owning a whale as pet. "Can you believe this?" Jill said, running ahead. "Maybe we can get in through the basement."

The backyard was brick-walled on the street side. The wall extended sixty feet or more and had two decaying wood gates. We entered through the first and were surprised by the mess. The junk-cluttered yard was on its way to becoming a dump. There was so much lumber and broken furniture crammed under the porch, it'd take half a day to pull it out. We inspected the waterless hot tub and its load of garbage: a beer keg, a rusted seatless bar stool, a narrow cabinet with a louvered door, pulpy cardboard boxes, and other dark things we weren't going to touch. Curiously, the weedy yard was riddled with heel-sized holes: moles, we decided. Or gophers. Yard work? We could do that. Neither of us imagined that these were rat holes.

Behind us stood a defeated-looking dogwood tree on one side of the yard and a tangle of old rose bushes hunkered on the other. The wood fence between us and the neighbor's yard was slumped under the weight of a long mound of ivy. Rats, I would learn, love to nest under ivy. At the far end of the yard was the brick carriage house. It was so large that it had a small chimney. Its win-

back yard detail &
first-floor porch (1999)

cloth awning

vintage hot tub

original basement
utility sink

"gopher" holes:
rats!

dows had long been broken out and boarded over. Had we gone inside the garage we would have found sixteen empty beer kegs piled next to a four-foot-tall dirty-white heap of Victorian tile—the ruin of the house's master bathroom.

But it didn't occur to us to enter the garage. We were distracted by the house's three-story wooden porch. It had once been glorious, with its multi-mullioned windows mounted in sliding wooden frames as big as garage doors. But now, its green paint was faded nearly to a pale blue and its striped canvas awning hung in shreds like the flag of a long-ago defeated people. Many of its old, wavy-glass windows were broken. The basement door was locked. So we hiked up the rickety porch stairs and gaped at the furniture and garbage on the other side of the glass. The porch door was padlocked—not that anyone could have opened it, so much junk inside was pushed up against it. Among the porch clutter we saw a big Deco-chromed 1940s refrigerator—maybe this was the original. Was the house filled with similar treasures?

This much was clear to me now: the house would go cheap. And no, it hadn't belonged to an old lady, at least not recently.

When I was a child, one of my biggest, private thrills was to come upon a gumball machine that had gone haywire and would, for a penny, keep on giving. I'd turn the key again and again, gumballs dropping into my palms until my pockets and cheeks were bulging. *Why hadn't anyone emptied the machine before me?* I'd wonder. Such magical moments helped me believe that luck is possible, that amazing things can happen—even to me. Finding this old house was a similar thrill. Maybe we had hit the jackpot.

A more cynical person would have had other thoughts. It didn't occur to me to worry about the condition of the house or all the work that this wrecked behemoth would demand. I had never done carpentry. I knew nothing about wiring or plumbing or plastering. In eighth grade woodshop, I had earned a "C" for making a pathetic, lopsided box as my final project. I had no patience for plans. I had no tolerance for the painstaking care our shop teacher demanded of us.

All I could think of now, as Jill and I gaped at the backside of this grand old place, was that I'd lucked out and found both the woman and the house of my dreams and, if I played my cards right, I'd win both.

2
SHIPWRECK

IT TOOK A WEEK OF PHONE CALLS to reach "Imperial Realty," which was selling the abandoned house. They weren't listed in the phone book. And the man I talked to didn't sound eager enough to be a realtor. He gave me the phone number of someone in the neighborhood who would show us the house. That someone was Rick, a short fellow with a silver mustache, a slight underbite, and sympathetic eyes. Jill and I met him on a misty December morning in front of the old house. Hatless, he was wearing a navy peacoat, like an old sailor. His ruddy cheeks suggested that he'd been standing in the cold for a while.

"I'm not a realtor," he announced jovially. "I'm just a concerned neighbor." Then, smiling from me to Jill, he added, "You two will do just fine!"

I was pleased that he thought us acceptable. But I was anxious to know what was going on. If Imperial Realty wasn't a realty company and Rick wasn't a realtor, maybe the house wasn't what it seemed.

"You're not the owner?" I asked.

"I assigned myself caretaker," Rick explained. He unlocked the chain around the door handles, then pocketed the padlock and pushed open the eight-foot-tall double doors. "Vandals were ruining this lovely Queen Anne. Oh, the things they stole!"

I exchanged a worried glance with Jill. It seemed we were about to witness the scene of an accident—a twelve-car pileup, say. Would there be blood? I credit my morbid curiosity to having grown up with two older brothers who enjoyed collecting animal bones and insect carcasses. They were fearless explorers. You couldn't keep them out of a cave or an abandoned house or a sewage tunnel, for that matter. Always, I tagged along.

Before going farther, Rick turned to face us. Breathlessly, he explained that the house had been owned for ten years by a fraternity. The fraternity had bought it—at top dollar—from a speculator who had bought it—for a fraction of its value—from Miss Wilson, who had lived in the house for sixty-eight years.

"When the fraternity bought it," he continued, "the Queen Anne was in *original* condition. You walked into this house, and you walked right back into 1897!" Rick swallowed, then regarded us with dewy-eyed regret. "What they've done to our Queen Anne is a tragedy." He could have been talking about the abrupt death of a loved one.

We were standing in the vestibule. Its oak paneling was painted bright blue, the fraternity's official color. I supposed I could live with a blue vestibule or repaint it. The terra cotta tiles underfoot were loose but all appeared to be present. There was no light fixture dangling from the exposed wire overhead.

It can't be that bad, I wanted to say. I was jittery for reasons I would not have been able to explain at the time. I was thinking that if the house was truly a horror show, then I would be off the hook and Jill and I would laugh about it later and shake our heads in disbelief: *Did you see. . . ? Can you believe. . . ? Oh my god!* I realize now that some part of me sensed that once I walked in, I would never walk out—that is, I'd be a changed man, maybe a trapped man.

Rick pushed open the red hollow-core door before us and the house opened up like Ali Baba's cave. The twelve-foot ceilings

made the place look enormous. My first guess was that they were fifteen feet high. "No," Rick corrected with a knowing smile, "just twelve."

The main staircase, with its massive mahogany banister, was just a few yards beyond the vestibule: in a straight line, its oak stairs rose gradually, pausing at a landing midway.

The floor just inside the doorway looked ruined beyond repair. The wood was black. "Water damage," Rick noted. "Nobody wiped their feet."

The floor was oak parquet throughout the first level—1,200 feet of it, all the way back to the kitchen. "This was the builder's house," Rick announced, "so it's wider than the rest and has some special features." In this case wider meant twenty feet instead of eighteen or sixteen. The true measure of a row house, though, is in its depth. The rooms of the Queen Anne opened one after the other for a depth of seventy feet.

To our right were two huge pocket doors, which miraculously were still in place and working, though the pulls and latches had been stolen. Through these was the living room, which featured the tower's big, circular bay. The Queen Anne had two other bays on each floor, which added considerable space and light. I favored the tower's bays because they brought to mind a ship's wheelhouse, an impression reinforced by the first floor's elevation over the sidewalk. Because it was narrow and long, the house reminded me of an old steamer run aground. *Did I want a shipwreck?*

The living room fireplace had no mantel and its remaining tile had been painted black. Apparently, the frat boys had painted over or removed everything that might have suggested the refinement of an earlier age. I recalled how, when I was twelve, I had put some of my mother's antiques in my bedroom—like the butter churn from her mother's farm—but painted peace symbols and stars on them to make them look less antique. I suspect that children fear old things because old things have a certain power that new things don't. Age gives them a history. Painting an old piece of furniture—or vandalizing it in some way—seems to neutralize the power of that history. The Queen Anne was evidence of this at every turn.

Rick directed our attention to the way the plaster walls curved up to the ceiling. "Cove ceilings," he said. "A very nice feature, don't you think?"

The old plaster ceiling, I noticed, looked like a relief map of the Rockies. It seemed ready to fall in big chunks. The original plaster medallion was missing—stolen—from the hole where the original chandelier would have hung. Behind us, the house opened into the music room, where a bamboo bar from some Hawaiian-themed bacchanal sat in the place of the piano that would have been here originally. Beyond the clutter of cheap, ruined furniture and teenage treasures, like stolen traffic cones, was the dining room, through another set of pocket doors. Here, too, the fireplace mantel was gone, the firebox piled with empty beer cans, wadded hamburger wrappers, and a mound of cigarette butts. Painted gold and blue, two huge fraternity insignias marred the walls like the murals of a long-forgotten tribe.

I glanced around me, then up and through a transom window's wavy glass to the staircase, with its broken balusters. The place was cold—we could see our breaths in little clouds—and it reeked of garbage and sewage. But it was grand too, with its parquet floors, high ceilings, and ruined fireplaces, like the lobby of a small European hotel.

"Can you believe this place?" Jill was saying almost giddily. Then she turned the corner and exclaimed, "A butler's pantry!"

"Oh, yeah," Rick said. He smiled back at me as if to say, *She likes it, doesn't she?* "You don't see many of those anymore," he added. "The great thing about this house is that it retains the original floor plan. Nothing's been altered."

"Well, not exactly," I said. "It's trashed." I was staring at the pantry's collapsed ceiling.

"Oh, that's nothing," Rick said with a wave of his gloved hand. "All of this can be fixed up—everything is *here*, that's what I'm saying."

"Ron, a *butler's* pantry!" Jill cooed.

The pantry had cabinets nearly to the ceiling on both sides and, in one corner, the original large enamel-over-iron utility sink.

"Where are the cabinet doors?" I asked.

"They might be around," Rick said optimistically. "The boys left a lot behind."

I glanced at the circa-1920 gas stove parked opposite the sink.[1] None of us dared open the huge refrigerator that had been shoved against one wall of the pantry.

In the kitchen we saw that a beam had fallen through the ceiling. Here was a cheap electric stove and another refrigerator. Just behind the kitchen was the sun porch, so crowded with junk we couldn't even step onto it.

The narrow hallway at the back of the kitchen, leading upstairs, could not have looked scarier: it was cave-dark and had faded floral-print paper peeling in long strips from its walls. Far above, in the gloom, hung an old Jimi Hendrix poster. This was the servants' stairs, Rick informed us.

There's no way we're going to take this house! I said to myself. It was a relief to make this decision so quickly and definitively. *Absolutely no way!*

Step by step, Rick was carefully educating—and testing—us, I realized. "Some people tear off the plaster to expose the brick walls," he observed as we made our way up the main staircase, "but that does injustice to the wonderful lathe and plaster, don't you think?"

Upstairs we found huge swaths of graffiti. The doors to every room had been fitted with deadbolts and most doors appeared to have been used as targets for dart- and knife-throwing. The master bath on the second floor had been gutted. A confederate flag—eight by ten feet—had been painted across the wall of the rear bedroom. There was a refrigerator in nearly every room. We opened none of them. Mantels were missing. Some walls had been hacked open as if the boys had been looking for treasure. . . or mice. They had tacked up some track lighting and attempted to

---

1. This was the house's second stove. The original would have been wood- or coal-burning.

graffiti on the third floor

install ceiling fans, all of which had fallen. They had also installed plywood sleeping lofts in the tower bays.

Rick pointed out the extensive use of Southern yellow pine on the trim and floors, the generous transoms over every door (for ventilation), the gas pipes in the shallow fireplaces. There were all kinds of captivating details, like the servant's call button in many rooms, the skylight over the main stairs, and the view from the third-story tower bay: the best view in Charles Village, he said, because it overlooks one of the finest blocks of Victorian row houses.

I asked Rick a lot of questions and felt a little sorry for him when he mistook my curiosity as a prospective buyer's interest.

Yes, the old Queen Anne was a wreck, he admitted, but anybody smart enough (*as smart as you or I*, he inferred) could see that

Jill making a face among graffiti & garbage, 1999

the clutter of frat boy furniture, refrigerators, and piles of garbage were inconsequential. The house was solid and whole—never having been cut up into apartments—and it could be turned around. That's the key. You can find plenty of ruined old houses in this country, but only a handful will be redeemable for the average rehabber. Here's the danger: if the house needs too much work, it will not only bankrupt you, it will drive you mad. Did Rick tell me this or did I imagine him saying it?

At every turn, it seemed, Jill was exclaiming her delight, wholly unfazed as we waded through waist-high heaps of garbage. Silly girl!

I had thought that we would find a house that needed only cleaning and painting—and maybe some basic repairs. I had thought that Jill was of the same mind. Seeing Jill's unabated enthusiasm gave me pause. I didn't want the house. But I wanted Jill. And clearly Jill wanted the Queen Anne. It was like one of those simple logic questions: if A = B and B = C, then A = C. Did I have to buy this house in order to win Jill's love? Even at this early phase of our relationship, I was certain that she'd love me regardless. But I couldn't shake the A = C of it.

In my head, I was keeping tally of the work to be done:

- clean out 4,500 square feet of old furniture and garbage
- dismantle three plywood lofts in the bedrooms
- dismantle a twenty-foot bar in the basement
- repair three fallen ceilings
- replace all of the plumbing
- rebuild the master bathroom
- rebuild the three-story wooden porch
- re-glaze sixty-four-plus porch windows
- replace the roof
- replace the water heater
- replace seventy-two finely turned, custom-made balusters that had been knocked out of the staircase
- repair or replace thirty-three windows (most of them the size of doors)
- refinish the wood floors
- rewire the house for electricity
- repair and refinish twenty-four to thirty doors
- repair and re-plaster every wall
- replace twelve glass-paned doors in the butler's pantry

- replace ten wood doors in the butler's pantry
- repair and re-plaster every ceiling
- install kitchen cabinets
- repair and refinish two sets of pocket doors
- find and install four vintage fireplace mantels
- find and install fourteen ceiling lights
- refinish and replace thirty-three sets of interior shutters
- paint, paint, paint
- what else?

In a storyteller's voice, wrenched with emotion, Rick continued the Queen Anne's sad tale. Had the failing Miss Wilson been able to confer with someone knowledgeable, she would have learned that her house and its contents were worth far more than the $60,000 she accepted from the speculator. Afterwards, the speculator sold off Miss Wilson's many antiques—including some of the house's unique fixtures, like the chandeliers and the servants' annunciator (call box)—and made more than he would earn on the house itself.

The neighborhood tried to block the speculator's sale to the fraternity—there were other interested buyers—but the speculator wanted top dollar and the fraternity was willing to pay. The neighborhood would forever resent the speculator because, in selling to the frat boys, he loosed a plague upon the block. For ten years, the neighborhood would endure the worst of fraternity life: rock bands in the Queen Anne's basement, beer bashes in the hot tub out back, kids shouting and pissing from the porches and roof, drug dealing, date rapes—you name it. Several times, the police raided the place. Rumor said there were bullet holes in some of the walls. It got so bad, the neighborhood sued for a litany of zoning violations; a city suit followed; nearby Johns Hopkins University barred the fraternity from campus; and finally, the fraternity broke under the pressure and stopped paying its bills. The boys lived in the Queen Anne for weeks after the city cut their water and power. Then they ran away.

Clearly, the boys of Delta Upsilon had never *seen* the house they lived in. It is very likely that they bought the place only because it was big enough to hold a fraternity. They might have been just as happy, even happier, in a warehouse. Unprepared for the high maintenance of an old Victorian, the boys failed again and again at home repairs until finally, they gave up. At that point, if anything broke—whether a shutter, a ceiling fan, or a lighting fixture—they simply tore it out, then threw it into the basement or the backyard. Fortunately for us, many original pieces remained in the house, albeit broken. Upstairs, above a cracked window, over which they had nailed fractured shutters, were the black-markered words: "Fuck this piece of shit house." It was an expression of failure and profound misunderstanding—and the saddest reminder of the boys' stay.

Rick's attachment to the old house made him particularly sympathetic. Like me, he felt protective of old things and indignant about their abuse. I hate bullies and it seemed the house had been bullied. The house was, without question, the best Jill and I had seen—it was nearly a mansion and could be had for the amazingly paltry sum of $125,000. Even in the winter of 1999, this was a bargain. True, it had to be bought "as is." But Rick was telling us that new owners—a young, energetic couple, like us, people with "vision"—would make the Queen Anne grand again.

It was an observation that played me in the worst way. I love a challenge. And I love to please. The neighborhood was holding its collective breath in anticipation of finding the right buyer. I was flattered that Rick felt us *worthy* of this mission. Taking on the house would make Jill and me local heroes. It would also be the biggest challenge of my life. If I succeeded, I'd be a better man—a successful man, at last.

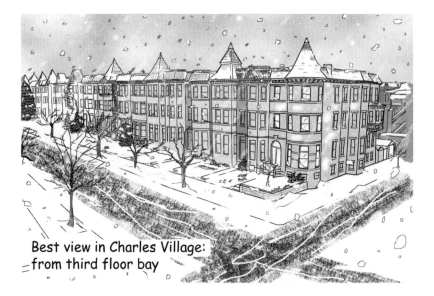

Best view in Charles Village: from third floor bay

I felt myself slipping, entertaining the possibilities of the impossible. It seemed I was feeling what better men before me must have felt as they hacked paths into unchartered jungles or climbed snowy reaches of unconquered mountains or flew small aircraft record-breaking distances. How often in the course of our modest lives do we get the chance to take on the impossible? *If it could be done,* I kept thinking, *imagine how your life would change!* I see now that I was in something of a giddy panic. Standing in that cold, cavernous, once-upon-a-time gorgeous Queen Anne, I saw something great—way off in the future: Jill and I triumphant and deliriously happy in a beautiful house. But I couldn't see anything else lying in the way of that fantastic vision.

Before I could second guess too much, cagey Rick invited us to his house down the street. "You have to see what we did," he insisted.

We met Charles, Rick's partner, who had the habit of smiling almost imperceptibly as he quietly told a joke. A slight, bespectacled man with the demeanor of an accountant, he was clearly the calming yin to Rick's energetic yang. Rick had recently retired as a drama teacher from the Baltimore city schools. In his spare time, he built sets for a local theater group. He had constructed grand floor-to-ceiling bookcases in his study and had built an elegant basement bar from pieces of a salvaged gym floor.

The minute I stepped into Rick and Charles's house, I was gasping my appreciation and thinking, *I want this!* On the newel post at the bottom of their staircase stood a bronze two-foot-tall Mercury, an orange flame-shaped light bulb in one upraised hand. In the hallways, old oil paintings hung one above the other all the way to the ceiling far above. There was a marble fireplace, topped by a six-foot-high gilt-framed mirror, in both the living and dining rooms. The furniture was fine antiques—a seven-foot mahogany sideboard, an eight-foot burlwood highboy—the scale of things only a mansion or museum might accommodate.

"It took twenty years," Rick reminded us more than once. "The house had been cut up into apartments."

Later that night, I kept saying to Jill, "I don't know, I just don't know."

We were sitting at the dining table in my apartment, Jill's grouchy old Basset hound, Harriet, lying nearby. My apartment was a spacious two-bedroom in a nicely restored 1920s building. It had large closets, high ceilings, and wood floors. Before meeting Jill, I had imagined spending years in the place. I thought: *I'm single, I have no children, maybe I can make a go of it alone for a while.* But then one afternoon I walked into an antiques consignment store and saw this ebullient, green-eyed woman with a girlish grin and a large tumble of curly hair. She was unpacking glassware behind the counter.

Now she reached across the table to take one of my hands: "What is there to know?" she said. "It's everything we've wanted!"

"But it's a wreck!"

"So it can be fixed up!"

"But I don't know *how!*"

"So you'll learn!"

Where did she get her confidence? I wondered. Or was she actually as foolhardy as I?

Harriet groaned as she stretched across my dining room rug. The rug would be too small for the Queen Anne. All of my furniture would fill no more than one of its rooms. I'd be swallowed in the belly of a whale.

Then Jill said what I'd been waiting to hear: "I'll help you, Ron."

"We'll do this together?" I asked. "You really think we can pull it off?"

"Yes!"

It almost sounded like a proposal. With Jill's help, it seemed I couldn't lose. She even had her own tool box.

3

THIS PLACE WILL
EAT YOU ALIVE

Nicholas, my realtor, said: "Don't do it, Ron. This place will eat you alive."

"I'm not afraid of the work," I insisted. "Besides, Jill and I want it."

Nicholas and I were standing in the Queen Anne's gloomy living room, battered abandoned furniture all around us and garbage nearly to our knees in every direction. It was another cold, overcast December afternoon. Rick and I had just given Nicholas the tour and now Rick watched us anxiously from the far end of the room, politely giving us space.

A tall, dark-haired thirty-something with wire rim glasses and the boyish good looks of the actor Robert Downey, Jr., Nicholas was someone Jill had run into a couple of years earlier when she had thought about house hunting. I was soon to learn that Jill knew all kinds of people around town who could be useful in our house rehab efforts. She liked Nicholas because he was flat-out honest. Sometimes this cost him a sale, but he didn't seem to mind.

"You've never done any rehab before?" he asked me.

"No, but I can learn."

"Everything in renovation takes three times longer than you think it takes."

"I've got time," I said. "I mean, what could get in the way?"

Well, I did have a job. That could get in the way. And Jill and I had only been together for six months. Maybe working on a house wasn't the best idea for a budding romance. And I didn't know anything about working on a house. There would be a learning curve, I supposed. It didn't matter what Nicholas had to say. I had already made the leap, following my old pattern. All I heard was the rush of wind in my ears.

Nicholas informed me that he had once been a contractor, so he knew all about the challenges of taking on a wreck like this: "A 203K rehab loan only gives you six months to bring the house up to code."

"What's *code*?" I asked.

He sighed. "It means the house is safe to live in—no peeling paint, no damaged plaster, no holes in the floor or ceiling, no visible hazards."

"I could work every day after teaching. Then, come summer, I could work fourteen hours a day."

"That's what you say now." Nicholas smiled politely across the room at Rick, who returned an uncertain smile. Rick had been waiting nearly a year for the right buyer. Obviously, if I could let my realtor talk me out of the house, I wasn't right for it at all.

I couldn't begin to explain everything that impelled me. The simplest explanation was that this house was my dream-come-true. It reminded me of Mary Jane's house. There wasn't another house like Mary Jane's in Winston-Salem, North Carolina, where I grew up. Built in 1920 from a French design, hers was brick, with a mossy slate roof and a two-story tower, where its crooked stairs rose. There was a broad porch that wrapped around to a sunroom, a large carriage house to one side, and a formal brick-walked garden in the back that featured a gazebo just beyond the rectangular goldfish pond. All of it was in an alarming state of decline because, while Mary Jane and her nerdy husband could lovingly restore any antique they had found, they never lifted a finger to repair their aging house.

As far back as I could remember, my mother and I had visited Mary Jane once a week. I never declined the offer to go. Like my mother, Mary Jane was married to an electrical engineer. Unlike my mother, however, Mary Jane had a math degree from Duke and was downright odd, always with a lit cigarette at the end of an antique cigarette holder (she had dozens) and never caring a whit about fashion. She rarely wore a dress or high heels, preferring black slacks and scuffed penny loafers, and all her adult life, her ebony-black hair remained the same—like a fat overturned bowl on her head. She also drank. A lot. Nothing but martinis, starting at two every afternoon.

Her house was crowded with antiques. The minute I'd arrive, she'd allow me to grab a handful of oatmeal cookies from a large green Depression-glass jar. Then I'd idle on her oriental carpet, marveling at its intricate design and the many strange objects she had collected from flea markets and garage sales, as she and my mother drank coffee, or, if later in the day, a cocktail.

Mary Jane's house was a portal to another world, a museum that honored the idiosyncratic beauty of one woman's fascination with old, odd things. Even at that young age, I sensed that this is what a house should be—not just a place to sleep and eat but a haven for fantasy, mystery, passion. Since then, I have sought out old houses everywhere I've gone and dreamed of owning one so that I could recapture that odd wonder of Mary Jane's house.

When I phoned my mother to tell her about buying the Queen Anne, she said, "Oh, Ronald, why would you want to do something like that?"

"It'll be just as cool as Mary Jane's house," I said.

I was learning that nobody thought taking on the wrecked Queen Anne was a good idea. Why couldn't they see what I saw?

Mary Jane's house

moss on roof

pink shutters & trim

Though my mother loved old houses and antiques as much as I, she believed my determination to buy this one was further proof that I always did things the hard way. In her estimation, life was a struggle and no one struggled more than her children. In part, she felt bad that my brothers and I had entered manhood without Dad's guidance. His death, at forty-nine, had shadowed all of us, and, for her, became a burden of guilt because she had no money to help us and, unlike Dad, no personal resources to draw upon: she was no handyman, no intellectual, no self-made success.

So here I was, her youngest—prone to mistakes, now over forty and still not settled down—announcing that I was going to cash in my retirement fund and buy a former fraternity house that my new girlfriend would help me fix up. What was there to worry about?

My modest retirement fund came from my previous job as an instructor. It wasn't anything I had planned. It was, actually, a fluke: it was a supplemental fund I had started because I thought my last job required this. I couldn't touch my current retirement fund but the supplemental was mine to liquidate. And so, just as I had liquidated the life insurance policy my father had opened for me years ago, I was ready once again to go for broke.

Unlike my brothers, I've never made much money and never been good with what I've made. I'm impulsive and too willing to spend instead of save. Dave and Mike had investments and healthy retirement funds and made enough to send Mom on vacations to Europe and Asia. I could barely make my bills, especially since the demise of my last marriage. Although I didn't resent my brothers' successes, I did regret that I couldn't do as much for my mother as they did. So, already, the wrecked house was becoming a point of desperate pride for me. I might as well have been a ten-year-old on the high dive waving to my family below: "Hey, look at me!"

"You're gonna love this place," I promised my mother over the phone.

"Jill's moving in with you?" she asked.

"Sure," I said. "Well, not right away. But soon—as soon as I, we, get the place stabilized."

"Oh, Ronald," she sighed.

I had taken Jill to meet my mother the first month we were dating. How's that for moving fast? To Jill's credit, she agreed to endure this test—which I took as evidence that she wanted me as much as I wanted her.

A Southerner, my mother believes a guest should make herself as helpful as possible. The truly gracious guest helps in the kitchen and offers to wash the dishes, and, generally, self-effaces so much that she nearly disappears. At the same time, the truly gracious host never lets the guest raise a finger to do anything and, at every turn, makes the guest feel treasured. So, in the typical Southern household, there's always a tug-of-war between the truly gracious guest and the truly gracious host:

Oh, let me help with that.

Nonsense, you just sit right where you are.

But it's no bother—here, I can do that.

No, you won't, dear. What you need is a drink—what can I get you?

The trick for the truly gracious guest is to know when to give in.

Jill had managed all of this remarkably well—better, in fact, than any woman I'd brought home. At one point she even maneuvered to the kitchen sink to wash a load of dishes. I had not enjoyed subjecting her to this trial. But, knowing it was inevitable, I wanted to get it out of the way. Also, as unfair as it was, I think I wanted to test Jill—in part because I couldn't trust my own judgment anymore. Was Jill really as great as she seemed?

I thought so. But now another question weighed in: If things got bad and the house turned out to be a terrible mistake, as everyone was suggesting, would Jill see it through with me to the bitter end?

4

FALLING FOR JILL

A FORMER HAIRSTYLIST TURNED GRAD STUDENT, Jill was the poorest person I'd met in a long time. I found her incredibly attractive—not because she was poor but because she didn't seem to mind being poor. Her poverty compelled her to be crafty, creative, and bold. She was always bargaining or bartering. It was fitting, then, that our first meeting was at Traditions, an antique consignment store so inexpensive that area antique dealers often shopped there to supply their own stores. The place occupied a sprawling, two-story 1920s auto showroom. I had come in to buy a vintage magazine stand for my new apartment.

"Who's the academic?" I asked, after seeing the *Chronicle of Higher Education* spread across the counter where Jill was working. Jill was wrapping antique wine glasses with it.

"That would be me." She grinned. A nice grin, I thought.

She wore an untucked lumberjack shirt and button-fly jeans. Her lipstick was too red, her hair a mass of curls that half-obscured her face, which was lively but surprisingly pale.

She was talking rapidly about rhetoric and literary theory, intermittently laughing at how silly it all sounded.

She was giddy and a little goofy, I decided. And maybe a little crazy.

She spoke with a distinct Midwestern inflection, flattening her vowels.

"You from Ohio?" I asked.

"My father's from Ohio," she corrected. "I'm from Detroit."

"Is that someplace I should visit?"

"No," she said. "But it's a great place if you like hummus."

"Really? I *do* like hummus."

"Detroit has the largest Middle Eastern population in the country."

"You're full of fun facts," I teased.

"I'm ABD in Rhetoric," she announced playfully.

She was writing her dissertation on the rhetoric of the Jerry Springer show, how Springer made poor people blame themselves for their poverty. "We live in a go-for-broke culture, don't we?" she said. "Everybody encourages you to make something of yourself but then if you *do* go for it and you *do go broke*, then everybody blames you for not knowing better—for failing at the American dream, which is supposed to be easy."

I could not have imagined anymore than Jill that, by the end of the year, this scenario would apply to me.

"You're a champion of the underdog, is that it?" I asked.

"I'm a champion of honesty," she said. "So much bullshit is dumped on the working class."

I glanced around: "So is this research?"

"No, this is my job," she said. "I also teach part-time at the community college."

I told her that I might be in a position to hire a part-time rhetorician in about six months, when my term as department chair would begin. She looked at me as if to say, *What does this mean?* At the time, I thought it meant nothing, since I was dating somebody else. I didn't call Jill for six months, though I thought about her. Maybe I was testing myself.

When Jill interviewed for the part-time job in my department, I knew I was in trouble. Since I was going to be her supervisor, I couldn't date her. This only made me want to date her more.

I hate that I'm this perverse. It's the rebel in me. I'm too eager to do what I'm not supposed to do. I've always been this way. Part of it comes from having two older brothers who always dared me to betray authority. As the baby of the family, I got a lot of practice being reckless and a lot of second chances, which only emboldened me. Also, as the youngest of three and a boy who was fairly small for his age, I developed a deep regard for democracy or my version of it, which meant I hated to be pushed around or bullied.

After Jill got the job in my department, I held back from pursuing her as long as I could. I lasted exactly one week. Then I asked her out on the pretense of introducing her to some colleagues who were meeting at a bar. She accepted with a shy smile. I offered to pick her up.

"I live in a funky place," she warned.

"So?"

"So I'm fixing it up in exchange for a rent reduction."

"Fixing it up?"

"It's a wreck," she said.

I was intrigued.

Her rental was a crumbling two-story row house in the ratty end of a working-class neighborhood. Though built of brick, every house on her block seemed to sag in defeat. Their windows were small, their interiors cramped. These were mill-workers' row houses, made cheaply a hundred years ago and never meant to last.

I was surprised by all that Jill had done inside. Her house was cozy and arty. Had someone from 1930 visited her place, he would have found everything—from the deco light fixtures overhead to the hooked rugs underfoot, even the aged books on their crowded shelves—comfortably familiar. She had decorated the place with old oil paintings and ceramics from flea markets and thrift stores; she had bought used appliances from Traditions. Her kitchen counter was a bench-top set across two office cabinets she had salvaged. She had found a fly-by-night electrician to fix some of the aged wiring and hang a chandelier in the dining room. Her Depression-era dining room table—which she had re-painted and re-glued—she had owned since her early twenties.

"It's so cute!" I exclaimed. It was exactly as I would have wished had it been my place. Room by room, I was falling in love.

"And who's this little princess?" I asked in sing-song as Harriet, her old Basset hound, trotted to me, tail wagging.

"Don't pet her," Jill warned. "She's old and crabby and she doesn't see well."

"I'm good with dogs," I said. "Look at those big paws. Can she shake?"

"She'll bite, Ron. Give her space."

"Can you shake, Harriet?" I was kneeling in front of the dog.

"Ron—"

"No, really, Jill, I—"

Harriet lunged at my outstretched hand and bit me.

"Jesus Christ!" I snatched back my hand.

Harriet yelped and trotted away as if I had smacked her.

"Are you all right?" Jill asked. "Let me see your hand."

I held it out and said, "She didn't break the skin."

"No, she doesn't bite hard," Jill agreed. "But she's a little—"

"Neurotic?"

"Old, like I said. She gets scared easily. She was always biting my ex." She smiled.

I raised my eyebrows skeptically. "Some consolation."

"She's almost eleven. You just have to give her space."

"She was *wagging her tail!*"

Jill laughed. "I know, that's a problem. She gets her signals mixed up."

I also met her sixteen-year-old cat, Charlie, who was senile and arthritic and often woke her with his yowling at night because he'd think himself lost in the dark. He wasn't too good at hitting the litter box either.

If Jill and I lived together, I reminded myself, Charlie and Harriet would come with her. A couple of quirky animals weren't such bad baggage. You could do a lot worse. And I like animals.

Jill and I sat for a while in the old upholstered chairs next to her fireplace. Her neighbors considered her a lesbian, she said, because she owned so many books, which they could see through the front window. One night, two drunken men pounded on her door, demanding that she come out. Harriet's barking discouraged them finally. Her neighbors to one side were a couple whose arguments often ended in fist fights. Her neighbors to the other side were into heroin, which meant Jill had to check her backyard for syringes everyday so that Harriet wouldn't get hold of one.

Everything about Jill's life appeared to be teetering on the precipice of ruin—she had a fifteen-year-old car, two decrepit pets, part-time employment, and a crumbling rental in a bad neighborhood—and yet she seemed undaunted, even fearless. I must confess that I am thoroughly drawn to strong, resourceful women. The woman I dated just before meeting Jill taught me how to rappel from a mountain and took me hiking in the desert, where we camped in the shadow of an ancient Indian cave dwelling. It would appear that I am looking for a mate who can help me survive the apocalypse, someone tough enough to mend my broken leg, and, if necessary, kill a snake for dinner. Actually, I was looking for competence—somebody who could take care of business. After my two failed marriages, and experience with people who could not or would not *take care*, I needed somebody solid, unshakeable.

Like me, Jill was a late bloomer and had done things the hard way. At seventeen, she dropped out of high school to become a hair stylist, rejecting everything her upper-middle class parents had tried to impose upon her. Years later, she earned her GED at night, after work. The only help she received from her father was with the purchase of a then-new Honda Civic. He bought it for her in lieu of paying for her wedding one day. That seemed to say everything about their relationship.

Jill and I agreed that antiques and old stuff offer a kind of comfort. It takes us away from the mind-numbing, cookie-cutter, middle-class world of our parents. Though we love the chaos of American life, we dislike shopping malls, fast foods, tract housing, top-forty radio, cable TV, Muzak, eight-cylinder engines, sealed windows, Styrofoam food containers, Formica countertops, and polyester. But we knew then, as we know now, that our love of old stuff is a kind of fantasy. We don't pretend that we should live in the Victorian age. It's not about returning to a so-called simpler time. The Victorian age was in no way more humane or generous than ours and certainly no less complicated.

Jill and I want the old stuff because it shows a respect for materials and workmanship that we seldom see today. A respect also for the consumer, who, it was assumed, would recognize quality. It even shows a certain respect for the people who made these things. By contrast, there's something thoroughly condescending and disrespectful about our throw-away, consumer culture today.

Jill's critique of modern life and her determination to live on the fringe appealed to the rebel in me. As a teenager, I was a long-haired war protester. After college, I traveled around the country, worked as a yardman, a door-to-door salesman, a messenger, a customs clearance clerk, and a secretary. Finally, I decided to become a professional musician. I would not settle down, and much to my detriment, would not listen to the good advice offered me. It didn't help that my father had died so young. I could have used the balance he would have offered. I remember moments of insight that I quickly ignored, like the afternoon I helped a neighbor move shortly after my father's death: she stood back and watched me as I packed her belongings into the back of my van. She said, "You'd make such a good father." Surprised and embarrassed, I said nothing in return. Had I listened to what she was saying, I might have heard this not as a compliment but as advice. *You have the makings of a good, solid man,* she was saying, *if only you'd slow down and show care, just as you are doing now.* I did not slow down. Too often I did not show care. I know now that I was running scared, afraid that if I stopped too long I'd get caught somehow—in a hateful job, a miserable marriage, an unredeemable life.

Ironically, I ran so blindly that I stumbled into the miserable marriage I most dreaded. My then-girlfriend and I had little in common except an insatiable appetite for one another. When I asked her to live with me, she balked. She said that if we were serious, we should get married. I had always claimed that I would live with my mate for at least a year before marrying her. It only made sense. But then, facing my girlfriend's nonnegotiable demand, nothing made sense except my need to be with this ravishing woman. So I said, *Yes, of course we'll get married!* Never mind that I was a musician without a steady gig.

We trudged through ten years of trying to make our mutual incompatibility work somehow. Then, exhausted, we divorced. Shamed and panicked by my failure, I rushed into a second marriage with a woman who was all but a stranger to me. When she left four years later, I grieved as badly as I had when my father died. What did I know about love? Forty years old, I began to suspect that some things just can't be saved.

Then I met Jill. I was trying to forgive myself for my failures but I was such a slow learner! As Jill and I sat together in her bedraggled row house that first night, she told me about breaking up with her ex and moving to this house. He didn't believe she'd be brave enough to set out on her own.

"You called his bluff?"

"It was more than that," she said. "We'd been together for thirteen years and every year he treated me worse. It's like he blamed me for all the disappointments of his life."

"Thirteen years," I mused. "You might as well have been married."

"He couldn't bring himself to do it."

"But you were unhappy, so why bother thinking of marriage?"

"I couldn't live with someone I wouldn't marry."

I told her about my two failed marriages. "I was moving too fast," I confessed. "I couldn't think straight."

"Are you thinking straight now?" she joked.

"Probably not," I admitted.

She laughed and seemed at ease with herself, as if she had nothing to prove. I liked that a lot.

5

A HORSE OF A DIFFERENT COLOR

NICHOLAS AND I MADE A BID on the house—$115,000, ten below the asking price—and Imperial Realty accepted it. Maybe my luck was changing. Nicholas reminded me that the house was still open to other bids until Imperial signed the contract. But neither he nor I could imagine that anyone would consider bidding on the wreck.

That Christmas, Jill and I drove to Cincinnati to see her father. Jill's mother had died of a stroke when Jill was in her twenties. We had that, too, in common—the early loss of a parent. Her father was happily remarried and lived in a new suburb. The ten-hour drive gave Jill and me plenty of time to trade stories from our lives. I learned that, as a teenager, Jill took refuge in a world of antiques. She worried her parents. She was very smart but very willful. While the other teenage girls looked like Madonna, Jill looked like a Gibson girl. Following a year of Jill's insistent pleas, her mother bought her an antique brass bed, which Jill still owned. After Jill left home at seventeen, she rented old apartments. In every apartment, she was determined to bring it back to its original condition, pulling up the old carpet to reveal the wood floors and taking down the drop-ceilings to reclaim the rooms' original dimensions.

Though Jill and I agreed that meeting her father and step-mother was no big deal, it felt like the preamble to an engagement. Not that their disapproval would have made any difference. We were too old for that. Still, I wanted things to go well. Jill explained that she had always been the black sheep of the family, so their expectations would not be high.

I explained to her that I've never felt legitimate around well-established people, especially lawyers, accountants, and retired ad executives like Jill's father. But I had nothing to fear from him, I soon discovered. All he saw was that I was driving a new car and buying a big house. He didn't have to know that I was leasing the car or that I was cashing in my retirement fund to make the down payment on a condemned property. Had he known, he would have thought me a fool. A mortgage of $170,000 would be all I could manage on my modest salary. But that would give me about $60K to do the necessary work. For that much, I could barely make the house livable, Nicholas said.

Jill's father's house was about ten years old, an expansive ranch with a full basement. It sat among similar houses, each with a two-car garage fronting the street, in a grassy cul-de-sac development called Twining Estates. Jill and I had never liked suburbia. Now, dreaming of our new life in the Queen Anne, we shook our heads in dismay at everything her parents' expensive house boasted: wall-to-wall carpet, hollow-core doors, spindly baseboards, low ceilings, flimsy hardware, and veneered cabinets made of particle board. Privately we reveled in our new-found snobbery: we were now members of an exclusive club—old house renovators. Never mind that we hadn't lifted a single tool to start the work.

Jill's father and stepmother were very nice to me. Maybe they saw how in love Jill and I were. They seemed relieved that Jill had found a seemingly stable, well-established man. Everyday, I was on the phone with Nicholas to see if Imperial Realty had set a closing date. I imagined this made me look smart and in control of my life.

* * *

Imperial Realty, we learned, was a bogus company set up by the fraternity to avoid further lawsuits. There was no company, in fact, there was only a single lawyer to shepherd the sale of the Queen Anne and absolve the fraternity of its debts. The lawyer seemed in no rush to expedite the paper work, probably because he wasn't getting paid—he was working only as a favor for the influential father of a fraternity member. So the lawyer let our business languish through most of January, as I grew more anxious. Then, at last, he set a closing for the first of March. The 203K rehab loan would give me six months to get the house up to code. Six months did not sound like much time. I had to get into that house and start work—sooner, rather than later.

When I told Nicholas my plan—to clean out the house before signing the papers—he said, "I wouldn't do that, Ron. It's not your house yet. You're not even supposed to go inside."

Well, I thought, *nobody has to know*. Nobody but Rick, that is.

Rick was delighted to see me when I arrived with a box of industrial-grade trash bags in one hand and a new pair of work gloves in the other. Initially, I thought he might want to help me. I see now that this was an absurd expectation, but it shows how I was thinking: wasn't the Queen Anne a neighborhood concern? Wouldn't every old house lover want to help bring the Queen Anne back?

Jill was not only teaching in my department but also working weekends at Traditions and trying to finish her Ph.D. in Rhetoric, so I was on my own for this first phase of the adventure. She didn't think me foolhardy for wanting to clean out the place. "Just be careful," she said.

Standing alone in the Queen Anne's junk-cluttered living room that first afternoon, I felt I was making my acquaintance with something huge, untamed, and wounded. The first floor was a yawning space. I heard the wave-wash of passing traffic outside, the wheeze of wind through the old windows frames, and nothing else—no mice picking through the garbage, no creaking of floorboards upstairs. I thought of realtors talking about "good bones" and "great potential" whenever they came upon a wreck of a house. But Nicholas, my realtor, had nothing good to say about the Queen Anne except that it'd be "a fine house for someone who knew what to do with it." He had no faith in me whatsoever.

Bundled in a wool coat, my father's watch cap, and an old scarf, I started bagging garbage. Each bag was the size of a dishwasher. When it was full, I'd twist the top, then tie off the end with duct tape. After four hours of garbage collection, I had five bags behind me and I hadn't left the living room. This gave me pause. Sorting through the junk was slow-going. I had to pick out the fragments that belonged to the house—chunks of the banister, splinters of balusters, fragments of molding, door knobs, shutter latches. I had begun to gather piles of these leavings. It felt like I was cleaning up after a plane crash.

It was nearly dark when I was startled by a banging upstairs. It sounded like someone was battering a wall. Could something or somebody be trapped? I bolted up the stairs, paused on the second floor, then glanced up to the third in the dim glow of the skylight. The banging had grown to frantic pounding. I trotted down the hall, then up the next flight of stairs, now breathless. Whatever it was, it sounded like something was about to break. I was too startled to call out a warning as I approached the racket.

The noise came from the third-floor front room. It was a window in the bay. The wind had picked up, whipping the window in its loose frame. The sash slammed the frame, and slammed and slammed again. I found a piece of cardboard to shove between the frame and the sash and finally the banging ceased. To catch my breath, I sat on the plywood sleeping loft the frat boys had erected in the bay. I heard my heart playing Big Ben in my head. *Just a loose window*, I told myself. *Horses, not zebras*. That's something my father would tell me whenever I began to think the worst: *when you hear hoofbeats behind you, what do you expect to see?*

Dad would have liked this project. He was an amateur carpenter and jack-of-all-trades. It seemed there was nothing he could not fix. He even repaired our television sets. I spent a lot of time in his shop, fingering through his well-ordered jars of nuts and screws and electrical parts. Not that I had any desire to fix things. My brothers and I built forts and dug tunnels in the woods behind our house and took hikes wearing Dad's old knapsacks and riffled through his trunks of World War II souvenirs, which included a Samurai sword and hari-kari knife, but we never showed an inclination to analyze and repair things the way Dad did. Still, Dad insisted on teaching us how to use cross-cut and straight-cut saws and a hammer and screw driver—all the basics, which I promptly forgot.

Dad grew up on farms and ranches. He was all about self-sufficiency. One summer, he showed us how to make ice cream with an antique, hand-cranked ice-cream maker, using rock salt and dry ice. When we picked blackberries, he showed us how to make blackberry cobbler. He saved pennies, nickels, and dimes in big jars he kept in his bedroom closet. He used his old shirts for rags. He shopped for tools in salvage shops and surplus warehouses. He never threw anything away. When I was five, he built our family a barbecue out of our old swing set. Is it any wonder that this fantastically impossible challenge—bringing a wrecked house back to its original glory—appealed to me? Though I didn't announce it, not even to Jill, I felt a deep satisfaction in taking on this challenge because it would allow me to channel something of my father, and, in a remote way, make him proud.

* * *

In the cold, gloomy house, I had no music, no distractions, just my thoughts, which circled through my recent past. I reviewed every detail of my second marriage, which was far more disastrous than my first. My poor judgment—the profound pain it could bring—frightened me.

When I first met Sarah, she was a graduate student in the English department where I was an adjunct instructor. Even though I wasn't her teacher and wasn't much older than many of her fellow grad students, it clearly wasn't a good idea for me to date her. Sarah was the program's star pupil. Doe-eyed, with long blonde hair, she was popular and pretty and had recently divorced her husband, who had declared that he was gay. The circumstances of her failed marriage seemed to absolve her from any fault. I see now that I was dazzled by everything she seemed to represent: vibrant, talented youth and a new start. She was twenty-four. I was thirty-five and so thoroughly confused and filled with doubt and self-loathing that I couldn't recognize the many ways Sarah announced her own confusions. She seemed to know what she wanted and where she was going. When she showed an interest in me, I didn't imagine that, like me, she was looking for a safe haven—a seemingly sure bet.

I looked pretty good on paper. Though I had failed at my first marriage, it wasn't for the lack of trying. I had given it ten years, after all. I had no kids and only one school loan to pay off. My career seemed to hold promise. I was still young. At a party the graduate students threw, I saw that Sarah and I were on a collision course, especially after she said to me, with a sly smile, "Chocolate is almost as good as sex, don't you think?" After the party, I walked her to her apartment. It was a 1920s building whose stairwell reeked of garbage; its broad hallways dim and unswept.

Sarah's apartment was the typical grad school dive: thrift store furniture, dirty dishes piled in the sink, an unmade bed. Sarah was into country music. I hated country music but liked that she played it despite my opinion. In fact, it seemed she was determined to provoke me in every way. We debated great books, reductive stereotypes of country music, and the benefits of colorizing movies. Sarah hated black and white films. Her resistance was very sexy. As I said, I love a challenge. I didn't expect that we'd go to bed that first night. But once we got started, I didn't know how to stop. We stayed up till dawn.

The next morning I had an appointment to keep; otherwise I would have stayed with Sarah all day. Light-headed from lack of sleep and buoyed by my conquest, I greeted the new day with more optimism than I had felt in years. It was as though I were twenty-four again. I wanted desperately to make this last. Immediately, I decided that Sarah and I would get married. Never mind that I knew nothing about her. She was a smoker, I wasn't. She liked the beach; I like the mountains. She didn't like animals and didn't want pets; I had Celeste, my cat from the divorce. Sarah didn't like old houses or antiques, both of which I adore. Apparently, she had no interests or hobbies beyond her own reading and writing.

After we started dating, the chair of my department called me into his office. He said, "Ron, I hear you might be seeing one of our graduate students."

I felt heat rise to my ears. "Yes," I said. "Sarah and I have been going out."

He seemed to stifle a grimace, then said, "People have been talking about that."

"What have they been saying?"

"It doesn't look good," he said.

He was just doing his job, I supposed, but his fatherly admonition was both condescending and infuriating. "I'm not her teacher," I reminded him.

"But you teach in this department," he said. "A department in which she is a student."

"What if we're in love?" I said. I wasn't sure if it was love. I *wanted* it to be love.

"You can't be seen dating one of our students," he said.

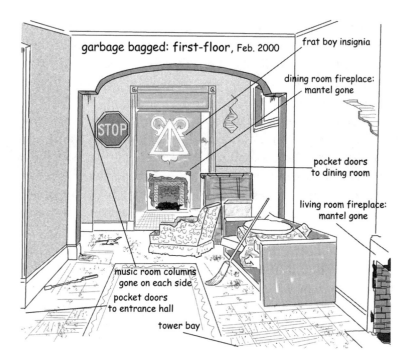

garbage bagged: first-floor, Feb. 2000

frat boy insignia

dining room fireplace: mantel gone

STOP

pocket doors to dining room

living room fireplace: mantel gone

music room columns gone on each side

pocket doors to entrance hall

tower bay

"So what are you saying I should do?" I asked.

"Stop," he said.

I nodded my head in agreement, though I knew I wouldn't stop. *Never tell me to stop.*

* * *

Every day in February, I got away from school as soon as I could and cleaned out the Queen Anne. Had there been electricity in the house, I would have worked late into the night. Some afternoons Jill would come by to check on me. Harriet happily nosed through the garbage and we had to watch her to make sure she didn't get hold of something toxic. Bassets will eat anything.

"This is progress," Jill exclaimed when she saw the nearly cleared living room.

"They said it couldn't be done!" I joked.

"If we invited a bunch of friends to help us," she said, "I bet we could get the place painted in no time."

"A painting party!" I said. "Great idea! And maybe neighbors will want to help too."

"Like a barn raising?" she laughed skeptically.

"Why not? Isn't everyone relieved and happy that we've taken it on?"

"That doesn't mean they'll throw us a ticker-tape parade."

By the time I was done gathering garbage at the end of the month, I had carted seventy-nine big bags to the city Dumpsters. This was only the light stuff—paper, cat litter, food spills, petrified leftovers, broken plates. There were carloads of other, heavier garbage to clear out before I got to the furniture and the loft beds upstairs and the twenty-foot bar in the basement.

To celebrate my completion of this initial phase, Jill and I went sledding with Harriet after a big snow. Despite her age and ill-temper, Harriet loved to sled. Jill owned a wooden toboggan (antique, of course), which we took to nearby Wyman Park. Jill would sit with Harriet in her lap, then I'd push off, our toboggan careening down the hill, Harriet barking excitement. Often we'd crash at the bottom, the three of us spilling over one another. We laughed and laughed, Harriet barking then shaking off the snow.

Through snowy Baltimore, we were driving Jill's new compact SUV, a Honda CRV. Ever frugal, she had saved enough for a down payment but needed me to co-sign for the loan. I was happy to do this not only because she was more responsible with money than anybody I'd ever met, but also because it was an act of trust on her part. Both of us agreed that even if our romance didn't work out, we'd be fine with the arrangement. This was bullshit, of course. Our romance was going to work out—it *had* to.

A week before the Queen Anne's contract was to be made official, I was relaxing with Jill at my apartment. Harriet lay nearby,

Jill and
Harriet

snoring. Then Nicholas phoned and, in a quiet voice he might have used to announce a death in the family, informed me that I had lost the house to another bidder.

He said, "I'm really sorry, Ron."

"Wait," I blurted. "Imperial already *accepted* my offer. I just spent *four weeks* cleaning out the place!"

"I *told* you, Ron."

"But it was a done deal!"

"Nothing's done until the contract is *signed*. You *knew* that."

He explained that a young couple—having just inherited a lot of money—had made a counter offer.

"Sometimes that happens," he said.

How could I have been so stupid? Would I never learn? Hanging up the phone, I was so depressed I could hardly talk.

Jill watched me carefully. She didn't know me that well yet and she could hardly predict what I might do or how she could best help me.

"It's gone," I told her. "A rich couple got the house."

"Have they signed the contract?"

"Any day now, I assume."

"But not yet?" she pressed.

"What does it matter, Jill—they're rich!"

"So?"

That night, too dejected to be with Jill, I phoned the most recent contractor I'd been talking to and told him that the deal was off. As I explained what happened, I felt cheated. Later, I thought about the other houses Jill and I had looked at. Nothing even came close to the Queen Anne. I imagined that every month of every year I'd drive by the old house—restored to its original glory by "the young couple"—and I'd think, *That was almost mine*. It'd be like losing Jill to another man. It was troubling to realize that already I was so attached. Sure, I'd spent a month cleaning the place. Sure, I was an idiot. But life goes on, right? It was just a house, right?

Well, no. A house is never just a house. When I graduated from high school, my father bought me a used VW van and outfitted it as a camper. I marveled at how he, an engineer, took measure of the small interior and made the most of it. I didn't imagine that I could do what he did. I'd never be an engineer. I lived in that van, slept in it, drove it around the country. My ideal was to never own a house. I boasted that I could fit everything I owned in my van and, within an hour, be on the road and as free as the wind. But I was deluding myself. After graduating from college, I took my big trip across America and I found myself longing for a house of my own. Everywhere I went, my eyes were open for that ideal piece of property. I don't think I've met any American who adamantly does not want a house. Growing up in this country, we are encouraged to think of homeownership as a God-given *right*. Among those of my parents' generation, you were odd if you didn't want a house and a failure if you couldn't buy your own eventually.

The historical truth is that house ownership was out of reach for most Americans until the late 1940s. In 1897, when the Queen Anne was built, you had to pay half down or more. Typically, you'd get a loan for twenty percent of the purchase price and you'd have to pay it off within five or ten years. When I bid for the Queen Anne, I didn't even have five percent to pay down. And I was asking for a thirty-year, fixed-rate loan. That's typical of my generation. Our expectations—supported by a number of federal programs and institutions, like Fannie Mae, that guarantee low-interest, long-term loans to people like me—would have seemed like presumptuous delusions to nineteenth century homebuilders. But after 1945 and the hard fight to win freedom for the world, Americans insisted that everyone of middling means would have a house on a separate plot of land and a new car to put in its garage. This norm was irrefutably reinforced by every TV series we watched growing up. Start with "Father Knows Best" and track it down to the present. Who doesn't own a house on TV?

My favorite shows as a child were "The Munsters" and the "Addams Family" because, you guessed it, these families lived in cool old houses. Big Victorian houses. These houses were exotic, idiosyncratic reflections of the people who owned them and, in their way, represented the American ideal: you're supposed to make your house your own. Even though homeowners in the subdivisions of my childhood years were discouraged from altering the exteriors of their houses (I recall the scandal created when someone painted his house purple), every man was expected to customize his den or basement or family room. For us children, the novelty of visiting a friend's house was seeing how his father had altered the interior. You couldn't tell from the outside of these cookie-cutter houses what the inside would look like. Thumb through the do-it-yourself magazines of the 1950s and 1960s, like *Popular Mechanics,* and you'll see pages and pages of homeowner modernizations and innovations. Fixing your house, *changing* your house, was a way of taking possession, taking charge, making your mark. (I think of dogs peeing on trees.) Though most of these early do-it-yourself house projects are hideous by today's standards, they all make the same point: a house is not just a house. Your house reflects who you are or who you hope to be.

If the once-grand Queen Anne represented what I hoped to be, I'd have to confess it was a fantasy built on stubborn pride. Getting hold of this potentially valuable property would prove that I am lucky and smart. It would mitigate my many mistakes. Yes, the Queen Anne was the hard way to go, as my mother rightly lamented. But it also seemed the only way to go. If I was going to turn my life around, if I was going to break through my bad luck, I needed to win big. Without a big win, without this seemingly heroic start, I'd be relegated to getting a modest house, a normal house, a house that no one would think twice about. Worse, I'd start my life with Jill by sharing the profound disappointment of having lost the Queen Anne. This would set us up for more disappointment, I was convinced. It wasn't the way I wanted to start over.

When I phoned Rick and told him the bad news, how heartbroken I was to have lost the house, how I'd been looking forward to working with him, how I couldn't believe this wasn't going to happen, he commiserated as if we had lost a mutual friend.

Then I phoned Jill to commiserate some more.

"Counterbid," she said.

"They'll just outbid me."

"You don't know that. Make an offer!"

"It seems hopeless," I sighed. But I knew she was right. The young couple's determination to have the house was proof that the house was worth a fight. What did I have to lose?

6

CAREFUL WHAT YOU WISH FOR

IMPERIAL'S LAWYER SAID he would accept my counter-offer of ten thousand more if the couple did not show up by noon Monday for their signing.

Today was Friday.

Jill and I spent a nerve-racking weekend speculating: *Was my bid higher than the couple's? If not, then why would Imperial go with me? Maybe the lawyer mistrusted the couple because they had come in at the last minute—they hadn't even had an inspection done.*

Monday morning, Nicholas went to the bank to wait it out.

I might as well have been waiting for news of landing a new job.

Nicholas phoned at eleven to say that the couple still had not shown up. I then phoned Rick to see if he had heard from them over the weekend.

Charles answered the phone. He said Rick was with the couple at this very moment, showing them the house once again.

Again?

"Yes, right now. This time with an inspector."

"Charles," I said, "please get over there and have Rick stall them. Stall them as long as he can. The house is ours if they don't show up at the bank by noon!"

Charles said he would do what he could.

Had I been thinking clearly, I would have been relieved that I was about to lose the Queen Anne. But I wasn't thinking clearly. I *had* to get that house—if for no other reason than to keep from feeling like a fool for having spent four weeks cleaning it out.

Nicholas had dutifully followed my instructions but made it clear that he thought me crazy. That's why he had accepted the couple's counterbid as the end of the story, as if to say, *You got off lucky, Ron. Really.*

Nobody would regret our loss of the old house.

Even this made me want it all the more, as if everyone's doubts were actually doubts about the prospects for Jill and me as a couple. We had something to root for now—our future. If we lost the house, I wasn't sure that anything would be the same between us.

As we waited for Nicholas to call, Jill made some tea. The recent snow had melted and Baltimore was soaked. The park across the street from my apartment looked like a marsh, the bare trees black from the damp, the sky a marbled charcoal. I was pacing the carpet, careful to avoid Harriet sprawled in a nap.

"There's nothing we can do," Jill said. "Want some tea?"

"How stupid am I?"

"Come on, Ron. Who could've known that somebody would come in at the last minute and steal your house?"

"*Our* house!"

"Our house," she corrected.

The kettle whistled. I stared at Jill's back as she poured her tea. Was she already putting distance between us because this deal was falling apart? Because nothing good can last? Because it's zebras, not horses?

My cat, Corona, squeaked at me from the top of a nearby chair. "What?" I snapped. "What now?"

"Oh, leave Corona alone."

"She's importuning."

"She knows you're upset."

"What are we going to do if we lose this thing?" I asked.

Jill shrugged, then blew the steam from her tea. She looked glum. I wanted her to play brave and talk happy talk. But she didn't like bullshit. "It's a real drag," she said. "We'll never find another house like the Queen Anne."

I continued pacing: "Had that damned lawyer gotten off his fat ass we could've signed the papers a month ago!"

"Maybe this is why he took his time."

I stopped in my tracks. "You think he courted another bid?"

"I don't know. We're driving ourselves crazy, aren't we?"

I looked at her for a moment. I felt woozy, as if I'd just stumbled from a car wreck. "Are we going to find another place, Jill?"

She put down her tea. "We're going to have to."

I wanted more enthusiasm from her but, then, I always wanted too much, didn't I?

Nicholas phoned at 12:30. "You got the house," he said.

"They never showed up?" I gasped.

"They *did* show up," he said, "but we had already signed."

I was so stunned by my sudden luck, I started weeping with relief. I handed the phone to Jill.

What happened to the young couple was a mystery. Nicholas didn't know. I imagined they would regret their delay for a long time. About two weeks later, they sent me the inspection report they had paid for. Why would they do that if they had tried to outbid me? It seemed I was missing a large part of their story.

The big surprise of winning the house was that Nicholas offered to be my contractor if I would pay for his contractor's license, which had lapsed.

The 203K rehab loan demands that the homeowner hire a licensed contractor to oversee the work—to make sure that everything is up to code. Until the rehab is complete, the bank will not release the house to the mortgage holder and, worse, the mortgage stays at its probationary rate, which in my case was nine-and-a-half percent when the going rate was already down to eight percent and dropping. So I had been phoning contractors nearly every day. One told me he couldn't undertake the job unless he was guaranteed $15,000 for his services. That was one quarter of my budget! Nicholas said he would *not* demand a minimum cut but, instead, would charge only by the hour for his work. A huge break for me.

Nicholas had been convinced that the house wasn't right for me—and that I wasn't ready for the house. But now, seeing my determination, he seemed encouraged and no doubt curious to see if I could do it. Perhaps, too, he felt a little protective of me.

The day of the signing, the Imperial lawyer did not show up. In his place, stood one of the fraternity boys. A clean-shaven regular guy wearing slacks and a dress shirt, he couldn't have been older than twenty-five. Surely he had lived in the Queen Anne. Was this Alex? Alex was the most popular name in the graffiti throughout the Queen Anne. *Alex sucks big titties!* the boys had scrawled in many places. This young man seemed both clueless about the legalities and awkwardly quiet through the signing, as though he'd been put up to this.

Afterwards, Nicholas clapped me on the back and grinned: "Isn't it great," he exclaimed, "you got the house!"

I wanted to feel great—this should have been a celebration—but I was scared. I would have felt better had Jill been there. But she insisted that she didn't have to witness the signing. "That's for you and Nicholas," she'd said. Now I wondered if it was her way of keeping some distance between her and the house—*my* house, not *our* house. At that moment I felt the way I had when the preacher had pronounced my first wife and me married. We had conducted the ceremony on a windy hill of the Marin headlands, overlooking the San Francisco Bay. We'd had no rehearsal, so the preacher was unprepared to orchestrate the reading of our vows, which we'd written ourselves. He read his part wrong and had to repeat it twice. In attendance were my fiancée's parents and two siblings and my mother, brothers, and grandma Nana. Though a sunny day, it was cool enough to raise goose bumps on my neck. The wind made the tail of my fiancée's lavender dress stutter and snap. It should have been a happy occasion but I wasn't happy. I was frightened and already brimming with regret—we had rushed it, we hardly knew each other after our eleven-month romance, and there were too many differences we hadn't worked through. Years later, my mother would tell me that she had known it wasn't going to last because the week of the wedding I forgot to pick up my wedding pants from the cleaner's.

Just as the preacher pronounced us married, my wife embraced me. Over her shoulder I saw a horde of German tourists hiking towards us, a tour bus having just disgorged them at the bottom of our hill. Suddenly we were surrounded by strangers. The grinning preacher—himself a stranger—was shaking my hand. I felt light-headed and scared. As I pushed my way through the crowd, my new wife at my heels, I kept saying to myself, *What have you done?*

Now, standing in the parking lot of the real estate office, my signed contract in hand, I realized that I'd barely be able to meet the monthly mortgage. I was house poor and bound to the bank's deadline and nobody but Jill and Nicholas were happy for me.

7
WHAT WAS AND WAS NOT HERE

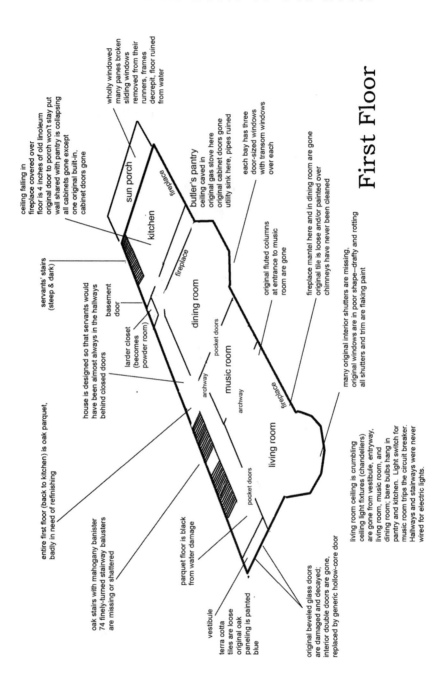

First Floor

ceiling falling in
fireplace covered over
floor is 4 inches of old linoleum
original door to porch won't stay put
wall shared with pantry is collapsing
all cabinets gone except
one original built-in,
cabinet doors gone

wholly windowed
many panes broken
sliding windows
removed from their
runners, frames
decrepit, floor ruined
from water

sun porch

kitchen

fireplace

butler's pantry
ceiling caved in
original gas stove here
original cabinet doors gone
utility sink here, pipes ruined

each bay has three
door-sized windows
with transom windows
over each

fireplace

servants' stairs
(steep & dark)

basement
door

dining room

larder closet
(becomes
powder room)

pocket doors

original fluted columns
at entrance to music
room are gone

fireplace mantel here and in dining room are gone
original tile is loose and/or painted over
chimneys have never been cleaned

house is designed so that servants would
have been almost always in the hallways
behind closed doors

archway

music room

archway

fireplace

entire first floor (back to kitchen) is oak parquet,
badly in need of refinishing

living room

pocket doors

many original interior shutters are missing,
original windows are in poor shape—drafty and rotting
all shutters and trim are flaking paint

oak stairs with mahogany banister
74 finely-turned stairway balusters
are missing or shattered

parquet floor is black
from water damage

vestibule
terra cotta
tiles are loose
original oak
paneling is painted
blue

original beveled glass doors
are damaged and decayed;
interior double doors are gone,
replaced by generic hollow-core door

living room ceiling is crumbling
ceiling light fixtures (chandeliers)
are gone from vestibule, entryway,
living room, music room, and
dining room; bare bulbs hang in
pantry and kitchen. Light switch for
music room trips the circuit breaker.
Hallways and stairways were never
wired for electric lights.

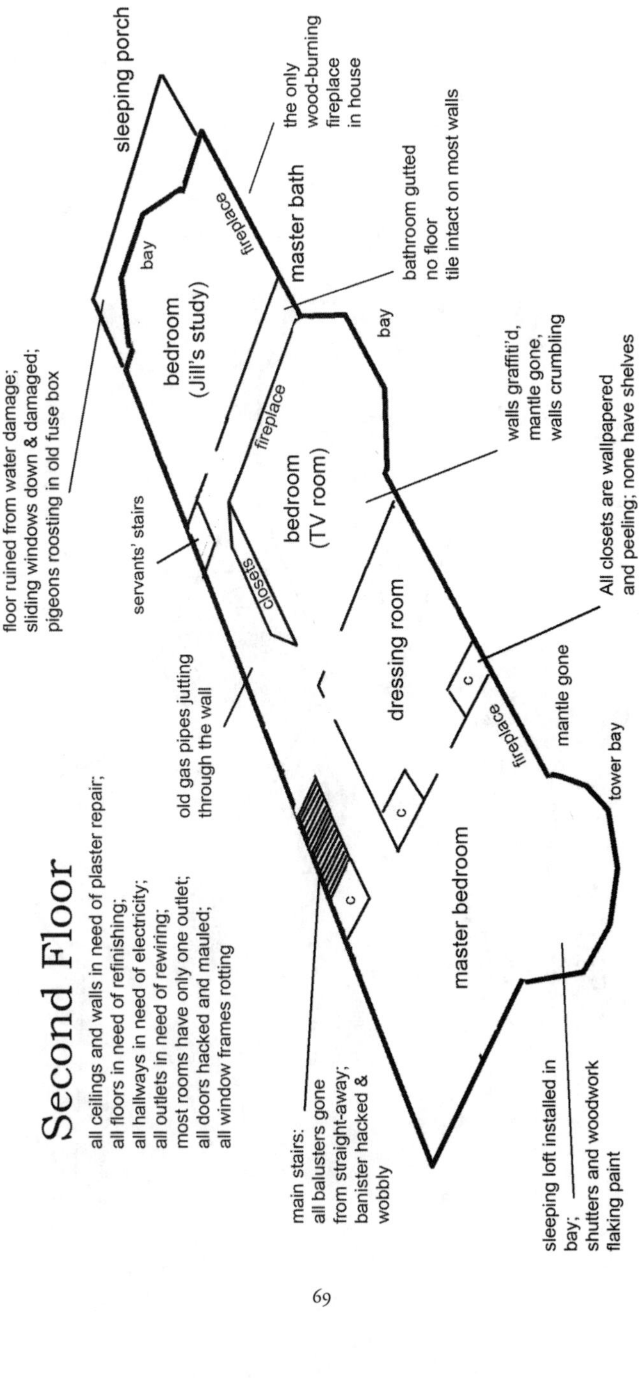

Second Floor

all ceilings and walls in need of plaster repair;
all floors in need of refinishing;
all hallways in need of electricity;
all outlets in need of rewiring;
most rooms have only one outlet;
all doors hacked and mauled;
all window frames rotting

floor ruined from water damage;
sliding windows down & damaged;
pigeons roosting in old fuse box

sleeping porch

bay

fireplace

the only
wood-burning
fireplace
in house

master bath

bathroom gutted
no floor
tile intact on most walls

bedroom
(Jill's study)

bay

servants' stairs

old gas pipes jutting
through the wall

fireplace

walls graffiti'd,
mantle gone,
walls crumbling

bedroom
(TV room)

closets

main stairs:
all balusters gone
from straight-away;
banister hacked &
wobbly

dressing room

c

c

mantle gone

All closets are wallpapered
and peeling; none have shelves

fireplace

c

master bedroom

tower bay

sleeping loft installed in
bay;
shutters and woodwork
flaking paint

69

Third Floor

all ceilings and walls in need of plaster repair
all floors in need of refinishing;
all hallways in need of electricity;
all outlets in need of rewiring;
most rooms have only one outlet;
all doors hacked and mauled;
window frames rotting

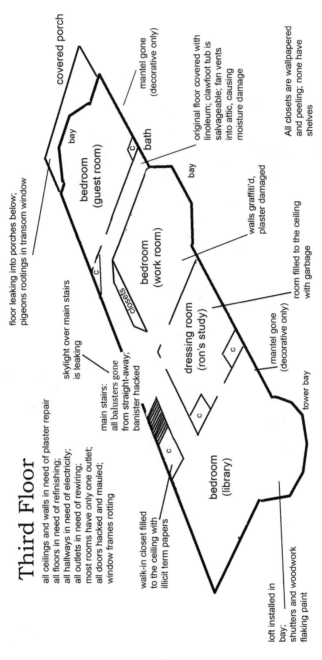

covered porch

floor leaking into porches below;
pigeons rootings in transom window

skylight over main stairs
is leaking

main stairs:
all balusters gone
from straight-away;
banister hacked

mantel gone
(decorative only)

bay

bedroom
(guest room)

c

bath

original floor covered with
linoleum; clawfoot tub is
salvageable; fan vents
into attic, causing
moisture damage

All closets are wallpapered
and peeling; none have
shelves

c

bay

bedroom
(work room)

closets

walls graffiti'd,
plaster damaged

room filled to the ceiling
with garbage

dressing room
(ron's study)

c

mantel gone
(decorative only)

c

bedroom
(library)

tower bay

walk-in closet filled
to the ceiling with
illicit term papers

loft installed in
bay;
shutters and woodwork
flaking paint

70

Basement

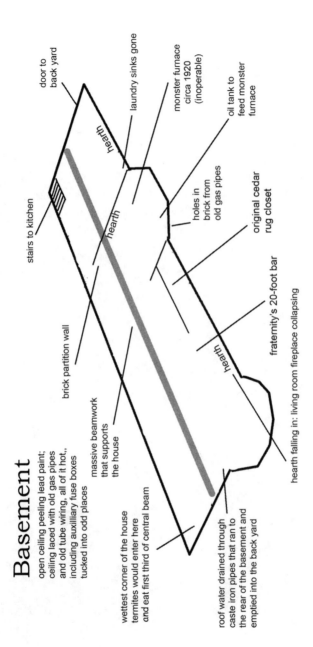

open ceiling peeling lead paint;
ceiling laced with old gas pipes
and old tube wiring, all of it hot,,
including auxilliary fuse boxes
tucked into odd places

stairs to kitchen

door to
back yard

laundry sinks gone

hearth

hearth

monster furnace
circa 1920
(inoperable)

oil tank to
feed monster
furnace

holes in
brick from
old gas pipes

brick partition wall

massive beamwork
that supports
the house

original cedar
rug closet

fraternity's 20-foot bar

hearth

wettest corner of the house
termites would enter here
and eat first third of central beam

hearth falling in: living room fireplace collapsing

roof water drained through
caste iron pipes that ran to
the rear of the basement and
emptied into the back yard

8

CLEANING HOUSE

JILL AND I GOT TETANUS SHOTS, bought work boots, then
scoured the flea markets for tools. We didn't know what we'd
need. I was hoping I wouldn't have to buy any big scary tools, like
a band saw or a table saw or a router, whatever that was. Nothing
bigger than a circular saw. This was a one-shot deal, I insisted.
No need to go overboard. We'd fix the house and be settled in six
months. Then we could live happily ever after. Silly as it sounds,
that's how it seemed at the time: just one big push—like ventur-
ing into the jungle to find a downed plane and rescue the pilot.
I promised Jill I'd be careful. I wouldn't lose a finger or a hand or
dangle from the roof. No, in fact, we'd hire people to do the big
stuff and the bad stuff. Nicholas was going to help me make the
arrangements. It would be nothing more than cleaning and painting and hammering for Jill and me.

When Jill and I surveyed the fraternity's abandoned belongings, we tried to be realistic. Okay, sure, there was a lot of junk
to get rid of. Forty-five hundred square feet of junk, to be exact.
Fine, we'd need a Dumpster. But just one. All right, a big one. The
weekend before the Dumpster arrived, Jill and I took an inventory
of the junk and concluded that we had one impediment: the huge
hot tub sitting in the backyard. That alone would take up a third
of a Dumpster.

"I could chop it up," I offered.

We were standing in the cluttered yard, where recently I had filled all of the so-called gopher holes. *Those aren't gopher holes*, Nicholas had told me a few days earlier. *Those are rat holes, dummy!*

As the new owner of this eyesore, I was liable to get cited and fined by the city if I didn't clean things up immediately. In Baltimore, a single broken window can get you a citation, as can litter and rat holes in your yard. But the city had agreed to wait and see what we did with the property. It seemed everyone was waiting.

"No, it'd take too much work to chop up the hot tub," I concluded.

"Put an ad in the paper," Jill said.

I turned to her in surprise. "Sell the hot tub?"

"No, give it away to the first person who can haul it out!" she said.

"Brilliant!"

Two mornings later, three young men were rolling the hot tub like a giant wheel over our backyard wall and into their pickup truck. Their leader was a collector of vintage hot tubs—and this was an especially good find, he said: a *1984 Satellite Deluxe with dual turbo-jets.* Jill and I waved them off, then looked at each other giddily: *collector of vintage hot tubs?*

I kissed her on the forehead. "You're a genius!"

She grinned. "Stick with me, lover. I will make your life a breeze!"

As we returned to the yard, I tried to pull the wooden gate closed and a piece of it came off in my hand. "I've got to fix that, don't you think?" I joked.

"It looks like you'll have to make a new one," she mused.

The wooden gate was a big green paneled door with an artful peak on top, a wrought iron pull and old iron strap hinges. It had an ornate iron grill over the small opening that allowed passersby

Garden Gate

to peek into our walled yard. The other gate was identical. Both were rotten beyond repair.

"We'll figure something out," I said.

"It'll have to look just like that," Jill pressed. "We want to retain its historic integrity, right?"

"Sure," I said, "of course." I didn't know how I would build new doors to replace the intricate old ones. It occurred to me that *all* of the doors inside needed repair too. I hadn't counted them but there were at least eighteen. Or twenty-five.

"Oh, Ron, look at that." Jill said this in a tone of voice I would soon come to dread: it meant, *This is trouble!*

In the damp circle of dirt that marked the circumference of the freshly uprooted hot tub, we saw two fist-wide burrows.

Rat holes. Unlike all the other holes I had filled with gravel and poison, these were fresh and very close to the house.

"If I fill them," I said, "the rats will just dig themselves out and nest somewhere nearby."

"Yuck."

"I'm gonna have to dig them up," I said.

"Oh, god!"

"What choice do we have?" I asked, hoping she had another inspiration.

"I don't know," she said. "We've got to get rid of the rats in the yard." Now she looked at me with alarm: "Are you gonna kill them?"

"Not unless they attack me!" I said. "Do rats attack?"

"I don't know!"

We groaned in unison, then backed away from the holes. "Maybe they're empty," I said. "We could get lucky."

"They don't look empty," she said with a grimace. "Do we have to do this now?"

"Before it's dark," I said. "If there are baby rats in there, the mother will move them."

"Baby rats!" she wailed.

"Let's come back later," I said.

We spent the day making and moving piles of junk inside. There was so much stuff—couches, chairs, desks, dishes, tables, lamps, clothes, file cabinets, books, especially library books many years past due, papers, a walk-in closet stacked to the ceiling with term papers the fraternity had banked for ten years, buckets of paint, half a ton of lumber from the lofts and the twenty-foot bar I had dismantled over the course of a week, every kind of pillow, colorfully painted initiation paddles, each emblazoned with a bright blue "DUH!," the boys' fond acronym for Delta Upsilon, window fans, ceiling fans, floor fans, track lights, uprooted toilets and sinks, five refrigerators, the biggest of which was the size of a

Volvo, shelving, book cases, curtains, running shoes piled up like a heap of gutted crab shells, folding chairs, full-length mirrors, bricks, end tables, beer mugs, tumblers, shot glasses, traffic signs, traffic cones, beer kegs, soft balls, Frisbees, baseball bats, and posters, the oldest of which was a vintage Jimmy Hendrix in day glow, circa 1970 and hanging twenty feet up the rear stairwell. So much stuff, all of it crumpled, dirty, broken, ripped or otherwise nearly worthless, I was beginning to suspect that we'd need more than one Dumpster.

At the day's end, Jill and I returned to the backyard. It was dusk, a cold and gloomy evening. She looked at me with concern, as if to say, "Do we really. . . ?" Standing near the two rat burrows, I looked back at her and shook my head sadly: *yes.* I am by no means brave, but I am stubborn. As a child, I'd force myself to open closets and peer under beds just to make sure no ghost or goblin was lurking in wait. If I'm in trouble, I want to know it sooner rather than later. So I took up the one rusted shovel we'd found among the fraternity's junk and I began to dig.

Wearing a dirty sweatshirt, tattered jeans, and her new steel-toed boots, Jill stood behind me, hugging herself against the cold. "Oh, god," she murmured, "be careful."

I felt like I was digging up a vampire. I imagined rats pouring from the burrows and swarming over my feet.

I began to unearth strips of plastic bags. That seems to be the rats' bedding of choice: handfuls of shredded grocery bags, with a smattering of chewed-up paper and shards of Styrofoam.

Two feet down, I got to it at last.

"What's that?" Jill yelped.

"It's the pups," I said.

Four of them. They looked nothing like rats.

"Pups?" she said. "That's what they're called, *pups?*"

They looked like dog pups, with stubby snouts and puckered eyes not yet open. And they whimpered.

Behind me, Jill began a chorus of regret: "*Oh my god, oh, god!*"

"I know," I said. "It's awful."

"What are you gonna do?"

"What *can* I do?"

"I don't know, *put them somewhere!*"

"Get me a garbage bag," I said.

"Oh, my god!"

"*Please*, get me a bag!"

She handed me a heavy-duty plastic garbage bag. I scooped a rat pup onto my shovel. Then I eased it into the bag, followed one after the other by its siblings. Jill groaned as she watched.

"This is bad karma," she said. "Rats are gonna haunt our dreams for years."

"I know, I know," I said. "Let's just finish what we started."

I tied the end of the garbage bag, then lifted it with both hands.

"Oh, Ron!" Jill cried.

"Rats, Jill—these are *rats*! Dangerous, dirty, invasive, terrible—they're not pets." My hands were shaky. I drew a breath. Jill followed me into the alley, where we soon found a Dumpster. It was dark by this time.

Free of the bag finally, we returned to lock up the house. There was still no electricity, no plumbing, not even sufficient locks on the front and back doors, just chains with padlocks. Later, I did dream of rats but not as Jill predicted: There was a crowd of them around me. They were small, fat, and cute and yapping at me like lap dogs. It was as if I were the pied piper, only I had nowhere to take them. So I just stood there listening to their complaints and telling them I'd find them something to eat in the house. But the house was empty and every fridge I opened (there seemed to be hundreds) was as clean as an Arctic landscape.

9

DUMPSTERS

THE DUMPSTER ARRIVED on a brisk, sunny March morning. For the first time in ten years, the house was wide open and neighbors stopped by to see what had become of the old place. I had invited a few people in charge of a neighborhood fundraiser to take what they wanted from the abandoned belongings: a couple of couches, the antique gas range, one of the original claw-footed tubs (minus one foot), the 1940s Deco refrigerator from the back porch, some chairs, a few ice chests, etc. Jill had enlisted Les, the moving expert from Traditions, to head a crew of strong arms to clear out the big stuff. A sweet-tempered, compact bull of a man, Les could lift anything, it seemed.

Smiling like a proud father, Rick played Master of Ceremony, introducing us to the neighbors, our small front yard crowded with the curious. It felt like a celebration. As I fielded questions and described our plans, strangers came up to me and exclaimed, *So you're the one!* They looked at me with such wonder, I felt I owed them an explanation.

"It's the kind of house we've always dreamed of owning," I said.

"You and your wife?"

"Jill's my girlfriend," I corrected.

"When are you going to move in?"

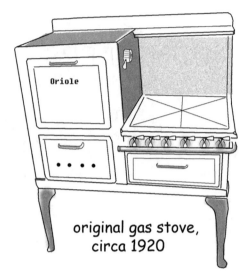

original gas stove,
circa 1920

"As soon as we can." I glanced to Jill for a reaction. She was smiling politely.

"How long's it gonna take to make this place habitable?"

I said, "The bank's given us six months." I heard gasps of disbelief.

"They're determined," Rick chirped. "They'll do it!"

"Rick's our inspiration," I said.

Everyone agreed that he and Charles had done a remarkable job with their house. Rick smiled proudly: "Took us twenty years!"

"And you're gonna do it in six months?" somebody asked.

"Just get it up to code," I reminded him. "The rest will take some time." Privately, I told myself I would *not* be working on my house for twenty frigging years. No way!

Soon the neighbors and onlookers excused themselves to attend to their own lives. I was tempted to call after them, "Hey, wait, don't you want to help?" I still clung to the fantasy that

dumpster #1,
March 2000

Jill carrying
illicit term papers

Ron wrestling
toilet

everybody would pitch in. Jill and I and Les with his three-man crew were left to fill the Dumpster.

You have to be smart about filling a Dumpster, I discovered. You don't simply drop a couch in there first thing, for instance; otherwise, the rest of the trash isn't going to lie down. While Les and his crew wrestled out the big stuff and Jill bagged things like pillows and clothing, I went after the things that were still screwed down, like the toilets. Later, Rick told me that when he saw me heft one of the befouled, reeking toilets into the Dumpster, he knew I'd make a success of the Queen Anne. Emptying the old house, I already felt successful, as if in clearing away other people's mistakes I was clearing my own too.

There were still surprises among the boys' garbage. The most unpleasant was a five gallon plastic paint drum, which I assumed was full of paint until I popped the lid. It was brimming with frat boy crap. Hastily resealing its cover, I carried the drum ever-so-carefully outside, then eased it into a tight corner of the Dumpster.

Nicholas came by when we were nearly done. I didn't understand why he was wearing a suit and still selling real estate. Didn't we have a house to work on? Where were his priorities? It took me weeks to understand that I wasn't paying him enough to be at the house every day. Far from detail-oriented, I wasn't thinking about money at all. Bringing the house back seemed a nearly noble undertaking that had nothing to do with money.

Nodding his approval, Nicholas smiled his boyish smile and patted me on the back. I was dirty and sweaty and the Dumpster was nearly filled. "You're gonna need two or three more of these," he said.

"Yeah, I guess," I said. "Let's see if we can do it with two."

Jill joined us. She was wearing her usual work outfit of tattered jeans, a sweatshirt, and work boots. No gloves.

"Aren't you two the cat's meow?" Nicholas said with a grin. "You're doing good work!"

Jill rolled her eyes. "You missed the fun part." She told him about the bucket of shit.

He winced. "Oh, man, let's hope there are no more surprises like that!"

"You know, with the junk nearly gone," I said, "the house is starting to look like a house, not a wreck."

Nicholas nodded politely and again patted me on the back. "I like your attitude," he said. "Let's stay positive."

After he left, I said to Jill, "He still thinks I'm crazy."

Jill smiled. "Is he wrong?"

Though it was reassuring to see Jill working on the house, she had yet to commit to moving in. This puzzled me. Weren't we thoroughly in love? Didn't she want to make a life with me? Wasn't this our dream house?

"I figure I'll move in as soon as the plumbing's good," I announced one evening over dinner at her place. "The start of May."

She set a steamy bowl of potato soup before me. "That soon?"

"Two months," I said. "The house should be in good shape."

She dropped a piece of dinner roll on the floor for Harriet—something I'd never do, but it wasn't my dog.

"May?" she echoed.

"Sure," I said. "By that time we'll get a ton of work done!"

I turned to Charlie, her ancient tomcat, as if for confirmation. Sitting on the table just beyond my bowl, he looked at me laconically. His white hair was stiff and matted. It seemed he had long forgotten how to groom himself.

Jill lit the candles on the table.

"What about you?" I asked.

"In two months I probably won't be in any better shape," she joked. "You know how much weight I've gained since we've met?"

"Because you're eating like a real person finally."

She'd been living mostly on rice and peanut butter when we met.

"Soup's hot. Watch it," she cautioned.

I took a sip. "Jesus!"

She rolled her eyes, then smirked. "Burn your tongue?"

"Damn!"

Charlie was sniffing at my bowl.

"Keep an eye on him," she said. "He likes potato soup."

I drank some water. The tip of my tongue would be numb for days. "When do you think you'd like to move in?" Though I asked this casually, deep inside me, I could feel a small winged piece of panic flying in circles.

Jill blew on her spoonful. "There's no rush, is there?"

As far as I'm concerned, in matters of love there is always a rush. Love is an avalanche, a headlong tumble. That pretty much described our romance. At no point—until now—had Jill ever given me the sense that she wanted to slow down.

"Is there something you're unsure of?" I asked cautiously.

At last she tried her soup. It was one of her specialties. Charlie extended a paw towards my bowl. Gently, I batted him away. I heard Harriet circling the table, claws clacking against the floor-boards. Outside, someone was playing a boombox, its bass thumping like a knock on the door.

"There's a lot going on," she said vaguely. "And you're really wound up."

"Wound up?" I answered. "You bet I'm wound up! This is the challenge of a lifetime. Nicholas tells me it will be impossible to get the house up to code in six months. Did you know he was that negative?"

"I think he'd call it realistic," she said. "He's your contractor. He probably knows what he's talking about."

"Yeah, but he thinks I'm going to punk out on him too. He doesn't believe me when I tell him I'll work on that house four-teen hours a day."

She stirred her soup. "It's not going to leave any room for us, I'm afraid."

"Sure it will, if we're working together—if we're *living* together."

I wasn't being honest. Ever since I'd gotten the power restored to the Queen Anne, I'd been on a blind run, working on the house every night until the early morning. Driving home at three or four A.M., I realized it made no sense to sleep at Jill's in the few remaining hours before dawn. I'd just wake her up. And then she'd wake me up as she left for work. It was better to drop into my own bed at my apartment and steal a few hours of sleep before I stumbled off to my job.

My sudden absence from Jill's life was a necessary evil, I had decided. And my neglect wasn't limited to her: I wasn't paying attention to my department either or looking after any other business in my life. I didn't like what had become of me, but it was just temporary. Taking on the Queen Anne was like taking on a sinking ship. I fervently believed that I'd get it under control soon. Six months—a year, tops. In the end, I insisted, it'd be worth it. A little pain for a lot of gain.

Now, I squinted at Jill across the table. Was it just the candle-light that made her look sad? The boombox outside moved away. Suddenly the house was quiet. I said: "Have you changed your mind?"

"I haven't changed my mind," she said quickly. "I just want to make sure we're in a steadier place than we are right now."

"And we're not in a steady place because . . . ?"

"Because the house has no plumbing, no ceilings, no useable closets, no locking front or back door, no heat—you want me to go on?"

"No, I see your point. But soon," I said, "all that will change."

Just then Charlie sniffed at one of the candles. Suddenly his whiskers were in flames. Jill and I leaped to smother the fire with our napkins. We quickly extinguished him. Charlie—now whiskerless—appeared unfazed. The room reeked of his burnt hair.

Jill stroked his head. Charlie uttered one of his croaky meows. She laughed: "He's so old, he doesn't know where he is."

"Promise me," I said, "when I'm that far gone you'll slip me a pill."

"We'll make a pact," she said.

There, I thought, *that's better: the future is ours.*

10

SUB-CONTRACTORS

THE SUNNY MARCH MORNING the sub-contractors arrived, I felt like the captain of a ship, making ready for a world voyage. Everything seemed well in hand. One crew was taking out windows, another was pulling out plumbing, and a third was clambering onto the roof. I myself was hauling the kitchen door into our small front yard, where I could strip it. Suddenly I heard a *whoop!* above me. Then I saw an empty six-pack beer container whirly-gigging from the roof. It was 10:00 a.m.

Over the next several months, I learned a lot about sub-contractors. Roofers seemed to be the most colorful. As far as I can tell, the typical roofer in these parts is a skinny thirty-four-year-old with long stringy hair, a brutal sun-wrinkled face, and a love of danger. Hard rock is his music of choice, which he'll blare from your rooftop, and Bud is his beer of choice, which he'll drink to excess—sometimes from your rooftop. He shows up wearing a dirty t-shirt and dirtier blue jeans. By the day's end, these will be black with tar. His fingers are permanently blackened from handling the stuff. He gets paid in cash. Some days he doesn't show up. Then he can't be located for weeks. When he does show up again, he'll offer vague excuses if you press him. If you're smart, you won't press him.

I discovered that the roofing company I thought I hired wasn't the roofing company that showed up—because many of the biggest and best companies sub out their work during the high season. My crew consisted of five men. The foreman was a slouched, pot-bellied, tousle-haired forty-something who looked forever puzzled. He had bid the job so low, he couldn't afford to rent a "cherry picker," one of those trucks with a mechanical arm that lifts a bucket up high. Instead, he sent his men to the roof on forty-foot ladders.

To appreciate the altitude of a forty-foot ladder, you'd have to imagine standing on a highway overpass and looking down. Now multiply that times two.

In addition to our huge flat roof, we also have the tower's shingled roof, as well as some other shingled areas at the front. Shingling a pitched roof from the top of a forty foot ladder is like trying to make a club sandwich while walking a tight rope. At forty feet, the wind can be three times the intensity of street level. And a sudden move can make the ladder heave and buck, even with two strong men anchoring the bottom.

On this particular morning, after the roofers had downed their breakfast beers, I found Nicholas standing on the sidewalk, hands on his hip, peering suspiciously up at the roof. He was wearing a flannel shirt and blue jeans, a tool belt strapped jauntily at his waist. My contractor.

"Those guys are insane," he said, shaking his head in disbelief.

I agreed.

Right now they were taking down the original copper gutters that had hugged the roofline for over a hundred years. It was beautiful work, the way the original roofers had mounted the copper with welded hooks so that it flowed smoothly around the tower's cap. I had assumed that we would try to replicate that work but now realized we weren't going to get anywhere near such quality.

The original gutters had run down the front of the house and into a cast iron pipe that sluiced the water—in seventy feet of five-inch pipe—through the entire length of the basement and out the

a sixty-foot ladder for a forty-foot climb

backyard to a concrete trough that diverted the water to another pipe, which sent the water racing under the sidewalk and into the side street. It had been a clever piece of engineering. Later, with my new reciprocating saw, I would cut that iron drainpipe out of the basement in heavy eight-foot sections. Our new gutters would drain directly to the sidewalk.

I didn't have time to watch and worry over the sub-contractors. I had just found the original kitchen door among the piles of junk in the basement. This door, which would open onto the porch, was to be my first attempt at stripping paint. I set the door across two sawhorses in our small front yard, turned on the electric paint-stripping tool, then went inside, because every five or ten minutes something or someone called to me from the house.

Rick had given me the heating tool he had used to strip paint in his house. It was his way of passing the torch, literally. The tool was no more than a plastic handle affixed to a loop of metal that was wired for heat and housed in an open tin box, which you would set on, or hold near, the surface you wanted to strip. Rick had also given me his paint-stripping tools, which were old, heavy-duty and very useful.

The heating tool covered as much area as a handprint and worked surprisingly well, the paint bubbling up fairly quickly. As I was just learning how to use it, I hadn't yet gauged *how* quickly it heated. And so, having set it on the door to warm up, I returned to the front yard to find the door in flames. Panicked, I knocked off the heating tool, then smothered the flames with my leather work gloves. As I muttered a curse, I heard laughing behind me. Standing on the sidewalk, silver hair neatly combed, his eyes gleaming, Rick could not have looked more amused.

I was beginning to realize that 1) Rick would always be watching, 2) Rick would always delight in my mishaps, and 3) Rick would never lift a finger to help me because, as he'd said in so many words, he had paid his renovation dues long ago.

It would have been helpful to have Jill around, but she was trying to make some money. If she wasn't teaching one of her three classes at the college, she was working at Traditions, where she also kept watch for things we could use in the house. Increasingly, I was cutting out on my own work and was beginning to feel divided, as if I was cheating somehow and was afraid to be found out. But I couldn't stay away from the house, there was so much to do.

When I next stepped outside I saw one of the roofers sitting on the edge of our small yard. He was hunched over in an odd way, sitting too still, one hand clasping the back of his head. I knew something was wrong. Had he taken ill suddenly? As he pulled his hand away, I saw that it was red with blood. At first I thought he had fallen from a few rungs of the ladder. I soon learned that a piece of the old copper gutter had just dropped forty feet and slammed the back of his head. None of the roofers were wearing a hard hat.

Five minutes later, the foreman drove the injured man to the emergency room at Union Memorial up the street and roof work stopped for the day.

The next day, the roofers did not show up, but Donald, my house painter, did. Most Baltimore row houses have ornate cornice work made of stamped tin around the perimeter of their roofs. Getting someone to paint the cornice is difficult and expensive because it's so high. Most painters told me they'd have to erect a scaffold to do the job. Scaffolding would cost thousands of dollars. The painter I hired, a Jamaican immigrant, gave me an offer I could not refuse. But now I saw why: he was going to paint from the top of a forty-foot ladder. To secure his safety, he had hired a burly young man to hold the ladder steady.

Donald was about forty and had a wife and two grown children in Jamaica and a girlfriend with a small child here in the States. A lanky, easygoing fellow with a *café au lait* complexion and a beatific smile, he called me "Mr. Ron" and assured me that his work was top-notch: I would not have to paint the cornice again for five to seven years. (He would be right about that: the paint still holds.)

He assured me too that he knew what he was doing—he would be fine on the ladder. As he began climbing, paint can and brush affixed to his belt, I watched him anxiously. His grimace of determination betrayed his own worry. Slowly, methodically,

he did the job—occasionally scolding his assistant for not paying attention to the ladder. By the day's end he had completed the
front of the house.

The next day, the roofers were back with *their* forty-foot
ladders. The injured man was back too, twenty stitches richer.
"Fuckers didn't warn me they were dropping," he said of the accident. Today they were going to tackle the outermost area of the
tower roof. The shingler, who looked the typical roofer to a tee,
boasted that every shingle he laid down would stay down.

I still had the plumbers to think about, and the window-in-
stallers and the floor-finisher.

When Nicholas showed up, today in his realtor's suit, he took
one look at the forty-foot ladder and the shingler readying for his
climb, and said, "That's it. We're stopping this right now."

Nicholas told the foreman you can't shingle a roof like that
from a ladder. It's too damned dangerous. They'd have to rent a
cherry picker. Nicholas agreed that we'd help defray the cost. At
that point I could see relief in the shingler's face, which mirrored
my own.

So the next day, the cherry picker showed up, parked on the
sidewalk in front of the house. Nicholas pointed out that they
should have laid a sheet of plywood under the machine's massive
wheels to disperse its weight. As they had failed to do that, the
machine's weight had cracked the sidewalk. That's when I learned
that, in Baltimore, the homeowner is responsible for sidewalk
upkeep, which includes not only shoveling snow in the winter but
also replacing broken sections of concrete. We have twenty-five
feet of sidewalk at the front of the house and 130 feet along the
side. Casually, Nicholas told me that routine sidewalk repair can
cost thousands of dollars.

By this point—just two weeks into the rehab—I was aware of a
disturbing pattern: so far the cleanout had taken three Dumpsters
instead of one; now the roof was going to cost hundreds more

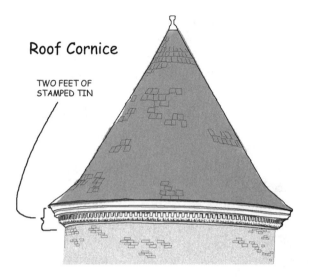

Roof Cornice

TWO FEET OF
STAMPED TIN

because the subcontractor had underbid the job; and my front sidewalk was cracked, which was going to cost me plenty.

Donald had convinced the roofers to let him ride the cherry picker to paint some hard-to-reach areas, including the tower's blunt metal pinnacle. I was glad to see him happy. By the day's end, the tower roof was re-shingled and it looked great. The cornice was done too. So I was happy, even though there was a lot more to do up there. We needed gutters, for example.

The next day, the roofers didn't show up. The huge cherry picker remained parked on our front sidewalk. For four days, at $200 a day, they let the machine sit idle. Eventually, the roofers returned to finish the job. Nicholas made them hang the gutter again over the back porch. This is the supervising contractor's job: to bully the subcontractors into doing the right thing.

* * *

Our plumber, Lou, could not have been a nicer guy. I had hired him because, unlike the others who had come by to make their estimates, Lou seemed to enjoy himself. A man of medium build, with curly blond hair and a Baltimore accent, he entered the house like a long-time neighbor, offering me a firm handshake. Then he glanced around and said, "Man, isn't this place cool?"

I gave him the tour.

"Oh, look at that—a butler's pantry," he said, shaking his head in wonder. "You don't see these anymore." Then he peered at the damaged ceiling. "We'll have to replace that cast iron. Shouldn't be too hard to pull out. PVC will be cheaper and last forever, though a little noisier."

Upstairs, he frowned at the makeshift plumbing that someone had tried to install for the boys. "They didn't know what to do with this short rough, so they raised the floor," Lou explained. "We don't want a raised floor around the toilet, Ron."

"You can fix that?"

"Oh, yeah."

Lou was full of suggestions, firing them off with enthusiasm: *we'll run your line down this way, pull a three-inch pipe behind this joist, might have to Fernco that coupling, but it'll be fine.* Nothing was too difficult for Lou, apparently. He almost made the work sound fun. When he rolled his eyes at another bogus frat house plumbing repair and said, "That's shit," I knew he was the guy for me.

His crew removed the old oil tank that sat in the basement, then they dismantled the old cast-iron furnace, which was as big as a bunker. I'd thought we'd have to live with that thing crowding the basement but Lou pointed out that old furnaces were made in sections that could be easily dismantled. So he recycled the thing.

His crew was fast and efficient. Within a week, we had our plumbing back. And now, at last, working toilets. It was time for me to move in—with or without Jill.

11
LOVE IN THE HOUSE

BY MAY 2000, the contractors were gone, my new appliances had arrived, and I was moved in. "Moved in" isn't quite accurate. I couldn't unpack my belongings because I had no place to put them. Like the rest of the house, the closets weren't ready for anything but major renovation. Readying the closets—plastering, painting, building shelves, and installing electric lines for lights—would take at least a full week of work. I didn't have a week to work on closets. I had to get to the really important damage, like the crumbling walls and ceilings. I couldn't set up any furniture because every room was a construction zone. I slept on a foam pad on the floor. Corona, my cat, didn't know what to make of all the space. She'd creep from room to room, close to the walls. Then she'd perch on the highest stack of boxes and watch me owlishly while I worked.

The company of my skittish cat hardly made the Queen Anne homey. As long as I worked myself to exhaustion every night, I was okay with my decrepit, too-big surroundings. But the minute I began to contemplate that I might live alone in this wrecked behemoth, I felt overwhelming dread. Though I trusted Jill and believed she would be honest with me, I feared that if I showed her how desperate I was becoming, she would bolt. Something was holding her back and it seemed she couldn't say what it was exactly. What was I missing?

Romantic love was a mystery to me. My mother frequently told us boys that love (meaning marriage) is "hard work." As a child, I imagined the work was like shoveling snow from the driveway: you had to do it to get on with life. But I also pictured romantic love as transformative and permanent—a life-long magic. My view wasn't far removed from the fairy-tale folderol we're fed as children. Boys are no less immune than girls to the fantasy that your loved one is somehow magical, and will, just by entering your life, transform your pumpkins into gilded carriages. My mother's own story was a kind of fairytale. She was an Appalachian girl in a rural high school when she met my father, five years her senior and a veteran of the recent war. He swept her away to California and a much better life. She often joked that had she stayed in Lenoir, North Carolina, she would have married a factory worker, grown fat on bad food, and lost all of her teeth by the time she was forty. This made a nice story but privately my mother suggested—with statements like, "it's hard work"—that their marriage, and by extension any marriage, was far from perfect.

Not long after I embarked upon my second marriage, I was standing at a urinal in a department store bathroom, where I saw these words scrawled on the tiled wall: "I love you, Mary Lou." It surprised me, this simple, penciled declaration, so different from the usual men's room offerings. More surprising was a second statement, printed in another hand (blue ink), directly below the first: "Then marry her, you fool." *Yes,* I thought, *marry her.* And automatically, I heard a childhood ditty singing through my head, "First comes love, then comes marriage. . . ." as if one naturally follows the other. That the bathroom wall advisor would call his advisee a "fool" suggested that this was a chance not to be missed, that it might be the chance of a lifetime because love—true love—is a rare thing. I suppose that most of us believe that romantic love is true enough if it leads to marriage. But what do we believe if

that marriage leads to divorce? Do we assume that our love, as hot
as it may have burned, was ultimately false?

I married Sarah, my second wife, because I was afraid of being
alone. At twenty-four, she was eleven years my junior and already
divorced. I refused to believe that she was as lost and desperate
as I. Against all good advice, we eloped. It was almost as if we
married on a dare. My mother was appalled. "Ronald, what *happened?*" she asked the next day on the phone. She might as well
have been asking about a car accident.

"We're married!" I said. "Isn't that great?"

"I don't understand."

"What's to understand, Mom? Sarah and I *got married!*"
I thought my mother would want me to get married again.

"You married that little girl?"

I was standing in the front room of the apartment that Sarah
and I shared. We'd been together for less than six months. When I
heard Mom say, "that little girl," I felt the old tug-of-war she and I
had waged since I was a teenager. It had always seemed to me that
my mother never understood who I was or what I needed. *You
know her name,* I wanted to snap, *and you know she's not a little
girl.* But I held back, because in recent years I'd learned that the
best strategy with Mom was to pretend I didn't hear what she'd
just said.

"We are very happy," I announced.

"It's so quick, Ronald. You could have taken *more time!*"

"What does it matter? We love each other!"

"Love?" she said. "I knew you were dating but you didn't mention *love.*"

I thought I was in love. I desperately wanted to be in love. And
I was grateful that Sarah seemed to feel as I did. Because she was
smart and accomplished and admired, I felt worthy by association.
Stubborn and painfully honest, she challenged me. She didn't like

bullshit. She could not abide happy talk or palaver. If you couldn't talk to her about something that mattered, she wasn't interested in talking. I thought she saw that I was running scared, that I was afraid of making myself vulnerable. I thought she was intent on exposing everything about herself and those around her—her gay ex-husband, her recent affair with a married man, her eating disorder (now under control). I thought she was going to make me a better person.

"I've loved her for a long time," I insisted, trying to disguise my irritation. "Wasn't that obvious?" A month earlier I had taken Sarah to visit my mother. My mother disapproved of her immediately and, in private, called her "a damaged little thing."

As Mom sputtered on the other end of the line, I added, "Just be happy for us."

"I *do* want you to be happy," she said sadly. "You know how much I love you."

"This is the real thing," I continued. "Sarah and I are on the same plane."

"What plane?"

"*Plane*—we're in harmony. She likes books and writing and. . . my pizza."

"Well, who doesn't like pizza, honey?"

"Mom, are you listening to me?"

"I don't know WHAT I'm listening to," she lamented. "You meet this young girl and then overnight you get married."

"She's not that young! And it wasn't overnight!"

"Twenty-four is *young*, Ronald."

"Well, it's not like she's a virgin. She's been married before."

"All the more reason to go slow," she cautioned. "I don't believe she's told you the whole story."

"I don't go slow," I said, defiant now. "I never go slow!"

My mother sighed. "Oh, I know that, Ronald."

Four years later, Sarah walked out without much explanation and even less warning. I begged her to stay. I wailed with grief. It was humiliating and devastating. Only later, after our divorce, did I learn that she was having an affair with one of her running buddies—the guy she had me sublet our apartment to during our separation. She married him a year after our divorce, then divorced him three years after that: the fourth divorce for her. What was Sarah looking for? True love?

Marriage, as we know, began as a business arrangement. Only in the last two hundred years did the question of love come up and then only among those who could afford to factor love into the arrangement. When friends saw Jill and me together for the first time, they took me aside and enthused, "Oh, you've picked the right one!" So what could I say about having picked the wrong one so many times? How can love, if you're in love, be wrong? As my mother generously granted after my first divorce, "Everyone's entitled to one mistake." Especially, she seemed to imply, a mistake of youth. In most states, a couple cannot marry until at least two or more days after purchasing their marriage license. A good measure to cool the impetuous, but apparently not good enough, given the divorce rates. And what about us repeat offenders? Perhaps we should be granted a writ of abeyance, something like a learner's permit.

For most people I know, both gay and straight, marriage seems to be the ultimate destination, probably because, for the longest time, marriage has seemed as basic a human urge as breathing or procreation. It's also been held up as the pinnacle of civilized behavior. One early nineteenth-century sage, writing in the first edition of the Encyclopedia Americana (1831), asserted that the institution of marriage rests "on the fundamental principles of our being. . ." Anthropologists have argued otherwise. There's nothing natural or inevitable about marriage. Faust's devil isn't far wrong when he describes marriage as a "ceremonial toy" that has little or nothing to do with love. As romantic love is a relatively new addition, can we really insist that it be the centerpiece of marriage? Sixty years ago, a French visitor to the U.S. noted in wonder that "in America the terms 'love' and 'marriage' are practically equivalent; that when one 'loves' one must get married instantly. . ."

Maybe we are shallow people. Maybe we are too scared to let love go its own way, and so we seal it up in the box of marriage. Two years before Sarah left me, her own mother left her second marriage of twenty years to marry the man who claimed to be her high school sweetheart. As it turned out, she and her long-lost had dated only a few times in high school. But they created for themselves a fantasy that was hard to resist. Within eighteen months, Sara's mother had divorced her second husband and married her third. It was as if she and her new lover could realize their fantasy only by making it legal. What would have happened had they decided to cohabitate instead of marry?

All I was asking of Jill was cohabitation—for now. Neither one of us had mentioned "marriage," though it was the elephant in every room. I was much too skittish about my judgment to talk of marriage. But I wanted marriage. We had to get married eventually. Despite all I've just said about love and marriage, I'm not bohemian enough or bold enough to attempt long-term love without the structure of marriage. Marriage is, for better or worse, a safe house.

This time, unlike the other times, I looked at my loved one first as a partner, because this time, unlike the other times, we were facing a mutual challenge: the wrecked Queen Anne. Maybe this put us in the greater, much older tradition of marriage, where a couple comes together not to make whoopee but, rather, to take care of business. True enough, much of our whoopee went out the window that first year. We were exhausted and distracted early on.

Working together gave us an opportunity to see each other in extreme circumstances and privately we both knew this was dangerous. We might fix up the house, but would we still love each other when it was done?

One morning, as we were driving on an errand, Jill—in the passenger seat—produced a bottle of unopened soda from her purse. One of those natural food sodas whose top you can't twist off.

"Got a bottle opener?" she asked.

Two hands on the wheel, I smirked at her. "Does it look like I have an opener?"

She started pawing around in the car—there was junk on the back seat: door hinges, nails, rusted screws.

"There's no opener," I insisted.

"This will do," she said, pulling up half a door hinge.

"That won't work," I scoffed. "You'll just have to wait."

Ignoring me, she hooked the hinge to the bottle top, then, in one fluid motion, popped off the cap.

"Ah ha!" she said with satisfaction, then proceeded to drink deeply.

This was the kind of try-anything attitude she brought to the Queen Anne. I loved this about her. But it scared me too because I couldn't *control* her. It was very likely that, like two stunt pilots flying in the same space, we would collide in midair.

The first meal I fixed for Jill in the Queen Anne was pizza from scratch, my specialty. We sat on a sheet of cardboard in the living room, surrounded by piles of shutters, stacks of two-by-fours, drums of paint, lengths of molding. Above us, on the walls to either side, were the fraternity insignias, painted in gold and blue. Harriet nosed aimlessly across the recently refinished parquet floors, which gleamed brightly in the glow of the single floor lamp I'd plugged in. The floors were the only thing that looked right.

I laid a small square of plywood over a five-gallon paint drum, then put down the hot pizza. "Someday soon we'll have a better table than this," I promised.

"It should be mahogany," Jill said. "That would be era-appropriate."

"A big table, I imagine."

"Twelve feet would do," she quipped.

"I'll add it to the list." I picked up a piece of pizza. We both love pepperoni.

"That looks hot," she cautioned.

"Very hot," I agreed. I took a bite. Then: "Damn!"

Jill shook her head and smiled.

My mouth half full and still smarting, I said: "What do you think we should do about the mantels?" Behind us, the fireplace was still crowded with trash—something we had overlooked in the clean-out. The mantel was gone and the surrounding plaster was crumbling.

"We should look around," she said matter-of-factly. "You'll probably want something pretty fancy."

I didn't like the tone of this, but I wasn't going to let my dismay show. "Marble?"

"Sure. If you can afford it."

What about us? What can we afford?

I wanted to tell her something fascinating about the house, something that would pique her interest and make her exclaim, *I can't wait to move in!* But all that came to mind was my suspicion that a bat was living in the attic. I hadn't *seen* the bat, exactly. I had sensed its flitting presence in the darkness above me on more than one occasion as I awoke abruptly from a fitful sleep.

Obviously, this wasn't something I was going to share now.

I chewed my pizza. Jill chewed hers. Harriet circled, claws clacking.

Jill said, "I love your pizza, Ronny. You could open a restaurant."

"Okay," I said. "I'll add that to the list too."

She eyed one of the frat insignias skeptically. "When do you think you'll paint?"

You'll paint. Your house. Your mantle.

"Soon," I said. "Maybe this summer. Our deadline is September, don't forget. I can probably get a good deal on five-gallon drums of off-white."

"Are you kidding?" she blurted.

"What's the matter with off-white?"

She laughed. "In *this* house?

"Off-white is classic," I said.

"It's so blah!" she said.

"You have some other color in mind?" I asked innocently.

"*Colors*, Ron. Mustard, celery, topaz! Oh, the possibilities!"

"It hadn't occurred to me," I said.

"Ron, the house would disappear behind all that off-white."

"I guess it would look a little boring, now that you mention it."

She took another bite. "Sometimes, it surprises me how conservative you are."

"That's why I need you around, Jilly." I kissed her free hand. She smiled.

Then I said, "Your piano would fit nicely in the music room, have you noticed?" I nodded in that direction.

"Yeah," she said, "I guess it would."

"We could get Les to help us move it."

"Yeah," she agreed.

"When do you think that'd be?"

She shrugged. "Hard to say."

Wearily I put down my half-eaten slice. "What's it going to take to get you to move in, Jill?"

"We're not ready."

"What would it take to make us ready?"

"For starters, I don't know why I'm moving."

"Because we *love each other* and *want to share a life*?"

"Yeah, I know that. But what is this house to me? What will I be, your renter?"

"I'd like you to contribute to the expenses, sure, but it's not like you'd be a *lodger*, Jill."

"Then you could kick me out at any time," she said.

I noticed that Harriet had sneaked away with my half-eaten slice. She growled when I glanced at her.

"*Kick you out?*" I half-laughed. "Why would I kick you out?"

"I'd have no guarantees! You'd have all the power."

"I don't get it, Jill. It's not like I can put your name on the deed."

"Why not?"

"What?"

"Why not put me on the deed?" she asked.

"Because you didn't *buy* the house!"

"But you tell me it's as much my house as yours," she countered.

"Jill, you didn't *buy the house!*"

"But I'd be helping with the mortgage."

"Yeah, you would."

"So I'd be just paying rent?"

"Okay, yeah, it'd be like paying rent," I said. "Surely you understand why I can't put you on the deed."

"Not really."

"Wow," I said.

"What *wow*?"

"I can't believe you don't get it, considering what happened in my last divorce."

"I *know*," she said. "Sarah said she wanted out and promised she wouldn't take anything from you if you let her go."

"And then she took me to the cleaners. You realize what I could have done with that money, how badly I need it now?"

"I'm not Sarah."

"But you want half my house!"

Jill smiled a crooked smile. "*Your* house. Right."

At hearing this, I felt my heart dive off a high bridge.

"You know what I mean," I said.

"Yeah," she said sadly. "I know what you mean."

"Jill, don't be that way."

She didn't seem angry. And I wasn't angry. But this was a fight, no two ways about it. And it was the worst kind of fight because we both thought we were right.

Jill stayed the night, but we hardly touched in bed. Harriet snored from her blanket nearby. Corona slept, as usual, at the foot of the bed. I lay awake and watched the darkness for bats.

12

SOME THINGS
I DIDN'T KNOW

JILL LEFT EARLY FOR WORK the next morning. I had taken another day off from duties at the college, so I lay in. When I awoke, it felt late but looked like dawn, long blocks of sunlight thrown across the room. I heard tapping, like someone rapping at the window. Except I was on the second floor. Corona wasn't around. Jill had taken Harriet. The tapping was insistent, as if to say, *Let me in!* I sat up, pulled on my jeans and boots, a sweatshirt, then stopped short of the stairs. The noise came from above—the third-floor skylight over the main staircase. Vandals? Mischief-makers? Peering into the opaque light, alarm pulsing at the back of my tongue, I saw that it was a. . . crow, tapping a bone against the skylight glass, no doubt trying to get at the marrow. Jesus. How fitting for a city that claims Edgar Alan Poe!

I had not been to the roof yet. In fact, I wasn't sure how to get there. A trap door in the ceiling of the rear room closet on the third floor opened to the attic. I'd never seen the attic. As I played a beam of light into its gloom, I was surprised to discover that it was no higher than a crawl space at the back but rose to nearly eight feet at the front. The floor of the attic was massive beam-work separated by dirty gray piles of Rockwool, an old insulating material. Mouse droppings were heaped here and there among the wooly mounds. I steered my light to the front of the house and the wide darkness of the tower. Suddenly, a bird—or bat—bolted with a startling smack of wings. Apparently, there were holes in the walls big enough for it/them to get in and out. Sunlight streaked through at the front. I wasn't in the mood to attempt a visit.

I tried the trap door to the roof, just above me. It didn't budge. I discovered that it was latched. Even unlatched, it was difficult to move because roof tar had nearly glued it shut. When it gave finally, I was in a shaft of sunlight and cool air. I clambered out. Our house has a flat roof, a huge tarred expanse that slants ever-so-slightly to the rear. Standing on it is like standing in the crow's nest of an old ship: there's a brisk breeze, the low clutter of Baltimore's horizon on all sides, the sun too bright, the sky too wide. It was both exhilarating and frightening. It seemed I was adrift without a crew. There were no more sub-contractors coming because I had run out of money to pay them. They had refinished the floors and replaced the plumbing, windows, and roof. The rest of the wreck was now mine to revive or bring to final ruin. I was just beginning to understand that I had pinned too much hope on Nicholas. He alone couldn't do all that needed doing, even if I had the money to pay him. I couldn't even be sure if he'd be by today. And Jill?

On the skylight, I found a scatter of chicken bones and one pork chop bone. I gathered them up. I noticed that the crow and his cohorts were in the alley, picking through the buffet of Tuesday's garbage.

Later, downstairs, I stood in the bedroom bay and scouted the road for Nicholas. I saw Rick making his morning tour of the block, his head held high, his eyes inspecting every house, gate, and garden for trouble. His tidy silver mustache and pugnacious underbite made him look like a sergeant recently retired from a British regiment. Everyday, he would repeat his foot patrol two or three more times, nodding and waving if he saw me.

While waiting for Nicholas, I swept up and moved around piles of tools and buckets of paint on the first floor. When it looked like he wouldn't show, I decided to install new electrical outlets in the living room. When Victorian houses like the Queen Anne got electricity, usually between 1900–1920, there were few appliances to plug into a socket: a floor lamp and maybe a table fan. That's why each room had only one outlet. I knew nothing about working with electricity. But I was desperate. And I had seven how-to books to consult. Desperation would drive me hard, compelling me to do the most harrowing things. The prospect of working with electricity made me quake: either I'd burn down the house or kill myself. Or both.

I decided to start simply: just run the wire to a new outlet box. Don't even worry about the connections yet. But here's the problem: little things get in the way—a stubborn screw, a snagged wire, a brick. Cut a hole in the lathe and plaster wall, watch for the studs (sixteen inches apart), be careful the lathe doesn't pull away and more plaster doesn't fall off, now consider the two-foot hole you've created for an outlet the size of playing card: how are you going to hang the box in that hole? Oh, Jesus, it just goes on and on!

When Nicholas arrived finally, I was relieved. He asked what I was doing. I showed him. Gently, he explained that I was using three-wire cable for two-wire connections. It wasn't a big deal, it just meant I had an extra wire left over for every connection. I had wondered about that.

"C'mon," he said. "Let's do something else."

Another time, he came by to find me cutting two-by-fours with my new circular saw. Problem was, every cut was coming out crooked.

"What'd you do to the blade?" he asked, inspecting my saw.

"I put in a new one," I explained, "but it didn't help."

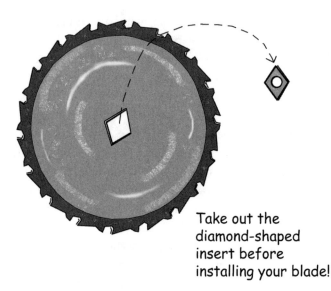

Take out the
diamond-shaped
insert before
installing your blade!

"Ron, you have to remove the diamond-shaped insert in the middle of the blade before installing it. See this? Otherwise it won't seat."

"Oh," I said, "I wondered why the blade kept coming loose."

Nicholas shook his head sadly. "You could hurt yourself," he cautioned.

My fund of ignorance was monumental and it embarrassed me nearly every hour of every day. When the new garbage disposal stopped working, for instance, I thought it was broken. Actually, it was just locked up. I knew only this much: every garbage disposal has an overload button on its undercarriage. If you make the disposal work too hard, it will automatically trip a switch so that you won't burn out the motor. All you have to do is press that little button underneath to get it working again. But mine wasn't working no matter how much I pressed the button.

An overfilled disposal, I learned, will not only trip the overload button but will also lock up the entire mechanism, too much

self-service
wrenchette

mashed food caught in its teeth. All I had to do was use the disposal's hex key to unlock it. Hex key? Every disposal comes with a hex key, which you fit into an insert under the disposal. This allows you to turn the carriage manually, which clears the teeth.

Scrawled on my little hex key is the descriptor "self-service wrenchette."

Some experts in the world of construction took pity on me. Donald, the Jamaican painter and wallboard expert, showed me how to use my new belt sander on the door I was stripping. "You let the machine do the work, Mr. Ron." He allowed the sander to glide easily under his hand. "You do not press down. That will burn out the motor, man." I would burn out three sanders.

An old plumber at the plumbing supply store, where a sign informs laymen that "the trade" will be served first, showed me how to put together the new faucet I'd bought at an online auction. All of the plumbers in attendance just shook their heads in dismay when they heard where I'd bought the faucet. Online

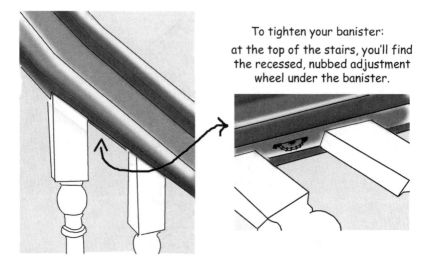

To tighten your banister:
at the top of the stairs, you'll find
the recessed, nubbed adjustment
wheel under the banister.

goods are notoriously undocumented (without instructions) and often shoddy. Almost as an afterthought the old expert cautioned, "And don't you put silicone on that rubber washer inside or you'll never get the thing apart again." How did he know that this was precisely what I had been planning to do?

When the expert behind the counter at another plumbing supply store claimed that he could *not* help me figure out how to create an odd angle for the waste line under our bathroom sink, one of the pros among his customers showed me how, patiently picking the right parts from the shelves and guiding me through the assembly.

I didn't know—until told by Jerry, an engineer who happened to be passing by—that you can't seal the gap between your foundation and the sidewalk with cement because cement is too rigid: it cracks and crumbles. You have to use a silicone or latex product that will both adhere tenaciously to the masonry and flex with the vibrations. Houses are always shifting and vibrating.

I didn't know—until Mark, the wood-turner, told me—that a tension rod runs through old banisters and can be adjusted via a recessed, knurled wheel under the banister itself. That's how you tighten wobbly banisters.

Not all experts were helpful. After examining our first floor parquet, the project manager from a local home improvement company proclaimed, "You try sanding this floor and everything's gonna come up because the sander's gonna pop off the nail heads." He'd already told me that the entryway, where the parquet was nearly black from water staining, was beyond repair and would have to be replaced.

"You mean I'll have to replace ALL of this parquet?"

"Looks that way, yep."

"That's twelve hundred square feet!"

He nodded. "Well, you could keep it the way it is."

"It looks horrible the way it is!" I exclaimed.

"Yep," he said.

A tall, clean-cut guy, about forty, wearing a flannel shirt, well-pressed khakis, and clean work boots, he seemed professional enough. And I supposed he was somebody's husband and father. But his definitive pronouncements, fired off after minimal inspection, made me suspicious.

When I took him to the porch for a look, he simply shook his head in firm disapproval. "Tear it down," he said.

I gaped at him in disbelief: "All three stories?"

"It all needs painting, you can see that," he said. "The wood's got a lot of age. It's sagging. I'd replace it with something new."

"What would it cost to replicate this porch with new materials?"

Without blinking, he said, "Forty thousand."

"That's two-thirds my rehab budget!"

He shrugged.

I couldn't get rid of this guy fast enough.

James, a flooring expert recommended to me by Sue and John across the street, was a broad-chested man who had the swagger of a running back and the winning smile of a preacher.

"What do you think?" I asked as he surveyed the water-damaged entry.

"It'll come up fine."

"You can save it?" I nearly croaked in disbelief.

"Sure, like I said."

"What about the rest of the parquet?"

"It'll come up fine."

"Won't you pop off the nail heads?"

"*What?*"

"Won't the sander pop off the nail heads?"

"This floor's never been sanded, anybody can see. You've got plenty of wood to sand."

At some point, you've got to have faith, I decided, so—without a third opinion—I gave the job to James.

* * *

I didn't know anything about windows until I met Marvin. All of the Queen Anne's thirty-three windows needed replacing. Most of them are three-by-six feet—as big as doors. Replacing them would be the greatest expense in this first phase of rehabbing, taking one quarter of the budget. In keeping with the historic restoration guidelines, the windows had to be the same size and style of the originals. But the new ones would be dual-paned and aluminum-framed.

Marvin was the third salesman I'd called to the house. A small disheveled man with thinning hair and big eyeglasses, he pulled up in a dusty fifteen-year-old Ford. He said he was the president of his company. On the one hand, this impressed me: how many company presidents peddle their own products door to door? On the other hand, this gave me pause: couldn't he afford to hire salesmen?

His sample was certainly top-notch, a suitcase that opened to show a cut-away corner of the window. Like the other salesmen, he pointed out the dual-paned efficiency, the ease of cleaning, etc.

Unlike the others, he was adamant about the superiority of his product. The minute he saw me hesitate, he started asking hard questions: *Look at the ratings for these windows. How much air is getting in? How much heat is getting out? Is the frame reinforced?* He seemed possessed of a simmering outrage at all other products, which—he explained in great detail—were poorly designed. He filled me with self-doubt. As he left, he said, "A house like yours deserves the best windows, Mr. Tanner."

When he phoned a few days later, I let slip that I was inclined to go with the second dealer I'd seen. "Have they shown you their NFRC figures?" he scolded. "Don't make a move until you've compared U-ratings and especially their air leakage numbers. I bet we beat theirs by double."

I admitted that I didn't know those figures. Still, I insisted, the competitor's product looked impressive.

"Their product is crap!" he snapped. "You *ask for those ratings.* I showed you mine. Do you need to see them again?"

"No, your figures were quite convincing."

"You've got to think this through," he said. "We're talking a lifetime investment."

Yes, yes, I agreed.

After I got off the phone, my ears were burning: Marvin either made me feel stupid or guilty, I couldn't decide which. I did some research on the internet. The National Fenestration Rating Council sets standards for window quality and all new windows should carry a sticker that displays the window's ratings for heat loss, heat gain, and light transmittance. More important, though, is air leakage: if this information is not on the NFCR sticker, you'll have to ask for it from the dealer, who is obliged to reveal it. Many won't be happy to.

I asked the second dealer to bring his specs in writing. When he did the next day, I saw that his windows allowed a whopping .3 cubic feet of air in per minute. The best windows allow only .01

to .06 cubic feet per minute, and Marvin's windows were within this range.

So Marvin got the sale, nodding his satisfaction as he filled out the paperwork that afternoon: *You see, Mr. Tanner, how quality wins out?*

13

JILL'S WAY

UNDER NORMAL CIRCUMSTANCES, I would have been the first to admit that a newly romanced couple should *not* rehab an old house together. But I had never owned a house. Having been brave enough to buy a big, ruined place against all good advice, and having won the bid against the interloping young couple, I felt I had done the hardest part. Now the fun begins, right? A little paint, a little plaster, some decorating. Then Jill and I would get married in a splendid ceremony that would celebrate both our good work and our wondrous love. We were going to be heroes of the neighborhood.

Up to this point, contractors had crowded the house and it seemed we were making tremendous progress: the floors sanded, the roof repaired, the plumbing installed, the appliances delivered. But soon everybody was gone and Nicholas was dropping by only every other day and Jill and I were alone together in that big wrecked house. We should have had a plan, obviously. We should have laid some ground rules. Instead, we simply walked into the house and started doing things. I don't know why I was surprised that we were at odds the very first day we began working together.

"I found the side panel to the original door!" Jill announced happily that morning. She had just stepped from the basement stairs into the kitchen.

I looked up from the wall that was crumbling in my hands. Every time I touched the plaster, it fell away. Soon, half the wall would be on the floor. How could I fix a house that wouldn't hold still for fixing?

"What side panel?" I asked.

Jill was wearing a black beret pinned to her hair, a tattered sweater, her jeans rolled to her calves, steel-toed work boots, and no work gloves. She refused to wear gloves.

For hours she had been rummaging through the piles of salvage we had gathered in the basement. It would take us years to sort through it all. Among that junk, we knew, were many of the architectural details the fraternity had stripped away: balusters and corbels and brackets and molding. I had told Jill—more than once—that all of this could wait. We had plastering and painting and general repairs to do.

But Jill had her own ideas. *To me* it seemed she was simply playing around, as if the house were a hobby. She didn't seem to appreciate the urgency of our situation—or rather, *my* situation: the bank deadline and my imminent financial ruin if I didn't meet that deadline. Had her name been on the deed, her attitude would have been different, she had already suggested. This made me quietly resentful. Sure, I could have put her name on the deed. But hadn't I done too many things too hastily already, all of it with ruinous results? Didn't I owe it to myself to hold back something? Jill and I had been together for eight months and already, in the name of love, I had made a dangerous leap and bought this old house. So couldn't Jill, in turn, take a risk too and move in without demanding that she own half the house outright?

"You must be mistaken about the side panel," I said.

"I'm not," she said.

I didn't know how to explain what I needed from her, not without making her feel bad. I reminded myself that she was with me in this ruined house and *working*, at least. I said, "I'm really busy here, Jill." More plaster fell into my hands.

She regarded me curiously. I attempted a smile, though I hardly felt friendly.

"Ron, it's part of the original door."

Later, to humor her, I pulled the panel out of the basement, carried it upstairs, set it in the door space and, sure enough, it fit perfectly—just as Jill said it would. She didn't gloat. This only made me grumpier. *Okay, fine,* I wanted to say, *you've found the side panel to the missing doors. So, in another year or two, when we replace those doors, then—THEN—I can put in the side panel. Now will you do something more meaningful, like help me keep this house from falling in on us?*

To make matters worse, Nicholas had disappeared. I didn't know where he was. He wasn't returning my phone calls. Apparently, he was out of town, probably on vacation. But I hadn't heard him announce his departure. He hadn't been by in three days. I felt abandoned. I had no backup. And my girlfriend might as well have been picking daisies for all the help she was offering. I had no alternative but to set my own agenda and learn what to do and learn it fast. *Do or die*, I told myself; I'd make the September deadline. I didn't care how funky the house looked as a result. I could correct the fast-fixes and the mistakes later.

Jill was of a different mind. She advocated the do-it-once, do-it-right rule. One morning, she showed up carrying a new tool: a "mutt," a thick broom-length handle attached to a straight-edged blade that allows the user to wedge it under boards or tiles, then pry them up.

"What are you going to do with that?" I asked.

She smiled at me. "Take up the kitchen floor."

Oh, Jesus, I thought, *here we go again.*

In my desperation to keep the expenses to a minimum, I had told James, the floor-finisher, to skip the kitchen floor, the pantry floor, and the servants' stairs. Since the kitchen floor was an inch thick with old linoleum, I suggested to Jill that we cover it with another layer of linoleum—as an interim solution.

"*No way,*" she said. "Now's the time to do it right, while everything else is torn up."

"Jill, we don't have time to strip off all of this shit."

"You're always saying we don't have time!"

"Because it's true!"

"There has to be time for *something!*" she said. "Just let me do it. Either the original 1920s linoleum will be good or the original wood under that will be salvageable."

Her persistence both irritated and impressed me. If I thwarted her every time she showed initiative, who would blame her for leaving? If I let her have her way every time, I'd never be done with the house. As I considered Jill's request, I stewed and steamed inwardly: *Why can't she get with the program?* It didn't occur to me that I hadn't *explained* the program, much less gotten Jill's input about the program that loomed so large in my mind.

"Okay," I sighed. "Go for it."

Another day, as Jill continued digging again through the clutter in the basement, she announced that she had found the original jamb to the still-missing vestibule doors. The jamb was a hefty post that abutted the side panel she'd found a couple of weeks earlier. It had been sawed in two.

"That's not it," I said. I was pulling thin electrical wire from a wall. The wire didn't look old—and it wasn't live—but there seemed to be a lot of it.

"Just try it," she said.

I wondered if I had been the one to cut that post in two. Moving very quickly in my work, I really wasn't watching what was what. That meant I might take the nearest piece of lumber at hand, cut it hastily, then use it as a prop, a buttress, or a door stop.

Jill & the Mutt

pencil to keep hair in place

prefers blisters to gloves

steel-toed boots

the Mutt!

"Jill, I've got my hands full right now." Then I caught myself and turned down my irritation a notch: "Maybe later."

"Okay," she said. "Later."

Later, Jill held the upper piece of the jamb in place, I held the lower. The jamb fit perfectly. I sighed. Jill smiled at me as if to say, *Isn't this great?*

No. It seemed I couldn't do anything right: I kept getting my shirttail wound up in the belt sander and soon I burned out its

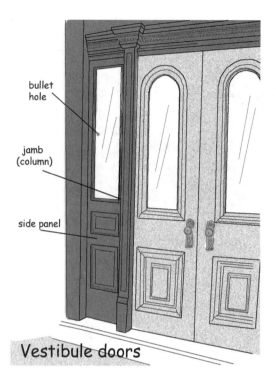

bullet
hole

jamb
(column)

side panel

Vestibule doors

motor; I couldn't cut a straight line with my new circular saw to save my life; I used three-wire cable for two-wire electrical connections; my first plaster job looked like a badlands relief map.

After a particularly arduous week of my plastering, Jill pointed out that I needed to reset the electrical outlets and switch plates so they'd be flush with the new plaster.

"You can hardly see them because they're sunk into the new plaster," she said.

"I know," I said, "but it can't be redone."

"It can't?"

"No, it's got to stay as it is."

What I really meant was that I didn't want to fool with the outlets and switch plates *now*. I meant to *imply* that we could deal with such details later. But it *sounded* as though we didn't have the option, that I'd done these things the only way they could be done. Increasingly, after these exchanges, Jill was watching me with skepticism. I was sounding imperious, uncommunicative, and mistrustful.

A week later, when I attempted to wire the hallway with a single-switch ceiling light, Jill said, "We need two switches."

"That's complicated," I said.

"But it has to be done," she insisted.

"That means I'll have to cut *a channel* into the plaster to run an electrical line all the way down the stairs to a second switch."

"So?"

I sighed. It seemed so easy for her to tell me what was wrong and what I had to do. None of our hallways had ceiling lights; they had been illuminated by gas jets. Running new electricity was beginning to look like months of work. But it would have been silly to have a switch only at the top of the stairs. So I did as Jill suggested. After it was done, I knew it was right. But I couldn't admit it.

Jill's call to do-it-once-do-it-right eerily echoed my father's. I can't count the number of times he'd said this to us boys as he made us redo our chores of weeding or shoveling or scraping. Dad's abilities were impressive and I never thought I'd measure up to his accomplishments. That's why I spent a good deal of my adult life avoiding the things he did so well. Rehabbing an old house put me squarely in his territory and, hammer in hand, set me up for a devastating failure. I couldn't run away or hide or make excuses. Either I was going to make this renovation happen or I was not. The situation was as straightforward as pounding a nail into a two-by-four. Every fault Jill corrected, every good idea she discovered, every "suggestion" she offered seemed a diminishment of my efforts and revealed what I already knew about myself: I wasn't good enough to succeed at this. But I was afraid to tell Jill, afraid to give her reasons to doubt me. As a result, my self-doubt boomeranged into resentment of her efforts: *Easy for you to stand there and point out what needs doing,* I often thought. *You're not the one who has to run the wire, repair the plaster, pay the bills, meet the deadlines. . . . Tourist!* Intellectually, I understood that she was only being helpful. But in the moment, my fingers caked with wet plaster or my arms up inside a wall and flailing after a missing electrical cable, I had no patience for her "help." She just pissed me off.

Would nothing be easy? I wondered with alarm. The physics of home repair confounded me. On paper, it looks straightforward. There's only one way to wire an outlet, for example: you get three wires to attach to three screws. That's it. Wet plaster will set up in ten minutes. Wall paint will dry in four hours, sub-floor glue in eight, caulk in twelve. But nothing was going as planned. I'd start priming a wall, thinking it looked good enough—"good enough" was my increasingly desperate measure for moving ahead. But then, I'd discover that the plaster was crumbling under my paint brush. And then, upon further inspection, I'd find that it would keep crumbling until I was staring at a door-sized hole in the wall, the wood lathe exposed like the house's skeleton. It was like a cruel joke. There was never enough time. My life was spiraling out of control: I was ignoring my job and my friends. I was getting no more than four hours of sleep a night. The only time Jill saw me was when she came by to help. After one month of clean-out, another month of contractor work, then a third month of Jill and I working on the house, it was still a wreck—and Jill had yet to move in. I understood her reservations only in the abstract: yes, the house was a mess and I was a mess but was that any reason *not* to move in?

When I pressed her about this over lunch at her place one afternoon, we argued. Loudly. She said I acted like it was my house, not *our* house. "Well, it *is* my house," I said. "I pay the mortgage!"

"So where do I fit in?" she asked.

"Right next to me," I said. "Isn't this our dream?"

"But it's YOUR house!"

"You've got as much say about the house as I do!"

"IT'S NOT MY HOUSE!" she said.

Jill and I weren't really arguing about the house, of course. We were arguing about control, boundaries, respect, trust. Putting her on the deed was only the most superficial of the requests she was making. At bottom, she was asking if I was man enough to give her my heart, not my house. She and I had been working side by side for a month and the results were far from impressive. I had grown resistant and resentful. She had grown mistrustful and disillusioned.

Finally she said, "Ron, I'm tired of talking like this."

"But aren't you happy that I'm *willing* to talk?"

"I can't reach you," she said.

"Reach me? Here I am, sitting knee to knee with you at the table!"

She started crying.

"Jill?"

"Go home," she said.

"Jill?"

She left the dining room table and headed for the stairs.

"Jill, we can work this out!"

"Go home, Ron!"

"Jill, please—"

"Will you *leave me alone!* Just get out!"

Then, weeping, she ran upstairs.

For the longest time, I sat at her dining room table. Charlie, her old tomcat, licked at his paws, then blinked at me blandly.

Grumbling with effort, Harriet hobbled up the stairs after Jill. Jill's weeping resounded in the small house.

This seemed like the end. We had never argued this loudly. Jill had never told me to "get out!" It sounded definitive. Had I alienated her that much? I knew I had been stubborn and uncooperative. This, too, is part of my father's legacy—though a kind and gentle man in many ways, he was also proud and hard-headed. He never admitted to faults. His determination, his unyielding pride, allowed him to rise from the most humble of beginnings. But I am not my father. Despite my insistence on doing things my way, I actually liked Jill's ideas. I liked that she had never read a how-to book while I lived in fear of misreading the instructions in the seven how-to books I referred to daily. Jill seemed to break all the rules. I wanted to break some rules too.

I suspected that if I left Jill to her grief, if I walked out of her house right then, she would not ask me back. It was as if we were standing on opposite banks of a raging river. One of us had to cross over. My heart lodged at the back of my throat, my fingertips throbbing, I walked upstairs. Jill's bedroom was at the front of her house, its windows bright with late afternoon sun. I heard children playing in the street. I smelled someone's cigarette smoke from the sidewalk.

Harriet was grumbling from her mat in the corner of the room.

I sat on Jill's bed. She was lying facedown, her head turned away from me. Muffled by a pillow, she would not stop weeping.

I laid one hand on her heaving back.

When she quieted down, I told her I loved her and that I would wait for her, however long that would take.

She didn't answer. There didn't seem to be anything else to say. So I just sat there and stroked her hair.

When I left her finally, she hadn't spoken a word. It was as if she'd been stricken and I had visited her sickroom. Scared and shaky with dejection, I knew we hadn't solved anything or come to any agreement. But I hoped Jill realized that, if she could be patient, I was willing to learn.

14

JILL MOVES IN

IN MID-JUNE, after three months of working with me on the house, Jill agreed to move in. Since our big argument at her place two months before, I hadn't said one word about her moving. I'm sure this helped. In deciding to move, maybe she wanted to show me that she could take as big a risk as I. Thoroughly grateful for her sticking by me, I had begun to change my work habits. Jill would make a suggestion, I would soundly reject it, then, a few days or a week later, I would follow her suggestion to the letter. Not long after she made her observation about the switch plates and electrical outlets, I pulled them out and reset them flush with the newly plastered walls. Instead of saying, "I told you so," Jill simply nodded her approval and thanked me for doing a better job.

It was a radical education in humility.

One afternoon, I came home to find Jill tearing up the fireplace in our bedroom. At some point—at least fifty years ago—somebody had tiled that fireplace shut. There was no need to disturb it, at least not now. It was well-tiled and perfectly fine, the only fireplace in good condition.

But here was Jill, hammer and chisel in hand, surrounded by a scatter of cracked tile and mounds of broken plaster. It was like a twisted wish come true: sure, my partner worked on the house, but every task she undertook was something that didn't need doing.

My first impulse was to shout objections, to ask her to think of me, for pity's sake, to please get with the program. But I knew better. Jill was marching to a different drummer. She couldn't hear my music any more than I could hear hers. So, stifling my irritation, I could only whine: "Jill?"

She turned her smile to me: "I thought there might be something hidden back here!" I saw flecks of tile and plaster in her curls.

"Jill, this fireplace was perfectly *fine!*"

"I wanted to redo it. This tile is second-rate." Her energy and enthusiasm gave me pause. I was thinking, *If only I could channel her to more productive tasks. . .*

Carefully I asked, "So you're going to re-tile this yourself?"

"Yeah, I've got some ideas."

As I pondered this, she added: "Don't you want to see what's back here?" She hammered at the plaster.

"It's a firebox," I said. "The old fireplace."

"I think this tile's original or close to it," she said, still hammering. "Why would they have closed up the fireplace?"

"Maybe they—" But I didn't have an explanation.

She stopped hammering: "Yeah?" Then she grinned knowingly.

"Oh, stop it."

"Does that mean I get to keep the treasure?" she teased.

"No, it doesn't." I took the hammer from her. "Let me have a whack."

What we found, after tearing into the wall, was *half* a fireplace. The builder had miscalculated the path of the flue below us and didn't leave enough room for a full firebox upstairs. So he simply tiled over this one. But it was no big deal. The house was full of mistakes, we were learning.

As her attempt to get behind the bedroom fireplace showed, Jill wasn't always right. I admired her following a hunch, but often

re-tiled by Jill

ornamental iron cover

master bedroom fireplace

as not her hunches led to dead ends. She toiled for nearly a week, stripping linoleum from the kitchen floor, at one point on her hands and knees scrubbing off the aged gummy mastic, only to discover that the wood underneath had long been ruined. It was too splintered to refinish. We had no choice but to pay for a new kitchen floor. Another time, she bought a broken lamp with the intention of gluing together its shattered ornate metal shade. She spent four painstaking days gluing it, only to have the whole thing fall apart when she put the glass in.

But when Jill was right, she was right on. Once the new kitchen floor was in place, Jill said, "We have to move the radiator to make more room. The fridge should go where the radiator is."

"We can't move the radiator," I said.

"Yes, we can."

"That's where it's always been," I said.

"So?"

It never occurred to me that this could be done. But we did it. Moving a radiator on the first floor is an easy job for a plumber because the pipes are readily accessible from the basement. Lou did it for us in a few hours. We traded our big radiator for one just as old and ornate but a third the size, which fit perfectly under the window near the sink. Then we had room for the fridge, which left one kitchen wall wide open.

What isn't possible with Jill? I began to ask myself.

* * *

Early on, I learned that Jill is no housekeeper. She refuses to vacuum, though sometimes she will sweep. She will launder but not iron. She hang-dries her shirts, whose fabric afterwards has a distinct warp. And she may let the dishes pile up in the sink for a week. If every dish is dirty and she needs one, she'll remove what she needs from the dirty pile and wash it. But she's orderly, sometimes too orderly for me: she insists that everything be put in its place. When she can't find something—usually because I have moved it—she feels helpless, even threatened, because she doesn't have good spatial memory, a trait she shares with her late mother. I, on the other hand, believe I have exceptional spatial memory and can find anything I've put down anywhere. In actuality, I can't. Not a day goes by when I haven't misplaced something in this house.

My misplacement of things drove Jill and Nicholas mad. Nicholas is the kind of guy who keeps his work shirt tucked in and, even in the messiest chore, hardly gets dirty. I, by contrast, will be untucked, untied, begrimed, and thoroughly dusty by the day's end. Nicholas and Jill learned very quickly that I have a terrible habit of leaving tools all over the house: if I am called away or distracted by another task, I'll simply set down whatever tool I'm holding, then promptly forget where I've put it. I have found my tools on top of the refrigerator, inside bookshelves, hidden in planters, snugged against stairsteps, lying on beams in the ceiling—virtually anywhere. I agree: it is absolutely maddening. My best strategy for finding these things is to look for something else I've misplaced. In doing so, I usually stumble across one of the tools I've lost, but not necessarily the one I'm looking for.

One day, Jill opened the refrigerator and laughed: "This is why living with you is an adventure!" She nodded to the wet sponge I had left inside the refrigerator.

"Oh, yeah," I explained. "I wondered what had become of that sponge."

Ten minutes earlier, I had been wiping down the fridge shelves, but then got distracted by putting away the groceries. Or, rather, in putting away the groceries, I saw that the fridge shelves needed cleaning. So I fetched the sponge and did *some* cleaning, but then felt compelled to return to the groceries. Then I forgot about the sponge.

To make matters worse, I create a tremendous mess when I work, letting the sawdust, wood scraps, tools, sawhorses, etc. accumulate until the task is done. Then, and only then, will I clean up. Nicholas—like Jill—cleans up along the way, sweeping his sawdust immediately after he's made his cut. Then he'll put away his saw and set aside his horses. Sometimes, when Nicholas arrived to help me, he would survey my mess with a grimace, then stifling curses, he would begin cleaning up—very fast and noisily, nearly knocking things over—until he felt the area was suitably under control. One day, he simply announced, "If we don't get organized, I'm gonna lose it."

So Jill agreed to move in on two conditions: I would make several closets useable and I would give her a tool drawer and a junk drawer of her own, neither of which I would be allowed to touch. On top of the chaos I created, we had no fireplace mantels, no kitchen to speak of, nothing was unpacked because there was no place to put it, all of the floors were covered with heavy pink "contractor's paper" to protect them from scuffing, bare bulbs hung from the ceilings (if they were even wired yet for electricity), and the walls were still painted black or blue or strafed with graffiti. We lived also with garish murals, including the ten-by-ten-foot confederate flag painted on one wall of the room that would be Jill's study. Our damp basement was crowded not only with salvage but also with furniture we couldn't set up. Tools and building materials—as well as more salvage—were scattered throughout the house.

Worst of all, plaster dust was everywhere because the only way to finish plaster is to sand it. Sanded plaster—gypsum dust—is as fine as flour but as abrasive as diamond grit. It will scratch everything from wood to glass. As I plastered my way through the house, white dust clouded the air we breathed and settled on everything, including the pets. We sneezed dust, we coughed dust, we tracked ghostly footprints everywhere we walked. In the end, my eyeglasses would be fogged from dust scratches. And most of our floors would need another coat of polyurethane.

Eager to please Jill, I took a break from this work to clean, repair, paint, wire, and shelve seven of our fourteen closets. I couldn't believe how long this took. Each closet seemed a house in miniature. By the time I was done, though, the closets looked great—each with an overhead light, broad yellow pine shelves, and cleanly plastered, white-washed walls. If I took my time, I saw, I could do good work. At last Jill moved in and we had a place for towels and sheets and shoes and shirts. I also set up Jill's bed so that we were off the floor. When we placed her table in our dining

the eyeball room

room, we laughed, it looked so ridiculously small. We had no choice but to put things wherever we could—always temporarily— and accustom ourselves to dusting off plates before we used them and shoving aside boxes of screws or bottles of solvent whenever we needed space.

Friends who stopped by to check on our progress were quietly appalled. They were polite and full of encouragement, but clearly worried. Jill and I were always wearing our stained, torn, and dusty work clothes. We looked exhausted. And the house looked like an abandoned wreck taken over by squatters. The banisters on the second and third floors were covered over with long sheets of plywood because they had no balusters. Every window frame and every length of woodwork was flaking paint. Although the plumbing was in, the bathrooms remained torn-up and untiled. Visitors were fascinated by the graffiti, especially in the "eyeball room." If nothing else, the Queen Anne had the appeal of a sideshow.

Jill's request for two sacrosanct drawers was as close as she could come to preserving a safe space for her sanity. Her mother had died, at an early age, of a series of increasingly devastating strokes and Jill lived in fear that this would happen to her too, that she would lose her memory as her mother had and then lose her mind. Looking back, I see that in living with me she was really testing her luck. In one drawer she kept her tools, in the other her everyday junk: scissors, tape, stamps, pens, etc. I was not allowed to remove or borrow any item from these drawers. I said Jill is "orderly." It goes beyond that. She is a compulsive clearer: she can't resist putting things away. If I had to psychologize it, I'd say it makes her feel she has more control of her world—a way to live in defiance of her mother's chaos. If I am cooking, she might put away the salt and pepper and spices I'm using while my back is turned. She doesn't even think about it, she just puts them away. She is a compulsive recycler too, which has caused us recurrent friction: "Jill, could you please, just once, let my newspaper lie around for more than an hour before tossing it into the recycling bag?"

If she feels she can't recycle it, she will stash it in one of the several sites she has designated as depositories: a basket in the kitchen, a magazine rack in the bathroom, another basket under the mail table. Even when I'm trying to help her recycle, she's still too fast for me. I'll set aside a pile of paper for recycling, then— the minute my back's turned—she'll stash it in a basket, thinking I've set aside the pile for reading. Then I'll have to dig these out of one of Jill's baskets to recycle them myself.

As we discovered our respective strengths and weaknesses, we established a set of separate duties: I cook, she washes dishes (eventually); I vacuum, she launders; I iron, she folds; I shop for groceries, she feeds the pets. Still, Jill found my messy cooking as frustrating as my messy construction. Usually my cooking works out but, in the process, I go through pots and pans and bowls and utensils like an ER surgeon going through gauze, sutures, clamps, and swabs.

"Couldn't you use fewer pots?" Jill would beg.

"Don't meddle with the maestro!" I'd joke. "Do you want a tidy kitchen or a great meal?"

"Both!"

I'd wave a spatula at her. "Life isn't that easy, my dear."

She'd roll her eyes, then carry another dirty pot into the pantry.

"Just let the driver drive!" I'd call after her.

We came up with this slogan because each of us is fond of telling the other what to do, especially in the car.

Nothing complicated our new household more than our pets. Harriet was a problem because she was always underfoot, waiting for food to drop. If Jill or I bumped Harriet or got in her way, she'd suddenly attack our foot, jawing at it angrily, then she'd rear away, yelping as if injured. This happened nearly every day. Worse, Harriet could abide no interference or interruption where food was involved. Occasionally when Charlie, Jill's sixteen-year-old tomcat, ambled in front of Harriet, Harriet would snatch him in her jaws and shake him from side to side as if he were a rag. Then poor Charlie would stumble off, slobber-wet and rattled. It would take him a day or two to recover, and yet he never learned to stay out of Harriet's way.

Charlie had his own set of issues, foremost of which was his attraction to Jill's clothes. Even though he was long neutered, he would take a piece of Jill's clothing—anything, even a t-shirt—then carry it away in his mouth, yowling a catty love song and pausing now and then to mount the clothing in a brief ecstatic bout of dry humping. This happened about once a week.

Unable to keep meat on his arthritic bones and long tired of grooming his matted white fur, Charlie was clearly living on borrowed time. At least twice a day and once a night, he would get lost in our house and begin to yowl, long and plaintively. He would often get "lost" simply by turning his back on us. It was clear that dementia was setting in. All we had to do was tap him on the back to remind him that we were still there, then he'd be fine.

Charlie also had the bad habit of peeing anywhere but in his cat box, which most of the time he couldn't find. He preferred to pee in Jill's big planters. Jill kept about a hundred potted plants going. They thrived mostly because she ignored them until they were nearly dead. She started potting plants not because she likes greenery, but because they give her an excuse to collect vintage pottery. We have gorgeous old pots throughout the house, the biggest of which Charlie regularly targeted.

If that weren't enough, Jill had brought home yet another cat, a fat tortie named Tess, which somebody had dropped off at the consignment shop. It was a surprisingly common practice for a pet to come in with a truckload of somebody's unwanted furniture. As it turned out, my cat, Corona, hated both Tess and Charlie. In fact, Corona hated all cats. But she didn't seem to mind dogs. She didn't know what they were, actually. Sadly, Corona began a campaign against Tess, once biting Tess so badly we had to get her stitched up. So finally, we sequestered Corona on the third floor. Tess took the first floor. And Charlie roamed aimlessly. We called Corona our "mad kitty in the attic."

Although I'm a pet lover, I never imagined having a houseful of them. Three odd cats and a demented dog seemed a bit much to me. But aged Harriet and Charlie wouldn't be with us long, I reminded myself. They were part of the deal. As baggage, they could have been worse, I supposed. The abrupt addition of Tess, though, illustrated that Jill could be as impulsive and willful as I. This was cause for worry. Somebody had to be the voice of reason. So I found myself cautioning Jill about reining in Harriet so that I could cook in peace and watching Charlie so that his random, aimless peeing would not ruin our newly refinished floors.

But we were very busy with housework and it's a big house and Jill simply couldn't keep track of Charlie. When I discovered that a week-old pee puddle under one of Jill's flowerpots in the first floor bay had blackened the parquet, I howled in protest. "We can't afford this!" I wailed. The stain was a perfect black circle the diameter of a dessert plate. Jill worked on the damage for a week, sanding, then bleaching, then refinishing the wood. When she was done, the wood was no longer black but it was no longer the same color as the rest of the parquet. "If we endure damage like this on a regular basis over the course of ten years," I reminded Jill, "our house will be one funky place. We've got to be careful!" Jill nodded in agreement, but nevertheless, we found ourselves cleaning up after Charlie, and sometimes Harriet, at least once a week.

That summer, just one month after moving in, Jill announced that she wanted a second dog. I tried to talk her out of it. Good sense was on my side. Or so it seemed. Jill reminded me that ten-year-old Harriet wasn't long for this world.

"All the more reason to wait," I countered.

"What's wrong with looking?" Jill asked.

I didn't want to be unreasonable. In fact, I was inclined to do just about anything to keep her happy. *How many women would put up with a man like me in a house like this?* I asked myself. Still, I was beginning to apprehend that when Jill sets her mind on something, she pursues it until she gets it. In this instance, I tried to convince myself that she'd be satisfied with window-shopping. Unlike her acquisition of Tess, getting this pet would demand a mutual decision. Time was on my side, I decided. I could stall.

After doing some research, Jill told me we needed a boxer, an American bulldog, or a pit bull. Immediately I saw the logic of this. We had never lived in the city and we had heard plenty of stories about thefts and muggings and worse. Something we didn't discuss but I worried about was Jill staying alone in the house. A few years before I met Jill, she was attacked in a university bathroom by a man who had hidden in one of the women's stalls. She managed to scream loudly enough and fight hard enough to make the attacker run. But she was bruised and hobbled for weeks. I don't think she was ever the same after that. Even now, if I come to bed late and adjust the blanket over her, she will wake with a violent start. And at least once a week, she'll wake herself from a nightmare with a gasp or a stifled scream. I've never met someone pursued by so many nightmares.

At the same time, I've never met someone so prone to laughter, especially first thing in the morning. One day, she woke herself laughing at the image of a big-bottomed wrestler sitting on his opponent's head. She couldn't stop thinking about this scene from *Cazadores des Espias (Spy Hunters)*, a one-dollar Mexican DVD we had watched the night before. Promising "luchas, robots, muchachas, y peligro"—*wrestling, robots, girls, and danger*—the 1960s movie was the kind of thing we enjoy on occasion. We also enjoy locally produced camp like "Lesbian Vampire Cheerleaders From Venus" and museums like Philadelphia's Mutter, where you can see cabinets filled with objects that doctors have extracted from children's stomachs and displays of such oddities as the largest human intestines in the world. When Jill found one of our mail carrier's press-on nails among our letters, she saved it to show me and laughed about it all day. I loved Jill's quirky humor, I loved that she was game for just about anything, including our messy

life in our wreck of a house. That's why I could not deny her a second dog.

So, taking breaks from our work, we drove to rescue shelters all over the state. We found PJ, a two-year-old pit bull. He was tall for the breed and, at forty-eight pounds, about ten pounds underweight. He had a beautiful face, wide mascara'd eyes, a sympathetic expression, and fawn-colored dapple over his white coat. He'd been at the shelter since he was a puppy and adopted once briefly but brought back because he wasn't housebroken. He wasn't particularly obedient either. The shelter said he suffered mildly from separation anxiety. Before I could pull Jill aside to debate the pros and cons of this important decision, she said we'd take him.

I sighed, shook my head in doubt, but could hardly complain, Jill was so happy. PJ sat on her lap all the way home. He took to Harriet right away, though she snapped at him. He seemed eager to please us, but he wet his bed often, usually when we'd leave him alone. When he wasn't with us, he was inconsolable. Sometimes we'd take him to a field and let him run. He was a reckless, fearless sprinter. He'd gallop from one end of the field to the other. It seemed he'd never tire. Always, it would take us a while to get him back. Fortunately, he shied away from strangers and would come only to us.

Though he looked formidable, he had the most fastidious personality and sometimes seemed downright shy around us, as if he didn't want to be a bother. He took biscuits from our hands so delicately, parting his lips slightly and waiting until we gently slipped the tidbit onto his tongue, Jill remarked. "It's like serving the Eucharist!" So she made a joke of it: "Body of Christ," she'd intone as she gave him his daily biscuit.

PJ turned heads when we walked him. One time I overheard a passerby say to her companion, "Que lindo!" *What a pretty dog.* He made us proud.

15

OUR FIRST SUMMER

THAT FIRST SUMMER, the neighbors on our block threw us a dinner party at Dan's house, a few doors down. A retired minister, Dan divides his time between playing cello in the community symphony and preaching for peace. Jill and I were pleasantly surprised by the diversity among our neighbors: a harpist, a bank manager, a graphic designer, a retired pipe-fitter, a lawyer, a realtor, a social security administrator, a movie location scout, a social worker, a journalist, a piano technician, and several retired teachers. One of the retirees was a famous peace activist whose cohorts had napalmed draft board records in the 1970s. His radical peace group—still active even in 2000—was so notorious that a right-wing think tank had relocated up the street just to keep track of him. Or so Rick told us. "There are spies in this neighborhood," he said with a serious nod. Rick himself had been in Army Intelligence during the Korean War. He was also an arch-Republican who had no reason to protect his radical neighbor. Jill and I were intrigued.

Our neighbors toasted to our success. And we toasted in return. Then we toasted some more. Then we stood around Dan's piano and sang show tunes until we were hoarse.

Later, as Jill and I described the work we were undertaking—and the looming deadline—the local historian said flatly, "You'll never bring that house back. It's too far gone." Maybe we seemed starry-eyed and he was trying to toughen us up. Still, it made us bristle. We wanted to prove him wrong. Rick counseled patience. He reminded us that it had taken him and Charles twenty years. *I'll have it done in two!* I thought defiantly. Never mind that it was June and we were so behind in our work that any clear-eyed observer could see that we would never make our deadline. I thought we'd be painting by now, but we couldn't paint until the walls were repaired and plastered. Every patch of plaster took twenty-four hours to dry and then had to be sanded and plastered some more. Then sanded and plastered some more—because I was just learning how to do it and doing it well took several tries. Virtually every foot of every wall and ceiling needed repair. It seemed I would never stop plastering, especially as Baltimore's summer humidity prolonged drying time.

But once the plastering was done, I told myself, we'd dispatch the rest of the repairs speedily. We'd catch up. We'd make our deadline. Just don't let up, that's the trick, just keep at it and keep at it. And keep at it. The long hours of labor made my elbows and wrists numb and my fingers cramped. Soaking in ice water helped keep down the swelling. During a fourteen-hour day, I might soak my wrists, hands, and elbows every hour—anything to keep the numbness at bay. At night, my arms would tingle so badly, the tendons swollen, the nerves smarting, I sometimes couldn't sleep. As it was, I got four hours a night, if I was lucky.

Jill got more, but she was working at full capacity too, spending much of her time stripping paint. When new, the Queen Anne featured shellacked wood trim of yellow pine, which would have looked honey-colored. By the 1920s, varnished wood trim looked old-fashioned—too Victorian—and so homeowners started painting their woodwork to make their interiors look more modern. The only woodwork that remained unpainted in our house were the doors, and those were scratched, hammered, scored, and pitted, their finish long having turned a dull, dark chocolate.

To strip paint, Jill was experimenting with chemicals and solvents. She never wore a mask. She never wore gloves. I badgered her about taking care of herself and reminded her that paint-stripping was low on our priority list. But Jill's list was often different than mine. I'd watch her working diligently on something I didn't want to do, her hands mucked with paint and solvents. Then I'd sigh in resignation. There were only so many things we could argue about.

Dogs—we argued about the dogs all the time. Maybe they were a stand-in for other problems. Jill put dog beds in the kitchen, the TV room, her office, and our bedroom. It seemed there was always a dog underfoot. And, of course, there was always a cat or two nearby as well. Every morning, I'd hear Jill in the kitchen, talking to the animals as if they were children. No matter what they did—Charlie licking the butter dish on the kitchen counter or Harriet snatching toast from her hand—they made her laugh. At least once a week, she'd make up a song about one of them, then sing it like a nursery rhyme:

> *Harriet's a crabby girl but we love her still.*
> *Harriet's a grabby girl—she never gets her fill.*
> *She growls and snaps and always complains,*
> *To hear her side she's always in pain!*
> *But we love you, Harriet, no matter how bad you are*
> *Because you're the doggiest dog—the crabbiest girl by far!*

Her singing would make the dogs bark and bark again, their tails swinging. Even when they broke into the garbage or snatched leftovers from the kitchen counter, she rarely got angry at them. I was less forgiving. I insisted that Harriet and PJ be tethered near their beds whenever we were working. Neither was truly housebroken. Their habits suggested an *acquaintance* with the concept, but they easily forgot themselves. Harriet was fond of leaving a turd or two on the rug in the entryway. PJ peed indiscriminately, spraying a chair one week, then a stack of my CDs the next. Sometimes, we wouldn't discover the mess for days. Jill said it was cruel to keep the dogs tied up.

"What's cruel about it if they're sleeping on their beds?" I countered.

Whenever I'd find the dogs loose, I'd take them to their beds and leash them to a radiator. "This is a construction zone!" I'd announce. Later, I'd hear the dogs padding about, free again. Then I'd see trails of tissues and Q-tips and half-chewed napkins leading to the bathroom or kitchen, after one or both had raided the trash bin. When the mail carrier arrived, Harriet and PJ would gallop to the front of the house, he barking, she howling. Then PJ would hurl himself at the door, clawing to get at the intruder.

Nearly every morning, their barking in the kitchen woke me from sleep. Jill got up at dawn, which was when I'd get to bed. One morning, my head pounding, I stood at the top of the stairs in my underwear and bellowed: "For god's sake, can't a man get even an hour's sleep in this god-forsaken kennel!" In the abstract, I understood Jill's indulgence, but in the moment—and there were too many moments—it infuriated me. Were the dogs more important than my rest? My sanity?

When I discovered that PJ had sneaked upstairs to the library (or what would become the library) and peed on the antique rug we'd bought for that room, I stormed through the house railing. Jill cleaned up the mess and promised she'd keep track of him. But then PJ did it again. Jill dutifully cleaned the mess and offered another apology. Then he did it a third time and I wouldn't speak to her for two days.

* * *

The Queen Anne was such a wreck, we weren't sure what we'd find hidden in its many folds and cracks. In stairway crevices we found Indian-head pennies and buffalo nickels. When we took off an original wall shelf in the kitchen, an array of Victoriana rained

from our collection:
a teaspoonful
every 2 hours

down: hat pins, a miniature tin mirror, rusted keys, a chewing tobacco wrapper, and a cigarette trading card of a pink ibis. When I broke into walls to run electrical cables or peeked into ceilings to make repairs, I kept coming across old patent medicine bottles. Evidently, the workers were drinking—medicating—on the job. After emptying a bottle, they'd re-cork it, then drop it inside the wall they were building.

Patent medicines were over-the-counter drugs. By the mid-nineteenth century, few of these were actually patented. Patents would have demanded a record of ingredients. Full disclosure was the last thing manufacturers welcomed, they made such bodacious claims for their potions. The primary ingredient in most was alcohol. Lydia E. Pinkham's wildly popular "Vegetable Compound," which sold for $1 a bottle as a cure-all for "women's complaints," contained eighteen percent alcohol. According to the label, its alcohol was "used solely as a solvent and preservative." Beer was only five percent alcohol. No wonder women had fewer complaints after a bottle or two of Lydia's.

Some patent medicines had as much as fifty percent alcohol; others contained opium or even poisons like mercury and borax. Coca Cola was invented as a patent medicine and first sold as a counter drink in 1886 for five cents a glass.

True to legend, it contained five ounces of cocoa leaf for every gallon of syrup, which gave it quite a kick. That's why my grandmother's generation called cola "dope." The most egregiously irresponsible medicines claimed to cure syphilis, cholera, and tuberculosis. The common folk flocked to patent medications because the so-called real medicine was prohibitively expensive and available only by prescription. It probably wasn't much better than the cheap stuff anyway. While medical science was making great strides in some respects, it was woefully inadequate in most. By 1897, there was only a rudimentary understanding of germ theory. Anesthesia was a new development. Occupational therapy was a century away. It's likely that most of the men building our house had been injured on this or another job and were in varying degrees of pain.

I could sympathize with their plight because injury dogged me daily. My great fear was that I'd hurt myself seriously—slip a disc or cut off a finger—and ruin my chances of completing the Queen Anne's rehab. I stapled my finger, hammered my hand, torched my arm, bruised my thigh, knifed my knuckles, knocked my nose, crowned my head, even fell five feet flat on my back (from atop a Dumpster), but never hurt myself badly. Week after week, month after month, I couldn't believe my good luck. I got used to living with splinters in my fingers. My hands were always cut or scraped. My arms, my wrists, my elbows, my fingertips were always half numb and tingling, flirting seriously with nerve damage.

I did some stupid things. Like hanging from the porch without a lifeline. Three stories up, I'd dangle from one side or the other, holding on with one hand while trying to scrape or paint with the other. A couple of times, I slipped but caught myself. Stupid? Then I went out and bought a mountain climbing harness. Because, after not hearing from the woodworker who was going to give me an estimate on replicating our missing stairway balusters, I phoned him and learned from his girlfriend that he had fallen from his roof while rehabbing his house. He toppled thirty feet to the asphalt. He ruptured his lungs, broke most of his ribs, and crushed several vertebrae. His survival was nothing short of miraculous. But now his career was over. Or so said his girlfriend when I stopped by to pick up the sample balusters I had left at his shop.

I remember thinking how lucky he was to have someone to take care of him. She happened to be a nurse, of all things. She looked so haunted with fear and exhaustion, I wanted to say some words of comfort but could think of nothing except, "Thank you. Take care."

* * *

In July, it was painfully clear that Jill and I weren't going to make our deadline, despite my fourteen-hour-a-day schedule. Jill was working at the consignment store and helping me at night. She was so exhausted, I could work around her while she slept. For three nights, I plastered the bedroom ceiling over her and she never woke up.

By this time, in my few fitful hours of early morning sleep, I started having a recurring nightmare. It didn't matter what dream I started with—I could be visiting the president of the United States or shopping in the world's best mall or sharing supper with friends—eventually I'd find myself facing a door. When I opened the door, and I always opened it, I'd be looking at the world's dirtiest bathroom.

The bathroom itself changed from dream to dream. Always, it had a tiled floor (which allowed water to pool) but otherwise it could have been any bathroom: as big as a stadium or as small as an upended coffin. What never changed was the degree of filth—as filthy as you can imagine, urine puddled on the floor, the toilet overflowing, I'd be ankle-deep in floating turds. My job, *which I never questioned*, was to make the bathroom spotless. It was clearly an impossible task. But I was committed to the challenge, and so I'd clean and clean and clean, knee deep in toilet water, turds bobbing all around me, my clothes wet and reeking of urine.

Then I'd wake up, feeling dirty and defeated.

One sunny Saturday morning, as I was sanding the Queen Anne's front doors, a young man approached me, his girlfriend in tow.

He called a greeting, then said, "Wow, you're fixing the place up, huh? You know, I used to live here!"

I looked up from my work, considered his smile, wondering—only for a moment—if he was one of the few frat boys who had *not* damaged the house. Maybe this was a good boy. The only good boy. He looked to be in his late twenties, clean-cut, smiling.

He wanted a tour, obviously. He wanted to see what I had done to his former home. He wanted to show his girlfriend what it had been like back in the day.

He couldn't have known that I was in a fragile state of mind. He couldn't have known that I was beginning to apprehend how utterly unprepared I was for all the work that lay ahead—that I was drowning. He couldn't have known that Jill and I had discovered that none of our friends, and none of our neighbors, was capable of helping us. They had their own lives and their own projects. The few who were inclined to help didn't know how to do anything we needed doing. Nobody, it seemed, even knew how to prep and paint a wall. And nobody had the time to learn what we'd learn. We couldn't blame them.

My Saturday morning visitor, this fresh-faced former fraternity boy, could not have known that—unable to thwart my wholly unrealistic and thoroughly impulsive optimism—I had invited my family to spend Christmas with Jill and me at "our newly restored house." Just six months away. Let me say that again: I HAD INVITED MY ENTIRE FAMILY TO STAY WITH US FOR CHRISTMAS.

"What are you thinking!" Jill gasped when I'd told her of the invitation. "You should have talked to me! We're not ready! We WON'T BE ready. We won't be anywhere NEAR ready!" She looked about to weep.

I felt my face grow hot with humiliation. This was something she and I still had to work out, my not consulting her on major decisions. Sometimes, carried on a wave of blinding optimism, I convinced myself that Jill would be delighted by what I'd decided in her absence. I *knew* I had no right to do this. But making sudden decisions—my attempt to fix things with magical speed—held me like an addiction. I *had* to change, as Jill's outrage and disappointment made clear every time.

"We will be ready," I insisted. "Christmas is several months beyond our rehab deadline. What's unrealistic about that?"

"Oh, Ron, what have you done!" she wailed, walking away, pulling at her curly hair. "Oh, god, it'll be horrible!"

"It'll be all right!" I called after her. But even then I could smell the smoke of doom. I could feel the flames.

"Ron, what were you thinking?" I heard her wail again from downstairs.

Now, looking at the beaming former frat boy, I saw everything that would not, and could not, be right.

"You," I snapped, "what you did!" I pointed my wire brush at the young man. "You should be ASHAMED. You and your frat boy friends nearly ruined this house. SHAME on you!"

Stunned, the young man backed away. I heard his girlfriend say, "Honey?"

"Shame on you," I said again, surprised at my own vehemence, but unable to stop myself. "Do you have any IDEA what you DID?"

The young couple backed out of the yard.

"DO YOU?" I shouted.

They retreated to the sidewalk, their wide eyes trained on me.

"This place is a WRECK, do you understand what I'm saying?" I called. "THIS PLACE IS A WRECK!"

They strode away, not quite running, but glancing back more than once to make sure I wasn't chasing them. As I stood there seething, I heard a ringing in my ears like a distant alarm.

* * *

In August, Jill said she was worried about me and insisted that we go away for a week. I was so exhausted, I could hardly protest. She took me to an old farmhouse she had found for rent in upstate New York. She drove most the way, while I stared out the window and napped intermittently. What a tremendous relief to be away from the Queen Anne! The farmhouse Jill had rented was small, just off a two-lane road outside a village in the Catskills. It had recently belonged to somebody's grandmother. We found the old lady's dresses, hat boxes, and trunks crowding the upstairs walk-in. The newest piece of furniture was a circa-1960 space-aged couch with nubby, sparkly fabric. The refrigerator was a big white 1955 GE with lots of chrome—the equivalent of a fin-tailed Cadillac. Everything about the place was reminiscent of visiting one of my country relatives.

Jill and I walked our dogs through the large, now-abandoned dairy barn. They nosed, poked, and pawed, then rolled in the manure-pungent hay, reveling in the smells. Outside, we had 250 acres to ourselves. PJ tore through the tall grass, Harriet bounding and barking after him. For a week, we let them run happily through the pasture while we lolled behind, pausing at the low stone walls where blackberry bushes grew, drooping with ripe fruit. I began to accept then what Jill had been telling me for months, that we would fail our inspection in September. Only vaguely did I apprehend what a disaster Christmas would be, when my mother and brothers and in-laws would show up at a house that wasn't even up to HUD standards. Our old house was literally condemned property.

In the rented farmhouse, I slept till noon everyday. After breakfast, I'd stretch out on the grass in the side yard and sleep some more. It felt like I was growing an extra pair of arms, so much was changing so fast in my life. I was beginning to admit to myself that I couldn't predict how the house would turn out, much less how I would. It scared me and I was quietly amazed at how desperate I was for Jill's love, that I'd destroy myself to prove myself worthy.

In taking me away, it seemed Jill was telling me I didn't have to try so hard, that we'd be okay. I still didn't believe it. I needed a win, it was time for a win, I refused to shoulder yet another loss. She and I were far from secure in each other. We argued too much. Too much was up in the air. She was still pushing for a share of the house. I wouldn't even talk about it. In truth, we were hardly talking. It was all work.

Except for this single week away—and even here—we were mostly quiet in each other's company. The nights at the farm were cool, sometimes punctuated by the cautious hooting of an owl. Jill and I made blackberry pies for dinner; we read novels on the space-aged couch. We saw no one. When we let the dogs out for their evening pee, we stood in the yard and stared at the star-stunned sky. One night we saw meteors falling in white streaks. "This is good," Jill reminded me. "Nothing but nothing." I listened to the night birds, pulled Jill closer to ward off the chill, then gaped again at the stars and thought, *Sure, let the sky fall.*

16

AMERICAN DREAMER

THE SUMMER I GRADUATED from college, I packed my Volkswagen van, and in the company of an ex-girlfriend, set off across the country. For three months, we would travel a nine-thousand-mile zig-zag to the west coast. My father had just died and I felt liberated in a wildly unpredictable way. I fully expected something great to happen to me. All I had to do was set myself in motion. Martha, my ex, was attempting to escape everything that tied her to home and her stalwart fiancé of two years. That's right, she just up and left it all behind. Her fiancé promised to wait. I'm not sure if Martha promised anything in return. She simply had to go and see what would happen. We shared that and not much else.

I could hardly articulate the pain I was feeling over the loss of my father. I was far from good company. I spent most my time eyeing the horizon, eager to get to the next destination. I had my father's camera with me. Also his wool pullover and winter jacket and Navy watch cap—the items I took away from the pile of belongings my mother split among my two brothers and me just a few months earlier. My mother was pleasantly surprised that I would be traveling with Martha, who was smart and accomplished and came from a good Southern family. Privately, I shook my head in dismay at my mother's naïvete. Why did she think I would settle for the status quo? Hadn't I proven that I would always work against the grain?

Halfway through the trip, as tension between Martha and me mounted, and nothing much happened on the road, it occurred to me that great things might not be easily found. I was still convinced that they were out there, but apparently, I had yet to walk far enough, in ever-widening circles, until I felt their pull as a diviner might feel his divining rod pull him to a buried spring. The American dream for me amounted to nothing more than serendipity, happenstance, the blind luck of a prospector. What amazes me now is that nothing in my family history framed this golly-gee view of the world. My mother's people were Appalachian mill workers. My father's parents were migrant fruit pickers in California. They labored hard and lived thoroughly modest lives.

After getting out of the Navy, following World War II, my father failed at farming, then went to college and became an exceptional electrical engineer and was recruited quickly by Western Electric and Bell Labs. He was a formidable, self-made man. And yet I grew up thinking that I would simply wander into good fortune and a great life. Maybe my mother spoiled me (I know she did); maybe the post-war legacy of my parents' generation encouraged us baby boomers to expect too much. As it happened, my great adventure ended abruptly in Spokane, Washington, where someone broke into my van and stole everything I owned while I was staying at a friend's house. Martha returned to her fiancé in North Carolina and I limped south to live for a time with my father's mother in California's San Joaquin Valley. I had pictured the valley as a tropical paradise. What did I know of California? The San Joaquin, I learned, is an irrigated desert, a hundred miles wide at its widest, a flat expanse of black dirt criss-crossed with dangerously deep concrete canals, and bounded by the treeless scrub-covered coastal hills to the west, and the foothills of the snow-capped Sierra Nevadas to the east. Corporate farms claim most of it, growing soy, cotton, citrus, spinach, asparagus, and most anything else you can find in the produce section of your local Safeway.

Nana's house was a rental, a two-bedroom bungalow that had been made into a duplex, walled into equal halves, one door for each tenant. Nana's side had been the front of the house, graced by a shallow screened porch, where Nana grew a jungle of plants: that was my first surprise, her green thumb. She had been living in Exeter on and off for much of her adult life and had numerous friends in the valley: we were only twenty miles from the "ranch" where my father had failed with his crop of cucumbers.

I slept on the floor of Nana's front room. I thought finding a job would be easy. Everyday, I drove through the depressed sprawl of farms and farming towns where most workers were Latino and most jobs were so menial I couldn't bring myself to apply for them. After a week of this, I stopped by the local junior college, convinced that they'd be happy to have me as a teacher. It was a *junior* college, after all. Despite my initial confidence, I was so nervous that I kept rehearsing numerous introductions, expecting somehow to walk into the college president's office and say glibly, "Good afternoon, I'd like to offer my services. . ."

Eventually, as I wandered the mall-like campus—where both my mother and my father had taken classes immediately after his crop failure—I found my way to the personnel office. It was larger than I had imagined. A big rectangular counter blocked the passage beyond the plate glass entry. Cleary, I wasn't going to saunter into anyone's office. At the counter, the Administrative Assistant, a youngish woman with mousy hair, asked, "May I help you?" This immediately deflated me because I had planned to say, "I'm here to help *you!*" Still, I tried something that sounded like, "Hi, I'd like my services for your benefit to teach here."

The assistant blinked across the counter and said again, "May I help you?"

"Employment," I stammered. "A job. For teaching. I can teach English."

She smiled politely. "Have you taught here before?"

It occurred to me that I hadn't taught anywhere at all.

"No," I said, "I'm from North Carolina. I just graduated from college—the University of North Carolina." *Honors in English,* I wanted to add.

"Oh, fine," she said, handing me an application. "Fill this out, if you would."

Somehow I hadn't thought an application would be necessary. But, now that it was in my hands, it did make sense.

It asked the usual name-address information, which I started scribbling out, and then it asked for more: teaching experience, publications, awards, references. Abruptly I stopped writing, a shameful heat rising to my ears. I don't know how long I stared at the unfilled page before me. "Teaching experience (list dates and institutions, starting with the most recent), publications (list most recent first), awards, references (list mailing addresses and phone numbers of three)." All of this echoed in my head.

When I stood finally, I was dizzy with humiliation. Surely everyone in the office saw me for the fool I was. Affecting as much calm as I could muster, I told the assistant that I would complete the form later, then bring it back—as if suddenly I had been called away. The assistant offered me another painfully polite smile (how young did I look?), then I stumbled into the midday glare, woozy with the realization that life on my own might be harder than I ever imagined.

I ended up selling family photo plans door-to-door. Pay was strictly by commission. I thought it would be challenging. I bought a couple of neckties and some fancy loafers Nana thought were ugly, then I was on the road, driving through the orange groves all day and looking for the next sale from my lead list, which my supervisor updated for me every few days from the birth announcements in the local papers. Always, I called upon expectant mothers. If the baby had already been born, I'd spout my congratulations, then let loose the avalanche of questions that every new mother wants to hear: *boy or girl? how many pounds?* If the boy was weighty, I might say, "Holy cow, you're going to have a football player on your hands!" If the girl was weighty, I'd say, "Oh, she's healthy!" *Named after a family member? Is He/she/it sleeping through the night now?* When a mother showed me the inevitable snapshot of a small face that could have been a plate of calamari, I'd say, "Beautiful! Who does he look most like, do you think?"

Every question was an invitation into their lives. The opening line was always, "Could you help me?" in order to appeal to their good Samaritan impulse. I'd let the mom-to-be take a good look at me to see that I was harmless. This was 1977, when you could still knock on a stranger's door without rousing suspicion.

My trainer drove a late-model Mercedes and spoke effusively about the great blessing the Family Portrait Plan had been for him, a guy who had hardly made it through high school and now had a wife, two kids, and owned a three-bedroom ranch in a suburb of Visalia. When he was making a sale, he would never take no for an answer. If he couldn't sell the "gold" package, then he sold the "silver," and, if not that, then, the "bronze." If the prospective customer was especially stubborn, he'd say such things as "Aren't your children worth the best portrait plan?" or "How much are you willing to spend on cable TV every month? The Family Portrait Plan isn't asking for half that amount!"

I'm not sure how depressed I was about all this. For a brief time, it seemed like a game, but very soon—within a month or two—I was determined to quit as quickly as I could afford to. In the meantime, driving up to a hundred miles a day, I got to know the valley too well, from the tangy cow stink of Coalinga in the far southwest—where the treeless, oppressively flat fields could have been lifted from North Dakota—to the pungent citrus rot of the orchards to the northeast, where the steep-mounded hills began and Kaweah River sluiced down from the Sequoias. Some days I would drive and drive, unable to bring myself to knock on another door. Often, I cruised the best neighborhoods and admired the older houses and wondered when and how I could buy a house of my own. It seemed that if I owned a house, had something as solid as that, I would be all right.

When I'd get back to Nana's, she would be in her tiny kitchen, frying pork chops or breaded steak in a big black skillet, a pot of kidney beans boiling on the back burner, a beer in her free hand. She'd get me a beer too, and, as I popped the top, she'd smile at me with such love and adoration, I'd all but cringe.

"How'd it go today?" she'd ask, ever hopeful that my sales had taken off, that I was happy and determined to settle here with her. I was surprised, and a little dismayed, at how easily she and I fell into the parent/child dynamic. Her eagerness to give me cash, cook for me, launder my clothes, succeeded only in making me quietly resentful. At least every other day she called me by my father's name. Although I never corrected her, it creeped me out: I didn't want to be my father—not even to please her. I was, after all, barely a man, barely out of my parents' house, and desperate now to be my own person. My stay at Nana's was nothing more than a stopover, I told myself: I was headed for better places, bigger things.

That's why selling door-to-door seemed like playacting. And that's why my ultimate failure at it didn't shame me. What did shame me was the fact that I didn't bring home enough to pay a dime of Nana's expenses. I hated that she didn't mind.

Nana worked on the line at one of the local packing houses, where she stood for eight hours a day sorting oranges. The conveyor belt that carried the oranges was similar to a grocery store's, only twenty yards long. Women on either side picked through the fruit, sorting by size and, occasionally, tossing the battered ones down a nearby chute. Nana, like most of the women, wore white cotton gloves to spare her hands.

Every night we would drink—beer for me, whiskey for her—and watch her black-and-white TV: "All in the Family," "CHIPS," "Charlie's Angels." That was good enough for her. All the while, I was wondering what would become of me—after three months of living with her, I had gained fifteen pounds, I had given up looking for other, better work, and my future seemed as hazy as one of those hamlets I'd see on the dusty horizon when I'd drive a long, two-lane blacktop to another one of my morning leads.

Some days, the rare days, when the haze of farm dust cleared after a rain, I could see the hulking purple silhouettes of the Sierra Nevadas, their jagged peaks pinkish white with snow. For me, an east-coast kid who had seen nothing but the lowly, aged mounds of the Appalachians, the Sierras were the skyline of Oz. The sight of them was the only magic California seemed to offer.

College friends of mine were living on the coast, just south of San Francisco. When I visited them finally, I beheld a version of California that bore a faint resemblance to the hip Hollywood vision most of America believes. I knew I'd have to leave the valley as soon as possible. The San Joaquin seemed like the Ozarks by comparison. I realized that its hickishness appealed to Nana. Exeter was distinctly working class: wood-framed bungalows, salt-boxes, and shacks block after block, on tiny lots, though well back from the incredibly wide roadways. That's what made life in California different, I thought when I first arrived: there's land to spare—wide streets and plenty of open space, as if this might be enough for the hopefuls who came here.

It took me two weeks to build up the courage to tell Nana I was leaving. At seventy-four, she was still working a forty-hour week. She had friends in the area—people she'd known since before I was born—and she had her jungle of plants and flowers

on her front porch. And here, at last, she had companionship, the
stand-in for her only son. Her life couldn't get any better.

It was winter, a time when a gray-white mat of clouds settles
over the valley week after week without a break and thick fog
makes driving hazardous at all hours and intermittent drizzle
dampens everything. On cold nights, I could hear the thumping chutter of the propellered turbines whipping the air above the
orchards to keep the freeze off. These had come to replace the
smudge pots of old, which used to fill the orchards with smoke
and feeble heat. I could not imagine a lonelier sound than those
distant props chopping the night chill.

More than once, Nana had mentioned that we could get a bigger place if I helped with the rent. Each time I had only muttered
"maybe" in response or I had said nothing at all.

Finally, at breakfast one morning, as Nana was frying the
usual bacon and eggs in a skillet of grease, I said, "I'm going to
Montara next week."

"That where your friends are?" she asked, poking at the
bacon.

"They have a house that's big enough to share," I said.

"How long you gonna stay with them?"

"As long as it takes to find a job," I said.

Then she got it: "You're moving?"

"Moving" suggested that I had come to the valley to stay and
now I had changed my mind.

"I won't be far away," I said quickly. "I'll visit you and you can
visit me."

Stirring the pan, breaking the eggs, she said nothing.

After I relocated, I was haunted by the image of Nana waving me off from her meager front yard, the carefully tended flowers behind her. I feared she would drink through the loneliness,
one long night after another. Much to my surprise, she adopted
Harold, the neighborhood's stray cat. During her first visit to me

in Berkeley, she couldn't stop worrying about the animal. "He might think I've run off," she said. I was relieved she had something to care for, someone to go home to. Later, she sent me a photo of Harold watching TV. "He likes to hear the president talk," she wrote.

One year later, I decided I was going to be a professional musician. Though I had some ability as a drummer, I didn't know how to do this. With the little money I had saved as a customs clearance clerk and warehouse messenger, I moved into a shared house in Berkeley. Then I rented rehearsal space in an old Laundromat that was crowded with broken-down pianos that a Chinese immigrant repaired and sold. I spent several days soundproofing my rehearsal room, then I began a regime of practice—as many as eight hours a day. I didn't know what I was doing, didn't really know how to teach myself everything a professional drummer should know. But I refused to fail. I was convinced that if I tried really hard and didn't give up, I could make something of myself. I told myself that my inspiration was Ringo Starr, the Beatles drummer. He wasn't a particularly accomplished musician. He couldn't even perform a press roll and he didn't know how to read music. Because he didn't know how to do things the right way, he did things differently. As a result, he was sometimes brilliant. His drumming was remarkable for its inventiveness. A lesser man would have been too self-conscious, too aware of his shortcomings and would not have tried.

I was a professional musician for six years. Nothing remarkable, but I made a living and was proud of that. I suspect that this modest accomplishment grew more from my appreciation of my father's work ethic and my mother's country girl optimism than from my admiration of a rock drummer. When later, I decided to go to grad school and fulfill my dream of being a teacher, I was terrified. I believed I'd be found out to be a dummy and unworthy of a degree. But I stumbled on because I believed I had no choice.

"Failure is not an option" sounds arrogant and presumptuous, but in the context of my family's history and especially my father's example, it was the only story I knew. This is why my failures hit me so hard later. And this is why, when I came to the Queen Anne finally, I would not give up.

17

FAILURE

IF JILL HAD NOT TAKEN ME AWAY for a week of rest at the end of August, I might have had a nervous collapse when September came and we failed our inspection. The house wasn't anywhere near up to code. I had imagined that the bank would repossess the house or put us on some stinging probation. But no. Missing a 203K rehab deadline is no big deal, we learned. It happens all the time. *Horses, not zebras.* I wished somebody had told me this beforehand. We filed for an extension on the loan, which was granted. Then Jill announced, "I can't do rehab work on top of two jobs. I'm sorry, Ron. I'll help you when I can."

Now that the university was in session again, she said I'd have to slow down too. "You'll end up getting hurt or sick and then what?" she cautioned. When I didn't respond, she added: "We've got to have a life, Ron."

"What about the high interest we're forced to pay until the house passes inspection?"

"So we'll pay it," she said.

"For years?"

"It won't be years."

"The way we're going, it'll take years." I drew a deep breath and secretly tamped down my panic. "My family's visiting in less than three months!"

Jill shook her head in dismay. "If you had asked me, I would've told you not to invite them."

"Too late," I said.

"Why not phone them and tell them we'll do it next year?" She attempted a sympathetic smile. "They'll understand."

"They'll understand that I've fucked up again," I said.

"This is no time for stubborn pride, Ron."

"It isn't just pride," I said. This was true. It was pride and desperation and obsession and superstition and blind fear all balled into one overwhelming sense of dread. "They really want to see the house," I continued. "And we still have time to make it good enough for a visit. All we have to do is paint and clean up a little."

"We're not ready to paint," Jill said matter-of-factly. "I don't know when we'll be ready." We were standing in the clutter of tools, supplies, and sheet-covered furniture in the living room. We hadn't set up furniture in a single room yet. She sighed: "Your family will understand if you cancel. Really, Ron."

"I can't cancel."

"It's not like you're stuck in a bear trap," she pleaded. "You have a choice!"

"Just do this for me," I pleaded in return. "We can make this happen."

"Your mother's going to be horrified. You know it's going to be a disaster."

"*Negative!*" I said this in sing-song fashion. It was one of the jocular watchwords we'd developed to check the other whenever the mood turned unnecessarily dark.

"*Realistic!*" she countered.

* * *

Nicholas came by once a week to do special work. He installed the salvaged, vintage double doors Jill and I had found at Historic York. So the side panel and jamb that she discovered came of use much sooner than I had anticipated. The vestibule, with its two sets of double doors, now looked very much as it had originally.

Nicholas was patient enough with my manic pace and I was deferential enough of his expertise that we worked well together. Occasionally, I would surprise him. When he saw some of my electrical work in the basement, he paused to admire it, then asked, "Who did this?" I was discovering that when I'm careful, I can do good work. However, Nicholas himself wasn't always careful. I didn't understand the significance of this until the day we were fixing the front stairs and Nicholas was nailing a loose baluster in place. The nail head bent, but he didn't pull out the nail or straighten it. Instead, he pounded it in the way it was. Sloppy work! When he saw my look of concern, he smiled and said, "That's good enough for this old house." I said nothing and we moved on. But his comment weighed on me because I saw that, like our neighborhood historian, he didn't think our work would amount to much. In his mind, we'd be lucky to pull the house together and get it up to code. End of story.

This had been my original aim—or the aim I had finally arrived at: just keep the house from falling in and be happy that we had such a cool, once-upon-a-time grand place to live in. I had imagined that, to save money and make it fast work, Jill and I would replace our seventy-two missing balusters with a wild mix of salvaged balusters of every style—anything that would fit the space. Same with the damaged doors and missing mantels and ceiling lights. Get cool old stuff, mix it up, and don't worry about historic accuracy or condition. Make the interior an arty, funky mish-mash. Wouldn't that be good enough?

But I'd been having second thoughts about this. The better I got at rehabbing, the more I wanted from my efforts. Why couldn't Jill and I bring the house back all the way? Although I was exhausted and thoroughly stressed-out, I was also on a radical learning curve and electrified by the possibility that maybe I could do work my father might have admired. I was starting to get a glimpse of what was possible: a gorgeous, state-of-the-art, thoroughly authentic Victorian. Forget the compromised, funky mish-mash. Jill was wrong about slowing down, I decided. If I slowed down now, I'd never see it through. When I was in high school, I ran a marathon for the first and only time. I did really well until the halfway point and then I stopped because I thought I needed rest. In fact, I sat down in the shade of a tree. And I fell asleep. When I awoke, I was so disoriented and so suddenly fatigued that I could do nothing more than walk the rest of the way. It was frustrating and demoralizing, and the resulting disappointment stayed with me a long time.

Already, Jill and I had met too many home-rehabbers who had stalled, their houses in perpetual disarray, their plans shelved, their energies exhausted because once stopped, they couldn't rev it up again. *Don't stop!* I told myself. That fall semester, after getting our 203K extension, I'd come home from teaching, eat a quick dinner with Jill, then go to work. I wouldn't get to bed until two or four in the morning. I did this seven nights a week. One afternoon, I forgot to tell Jill that I had removed some floorboards on the porch and covered them over with a piece of sheetrock to keep the cat from crawling into the open space. We had already lost Corona one day after she sneaked into the staircase where we had removed a tread. She was mewing in the recesses under the steps for hours.

As soon as Jill closed the kitchen door on her way out, I whirled around to warn her. But too late. The sheetrock snapped under her and she fell hard to the porch floor. She wasn't hurt badly but it shook her up and she began to cry. Legs sprawled, she looked like a skater just pulled from the cracked ice. Her beret had fallen from her head. I kneeled beside her and apologized twenty times.

She rubbed her bruised leg. "You have to be more careful!"

"I forgot!" I said. "I know I get sloppy."

"Careful with *me*," she said.

This sounded like a warning. "I'm *sorry*," I repeated.

"You're in ten places at once. And where am I?"

"You're right here, with me," I said.

"I mean *where am I in your life?*"

"You're the center of my life!" I said.

"No, this house is the center of your life."

"Well, sort of—for now," I admitted. "But it's only temporary."

She wiped at her eyes. We were still sitting on the cold, scabrous floor of the empty porch, which reeked of rat urine. Everywhere I looked I saw flaking paint and rotting wood.

"We never see each other," she said, "we haven't had sex in three weeks, and you're so tense you don't even recognize me when we pass in the hall at work."

Jill and I knew that, for the sake of professionalism, we couldn't act as a couple in the department. It was an awkward situation and a few colleagues didn't like it. I had given supervision of Jill's teaching to a senior faculty member. The dean didn't know of this. Had I been smart, I'd have resigned as chair so that Jill and I could come out of our closet, but my department was in the middle of a program review and I felt duty-bound to see that through. As it was, I hardly talked to Jill at work. And she was right: at home, I hardly saw her.

* * *

Our house was far from livable as Christmas approached. And yet I had told my mother and brothers that Jill and I had made great strides, that we were heroes of the neighborhood. One week before their arrival, I realized they would not be able to appreciate where we'd started. The house was such a wreck– despite all we had done—it just wasn't possible for them to imagine that it had been even *much more* of a wreck before we'd started work. So it wouldn't matter how far we'd come: we clearly had not come far enough. Jill and I had acclimated ourselves to a perpetual dream-vision. The Queen Anne would be splendid, it would be amazing—everywhere we turned, we saw it. But that kind of vision can't be argued or exhorted into somebody else's mind. We might as well have been missionaries plunging into the jungle to proselytize headhunters: when my family arrived, none of them would understand, much less believe, a word we'd say.

Unfortunately, I was a long way from putting a much-needed toilet on our first floor. So my mother would have to hike upstairs for a bathroom. And it was truly a hike. This was just one of many problems that announced themselves as I took an inventory of all that was wrong. The 2000 holiday season was bitterly cold in the northeast. Although our new windows were tight, their shuttered surrounds were not, and the cold wind pushed easily through the cracks and seams I had yet to seal. The front and back doors were even worse because I had not weatherproofed them. The back door—a big thin slab—was impossible to insulate or weatherproof, icy wind wheezing into the kitchen. And the basement, with its original casement windows, was hemorrhaging heat. It was impossible to keep the house warm.

In late December, the house was still nowhere near ready for guests. For weeks, I had worked every night until the early morning hours to patch and prime every wall. The walls were stark white. It would be another year before we would start adding color. On the first floor, we had replaced the missing mantels with modest wood ones, but each of these was simply hanging on its wall hooks. I hadn't yet repaired any of the fireplace hearths, so these remained crumbling and dirty. The windows were without shutters, so there was no privacy on the first floor. Our kitchen had a refrigerator, a stove, and a couple of funky cabinets that sat unanchored on the floor. For a countertop, we used a length of plywood that had been painted black, the paint coming up every time we tried to wipe the counter clean.

None of the bedrooms was ready for occupation. Everything was dusty from construction work, especially from sanding plaster. Our many boxes of belongings were stacked in corners. In the third floor front room, where my brother Mike and his wife were supposed to sleep, there sat fifty boxes of books. The room was going to be a library, but now it looked like a warehouse. Another room down the hall was crowded with tools and construction supplies. The basement—dark and damp—was nothing more than a cluttered storage depot. We had some furniture but not much. We were still using Jill's small table in our huge dining room and my much-too-small Mission-style sideboard. Nothing except the dining room table was set up on the first floor. We had put up a couple of ceiling lights, but bare bulbs predominated.

Two days before my family arrived, I had insisted that Jill stay up with me to finish tiling the master bathroom. We worked until 3:00 a.m. as I cut tile and Jill laid it. She was in tears as she finished, and I felt like a bully, but was convinced that the tile would make a difference. This seemed a metaphor for the year, how I would push so hard and Jill would give so much and still it wouldn't matter. There was simply too much to do.

Throughout the house, we still had long stretches of pink contractor's paper taped to the floor to protect the finish, only now there were plaster leavings, mounds of dog and cat hair, and all manner of other debris under the paper. And we could hardly vacuum the paper because the vacuum would suck it up. We had replaced none of the stairway balusters, so these huge gaps under the banisters were closed up with sheets of plywood, which made the house look like it was barely held together.

My hope to be nearly done with the rehab was an obviously laughable delusion. The family's visit was supposed to be a treat, an opportunity for me to express my love in a cozy big-tree, around-the-fireplace Christmassy fashion. Like one of those old Andy Williams Holiday Specials. I guess, too, that I had wanted to show my family that I was, finally, a success. It embarrassed me to think of my accomplished brothers walking into this house. They'd be polite and supportive but secretly they'd think: *well, that's Ron for you*. . . Here, I had done something unique and fun and I'd thought it'd be ready to share and celebrate, but now in a last-minute panic I saw that, as so often in my impulsive life, I had been wrong.

18
CHRISTMAS COMES BUT ONCE A YEAR

AS THE HOUR OF MY FAMILY'S ARRIVAL approached, Jill and I were nearly delirious from rushing to make the house tolerable for our guests. I had stayed up all night trying to clean and straighten and still nothing was clean enough. We hadn't had time to buy a Christmas tree. We hadn't even made the beds. And the beds were the only pieces of furniture that were usable. Everywhere, furniture was stacked in piles. Sue and John, our friends across the street, came over and spent three hours tidying up and arranging the furniture on the first floor. Then we were out of time. My mother was at the front door.

She's a small woman with a perpetually furrowed brow and a Southerner's expectations that everything be "nice." She stepped through the front door, took one look at the raw yawning space before her and said, "Oh!" as if bitten by a spider. Then she said something like, *You poor things, you're working so hard, are you getting any rest at all? Can't we get you some help? Why do you put yourself through all of this, you know we didn't have to have Christmas here . . .*

I installed her in the best, that is, neatest, room in the house. But, not five minutes later, Jill found my mother wiping down the bureau and saying, "Everything is so dusty!"

When my middle brother, Dave, arrived, he tried to pet Harriet and she promptly bit him, but—as usual—did not draw blood. "I'm really good with dogs!" Dave protested, examining his injured hand. Only eleven months older than I, he's my Irish twin and one of the few men I know who looks good with a mustache.

My eldest brother, Mike, arrived ready to convert us to a new life of raw foods. In six months he would be the same age my father had been when he died of stomach cancer twenty years before. Over the past decade it seemed Mike had been on a drive to find the key to longevity. He had lost thirty pounds and now seemed frail with good health. A pharmacist, he had been certified recently as a nutritionist and was in the process of setting up a business in nutritional therapy. Already, he had brought his sky-high 320 cholesterol down to a manageable 240. He did the same for Dave. My mother, who chain-smoked, was a harder case.

Then Lois, Mike's wife, got Multiple Sclerosis and the stakes were suddenly very high. Through a rigorous regimen of raw foods and vitamin supplements, he and Lois were able to stop the M.S. cold. She's had it for over fifteen years and it has never gotten worse. A hard-driving salesperson of medical equipment, Lois still works a fifty-hour week, traveling all over the Southeast.

His nutritional successes mounting, Mike was full of the latest research about raw foods and enzyme therapy, and so eager to share the good news that we could not get him to talk about anything else. We might begin a conversation about the Hubble telescope but he would end up talking about the amazing benefits of juiced barley grass and sprouted raw almonds. What made this all the more painful was that Mike is a soft-spoken, very sweet man—not a hard-pusher in any way. Had he been a hard-pusher, maybe one of us could have said to him: *Mike, will you please shut up!*

Ever the go-getter, Lois wasn't even unpacked before she was unloading my boxes of books on the third floor and helping me stack them into the wall of shelves I had erected hastily the week before. With Mike's help, we spent all afternoon putting up books.

When Mrs. King, Lois's mother, arrived from Birmingham, Alabama, she presented Jill and me with a bottle of her homemade scuppernong wine. Within a hour, paring knife in hand, she was scraping paint from the panes of our kitchen cabinets.

My mother called me to her room. "Ronald, what is that?" She held open the closet door.

"Did you find something?" I dreaded the worst. A dead mouse?

"It looks like a painting," she said with some concern.

"Oh, yeah, graffiti," I said, relieved. "There's a lot of it in the house. Or there was. Even in the closets."

"So what *is* that?"

"That," I said, "would be an eyeball."

"A *big* eyeball!" she said.

"Yeah, there were even bigger ones upstairs all over the walls. In the *eyeball room*."

She shook her head sadly. "You poor things."

To give everybody some relief, we went down the block to visit Rick and Charles, whose house offered everything you might expect from a Victorian Christmas extravaganza. They had a fully decorated Christmas tree in nearly every room, tinseled pine boughs draped from the archways between rooms, garlands wound around the banisters, candles flickering from the festooned mantels, a wood fire burning in their living room, and, in their gorgeous basement, Rick's massive Christmas train setup, its festive little cars clickety-clacking through miniature snowbound villages. My mother couldn't take enough pictures, exclaiming that everybody back in her retirement village was going to drop dead at the sight of such splendor.

She took no photos of our beat-up house during her visit. Even though Jill and I understood my mother's misgivings, I couldn't

eyeball in mom's closet

help being disappointed in myself for not having worked harder and faster to make our Queen Anne as beautiful as it deserved to be.

After sharing some mulled wine and apple cider with Rick and Charles, we went to our friend Scott's house, also in the neighborhood. A collector of antique Christmas ornaments, Scott has an annual display that is museum-worthy. Every year, he loads his tree with vintage ornaments, including 1940s bubble lights and even earlier electric decorations, like a circa 1900 Santa tree topper. His house is crowded with old Christmas displays and, upstairs, he has a roomful of cases for his rarest lights and decorations. I was happy to see my mother—a lover of antiques—*oh!* and *ah!* at his collection.

Scott took a picture of my family gathered in front of his splendid tree. In the photo, I look ill, like a cancer patient who has been let out of the hospital for his last visit home. Though smiling, I am pale, drawn, and downright skinny (I had lost twenty pounds), my stare almost dazed, bruises of sleep-deprivation under each eye.

That night, when Jill and I were alone at last, she said, "This is a disaster!"

"How can you say that?" I countered. "We've just started. I'm going out to get a tree tomorrow—and we'll make a good dinner. It's going to be great!"

We were lying on Jill's narrow, brass bed. Harriet and PJ were on their mats nearby. Charlie was at the foot of our bed, cleaning his paws. Tess was hiding somewhere on the first floor. Corona, upstairs, was quiet, thankfully.

Jill lay back and stared at the recently patched ceiling. "Ron, I heard her saying she was going to tell her friends that Rick and Charles's house was *ours*!"

"She wouldn't do that."

"I *heard* her!"

"You heard her say she *should* show those photos *as if* they were from our house," I said.

"Isn't that an insult?"

"Rick and Charles's house is splendid," I said.

"And ours looks awful," she said. "You know, your family thinks I dragged you into this."

"No, they don't!"

She turned to me: "Do *you* think I dragged you into this?"

"Why would I think *that*? Do you see how this conversation is going?"

Jill sighed. "Your mother thinks I'm awful—she wasn't here five minutes before she was wiping up dust!"

"Why is it your job to wipe up dust all of sudden?" Actually, dust-wiping was *my* job. "My mother *likes* you," I continued. "We've already been through that, remember?"

"No," Jill said. "This is the real test—this is what she's been waiting for."

"You can't be serious."

"You can't be so naïve," she said. "Our house looks horrible. We've let them down. Imagine what they're saying to each other right now."

"It's a cool house," I insisted.

She groaned. "That's *not* what they're saying!"

Secretly, I vowed to make this a great visit for everyone, Jill included. Somehow, everything would work out. Okay, the house was messy and run-down, but we could still have fun, couldn't we?

The next morning, I woke at dawn and knew immediately that something was very wrong. The house was freezing. When I got downstairs I discovered the problem: a cold gust was wafting up from the stairway to the basement, a stairway that so far was without a door. As I descended the basement stairs, it felt like I was entering a walk-in freezer. I discovered that I had failed to lock the basement door and, sometime during the night, the wind had kicked it open. All night, cold air had been pouring into the basement.

Jill could hear my curses all the way to the second floor.

After explaining the problem, I rushed out to buy space heaters. The night before, at dinner, both my mother and Mrs. King had mentioned how cold the house seemed. Without space heaters, our now-icy house wasn't going to warm up any time soon.

That afternoon, in the freezing backyard, I finished assembling the wrecked door to the basement stairs so at least I could block the basement's updraft. I also remembered to cut a cat hole in the center bottom of the door because we kept the litter boxes for Charlie and Tess downstairs.

Corona, I learned, was enjoying walking all over Lois and Mike throughout the night on their sleeper sofa. They were, after all, in her space.

Lois's mother, I learned, had taken to sleeping on the floor because her bed was too soft for her bad back.

winter view
from garden gate

The bitter cold would not let up, the day overcast, my mother and Mrs. King wearing thick sweaters over sweatshirts and hugging themselves most the day. Occasionally, I caught them eyeing the empty, useless fireplaces with longing. We might as well have been camping.

So much was going wrong so quickly, Jill retreated to the bedroom for a long, hard cry. The rest of us were downstairs in the chilly dining room. My bundled-up mother was nursing her third bourbon; Dave was playing gin rummy with Mrs. King; Lois was cleaning up—she couldn't stop herself, it seemed—and Michael was holding forth on yet another miracle: studies had proven that if you maintain a near-starvation diet, you will live longer.

Hastily I went upstairs. Jill was standing next to our bed, bawling quietly.

I took her in my arms. "Come on," I coached, "it's going well—all things considered."

"Oh, god!" She pulled away.

"No, really. They're being good sports about it."

She gulped for breath, wiped at her eyes. "So you admit that it's a little much for them?"

"Yes," I said. "I feel bad about it. Really bad." When she didn't answer, I continued: "I just thought—I don't know. I fucked up, I guess."

Shaking her head sadly, she began weeping again. "They hate us!"

"They don't hate us." I put my arms around her once more. "They pity us maybe."

"That's even worse," she blubbered. "If Michael tells me one more time how to improve my diet, I'm going to jump out a window!"

"Come on, we can do this."

"We don't even have a *tree*!"

"We'll have a tree—in just a minute I'm going out to get one!"

"It's two days from Christmas, Ron. The trees are *gone*."

"Nonsense," I said. "There are plenty left!"

Actually, there weren't. Everything I found was much too small. I wasn't about to bring home a laughable, spindly Charlie Brown tree. As I drove frantically from one tree lot to the next, I thought: *This is my life—everything's too late and on-the-fly, bolstered by promises I can't keep.* At last, I found a lopsided eight-footer

our first christmas

that looked worse for wear. It was so heavy I had to screw the tree holder into a three-foot square of thick plywood. But I was so harassed and tired, I failed to noticed that one of my screws had penetrated the back side. So, when I pushed the tree and its stand into place, I dug a seven-inch gash into our never-before-marred parquet floor in the first-floor bay. *Oh, well.*

Jill came down finally and helped decorate the tree. Although I thought the tree looked good—it was a remarkable last-minute find, I'd decided—it was, in fact, a most pathetic tree: a large version of the laughable Charlie Brown tree. But we wrapped a few strings of lights around it and hung a box of ornaments and then somebody snapped a photo of Jill hanging the star on top—the only photo of Christmas 2000 in our Queen Anne.

That night, for the second time during the family's visit, Charlie caterwauled. Arthritic, he could not walk down the stairs without making a loud thumping noise. Late at night, then early in the morning, we'd hear his yowl grow like the approaching distress of a small, damaged plane. When he was at full throttle, he'd begin to wander. Then, finally, we'd hear his thump-bump, thump-bump as he hobbled down the stairs, searching for us—or maybe simply for a warm place to die.

This went on for two more nights. By that time—cold, dusty, and sleep-deprived—our visitors were thoroughly miserable. Jill retreated a couple more times for more crying, once after Mike said she might have more energy if she ate raw beets and the second time after my mother said in passing, "I really don't know how you kids live like this, you poor dears." My mother was drinking a lot—and nobody was stopping her. I was almost tempted to let her smoke in the house too. Anything to make her happy.

They should have all gone to a motel. They had every right. But they knew that Jill and I would have been devastated had they abandoned us. So they stayed and tried to make the best of it. It was a tremendous show of love on their part and it deepened my debt to them.

Harriet was too often underfoot and managed to bite Mike on the hand.

"She was wagging her tail!" he protested.

"Are you bleeding?" I asked.

"She doesn't usually break the skin," Jill added.

"*Usually?*" Dave joked.

"Michael, didn't they tell you to leave that dog alone?" Lois scolded. "I swear you Tanner boys don't listen."

We were sitting at the dining room table for Christmas dinner. Our last meal together.

"She's right," my mother agreed, drink in hand. "Tanner boys are stubborn. You should have seen their father!" She chuckled. "He used to say, *I may be wrong sometimes, but I'm always correct!*"

"No," Dave said, "*I may be incorrect sometimes, but I'm never wrong.*"

My mother blinked at him: "Didn't I say that?"

"He wasn't more stubborn than *my* father," Lois said, "isn't that right, Momma?"

Mrs. King seemed to be daydreaming, staring into the distance across the table. Actually, she was hard of hearing.

"Momma?"

"What?" She looked like so many of the elderly women I'd grown up with: wire-rim eyeglasses, auburn-dyed hair pulled back in a bun, expression somewhere between a squint and a smile.

"Wasn't Daddy stubborn?"

"Oh," she answered, "Mr. King was stubborn, lord have mercy!"

"We tried to get him to stop eating white bread," Mike said. "It killed him in the end."

"Nearly everybody in my family's died of strokes," my mother announced somberly. She poured herself another drink.

"It's them butter biscuits," Mrs. King volunteered.

"Hydrogenated oils," Mike corrected. "We couldn't stop Mr. King from sneaking off to Trucker's Delight, his favorite cafeteria."

"And Krispy Kreme donuts," Lois added. "He loved his Krispy Kremes."

"But he died happy, didn't he, eating his Krispy Kreme donuts?" Jill said.

Though Jill said this humorously, I worried that she'd start an argument.

"No reason you can't be healthy and happy at the same time," Mike quipped.

I watched Jill carefully. Before she could answer, I blurted: "I used to be addicted to Krispy Kremes—I'd eat a dozen in one sitting!"

"Imagine that," Jill said in mock awe. "And here you are to tell the tale!"

"Ronald does the right thing," Mike continued, "juicing every-day. All you need to do now is to strain your juice, Ron, because that pulp slows down the absorption of enzymes."

Jill wagged her finger in my face: "Strain your juice!"

"Speaking of which," said Dave, "pass the ham."

What's Christmas dinner without a ham? My mother had asked when Mike balked at the suggestion.

There were also candied yams and turkey and canned jel-lied cranberry and creamed corn and steamed green beans. Our Southern mothers would not have had it any other way. At least three times my mother had come up behind me to turn on the burner under my steamed green beans after I'd turned it off. "You've got to cook them," she insisted. "Steaming *is* cooking," I told her. How many years had we had this tug-of-war?

The next day, after we took everyone to the airport, Jill slumped in the passenger seat—like a marionette with its strings cut abruptly—and said, "It's going to take me a month to recover."

I glanced at her: "Does that mean you don't want to do it next year?"

"Oh, you're funny, Tanner."

A week later, from her retirement village in Arizona, my mother vowed that she would never return to Baltimore in winter. It had to be, she said, the coldest city on earth.

19
LEVERAGING

THREE MONTHS LATER, at winter's end, after working every hour we could spare, we passed our final inspection. The house still looked a wreck but, officially, it was safe to live in. The bank locked our mortgage at 8% and at last we could breathe relief. So far we had filled three thirty-yard Dumpsters with garbage, 154 industrial-sized garbage bags with trash, made sixteen runs to the dump, used eight fifty-pound bags of plaster, ten five-gallon tubs of joint compound (more plaster), five five-gallon tubs of primer, fifty-two tubes of caulk, eighteen rectangles of sheet metal, and twelve sixty-pound bags of concrete and mortar. And we were only getting started. The banisters were still covered over with plywood, the mantels were still detached from the walls, the walls themselves were still unpainted, only primed—we had not found time to strip the shutters so we simply hid them in their recesses and the inspector didn't notice. In fact, the inspector hardly looked at anything.

One week later, after we paid the last of our big rehab bills, the hundred-year-old clay sewer pipe in our backyard burst, requiring a hand-dug trench and new pipe—at a cost of $2,000, all the money we had left. Then, in freezing weather, I poured a new concrete walk to replace what had been torn up for the sewer pipe. I kept the fresh concrete covered with a plastic tarp and warm with work lights for three days until it dried. It was like incubating a nest of chicks. Then, following a snow storm, our rear gutter collapsed under the weight of ice. Hammer in hand, I hung from the third floor porch and hacked out ice in twenty-pound pieces (the icicles were seven feet long and as thick as elephant tusks), then tossed them into the backyard, nearly forty feet below. Then, I spent two hours attempting to right the buckled gutter, like a sailor attempting to mend his mast in a storm. I ended up shoving my eight-foot ladder under it. The ladder wedged nicely—and at last the gutter was fairly level and the ice-water stopped spilling down the side of the house. Once I was inside and dry again, it took me about a half hour to thaw my hands. And another hour to warm them.

We were flat broke. I was barely making house and car payments from month to month. Jill was paying off her student loans and car payments and helping with utilities. Our heating bills were astronomical—numbers that made our friends gasp in disbelief. Only in America can you live like this, so far beyond your means. I was amazed at how eager banks were to give me money now that I owned a house. Jill and I could either hunker down and start paying off our debts or we could go for broke and finish the house. As it was, we couldn't renovate without spending money. We'd have to stop work and wait until we saved enough to do one project. Then wait until we saved enough for another project. At that pace, it'd take us twenty years. Just like Rick and Charles. I didn't see the point in waiting. My father died when he was forty-nine. I was already forty-four.

Dad was going to retire comfortably at sixty-five. His dream was to buy a big camper and travel the continent with Mom. Nobody was more frugal than my father. I recall those big jars of pennies, nickels, and dimes he saved. He was never in debt. Like so many of his generation, he was successful because he was careful. Maybe his generation made it too easy for us. Although I took summer jobs when I could find them as a teenager, I didn't have to work. Dad gave me a generous allowance for cutting the lawn and doing other chores. And he paid for my college education. I was grateful. I felt twinges of guilt for my privilege. And I wondered, when and if the time came, would I have the guts to live a hard life if I had to? I answered this question when, just three months after we passed our inspection, I took out a second mortgage on the Queen Anne.

Financial types call this "leveraging." Capitalize on what you have. If Jill and I could bring the Queen Anne back—I mean, really bring it back, make it a showcase—then we'd double our investment. Real estate prices were rising. We were riding a booming economy. Still, a second mortgage under our circumstances was risky. Our house remained a wreck and everything we planned to do relied on our staying healthy, staying together, and working very hard. One ill-placed disaster could ruin us, I knew. It's something my father would never have attempted.

Jill and I were obsessed by, maybe addicted to, our ongoing project. It centered us as nothing else could. When we were renovating, we seemed the perfect couple, complementary in every way. I'd do the electrical and carpentry, she'd do the paint-stripping and refinishing. She had an eye for detail and design, I had an eye for construction and mechanics (much to my surprise). We loved going to auctions and salvage warehouses to find mantels and lights and architectural hardware. But whenever we stopped working, whenever we weren't focused on fixing the house, we were at odds.

I'd come home at the end of the day and call for Jill, who got home before me, but she wouldn't answer. I imagined that she was self-absorbed. I'd picture her shopping online or reading her email. I was convinced that she just didn't care enough to look for me and greet me at the door. My misgivings went further than that, of course. Sarah had walked out on me. Then, my girlfriend after that had ended our two-year relationship because she said she couldn't sustain the love we had begun. Either I am too high maintenance or love, in most circumstances, is too heavy a weight to carry. Maybe both. When I'd come home and end up shouting for Jill, I'd think: *this isn't going to last, she isn't going to be here when I need her most.* Just the act of shouting made me angry. Jill explained that she couldn't hear me. I insisted that she wasn't listening—just as she wasn't listening when I asked her to keep the dogs quiet every morning. The dogs were never quiet.

Looming between us was an issue we had yet to resolve: marriage. To outsiders, this seemed a no-brainer: Ron and Jill were made for each other. We had just survived an impossible year together. We loved each other madly. What more was there to say? Plenty, but I couldn't say it. Jill's insistence that I put her on the deed scared me because it sounded as if she wanted a monetary guarantee, some kind of insurance. It echoed the demand Sarah made after I agreed to a divorce. Sarah insisted that I give her half of my modest pension fund. Never mind that I had supported her for four years. She said she'd sue me for the money if she had to. I didn't have money for a lawyer and I couldn't bring myself to fight. I was thoroughly demoralized, and it was all I could do to find a new apartment and try to start over. I struggled for years— with the help of two therapists—to forget about the bruising divorce, her secret affair, and my payment of $20,000 to a woman who had shared, reluctantly, four years of my life. I felt like a patsy.

Still, I continued to believe in marriage. I believe that faith in love—in the staying power of love—allows us to have greater faith in others: if we grant that we are lovable, then we grant that others are too. I like that marriage stands on the high moral ground of fidelity. I like that fidelity compels hard choices and compromise—the kind of work that makes us humbler and more compassionate. In other words, I had no doubts that I would marry again. I wanted to marry Jill. But I wasn't sure what my second marriage had taught me. It seemed nothing more than a stunning example of my poor judgment.

That's why I started talking about a pre-nup.

"A pre-nup?" Jill said. "You don't trust me?"

"Of course I trust you," I said, "it's just that I have to protect myself."

"Protect yourself *against me*," she said, "because *you don't trust me?*"

"It's not simply an issue of trust," I insisted.

We were sitting at our new, antique dining room table, which could seat fourteen comfortably. Slowly, we were growing into the Queen Anne.

"Either you love me and trust me or you don't!" she said.

"Things happen," I said. "No matter how well-meaning a couple might be, you can't predict what might happen."

"What could happen?"

"You could change! Something could come between us and you'd grow to hate me—then you'd want revenge. And you'd take the house."

Her face flushed. "I'm not that kind of person. You *know* I'm not like that!"

PJ, lying on the floor at her feet, groaned in sympathy. Harriet was snoring nearby.

"There's too much we don't know," I said. "I thought I knew Sarah, I thought that nothing could come between us but, in the end, I didn't know her at all."

Jill's eyes widened: "Are you saying you think you don't *know* me—even though, in your words, I'm the *love of your life?*"

"I know that I love you and that you love me," I answered quickly. "I know that you're a good person—"

"But *not* somebody you can trust for the rest of your life." She took a breath. "Ron, I will not steal this house away from you!"

"It's all I've got," I said.

"No, it's not! You've got *me*."

"I mean, if you left me. This would be all I'd have."

"What about me?" she said. "If you really loved me, you'd put me on the deed."

"Oh, don't start that again! You didn't cash in your retirement fund to buy this place."

"I don't HAVE a retirement fund!"

"EXACTLY!"

She sighed, then leaned over to pet PJ. "I am *not* signing a pre-nup."

Now I sighed. "Then we'll just live together the rest of our lives?"

She raised her brows at me. "Is that an ultimatum?"

"That's not what I said. It sounds like *you* were making the ultimatum."

"I guess I'll just have to wait till you're convinced that I love you as much as I say I do."

"I've made you angry. I'm sorry."

"Ron, you're making me crazy!"

It wasn't the house I was afraid of losing. I see that now. But the house seemed the only solid, certain thing in my life: I knew the house from top to bottom—and *I could fix it if it broke.*

* * *

Our huge basement used to be the fraternity's party room: 1,400 square feet of dank, dark play area. The windows had been covered over with plywood, black lights affixed to the paint-peeling ceiling joists, and a twenty-foot bar installed along one wall. It had taken me a full day to dismantle the bar, cursing with every screw I extracted from the massive plywood construction—I had never seen so many screws. A few of my former students recounted with glee some of the parties they had attended in our basement. "Oh, man," said one. "I was there when somebody set off some smoke bombs. It was nearly a riot, everybody running for the door!"

The basement was now crowded with all kinds of construction supplies and furniture. The concrete floor was very thin and had begun to deteriorate in places. The ceiling joists were flaking lead paint. Had the 203K inspector looked into the basement and seen this health hazard, he would have failed us immediately. The basement needed a new floor, the brick walls—painted the fraternity's royal blue—needed to be re-mortared, the ceiling needed to be finished, and the whole thing had to be dried out somehow. In other words, the basement still belonged to the fraternity and its ghosts. It was creepy.

I began to repair the windows in the basement's front bay when a small fold in a sill caught my eye. It looked like water damage. I poked it with the tip of a screw driver. The screw driver went through the wood as easily as it would have penetrated paper. I kept digging until I had chipped away most of the sill. The damage was old, I decided, either from water or insects, I couldn't tell.

I recalled seeing dead winged ants in the basement six months earlier. Lots of them. They were small and seemed to have flown stupidly into the numerous spider webs in the nooks and corners. *More power to the spiders,* I thought. No living ants, winged or otherwise, were visible now. Could they have been termites? This didn't seem possible, since 1) the inspector declared us termite-free before I bought the house, 2) the basement was made of brick, and 3) there were no signs of termites anywhere that I could see. Except this. I probed the next window sill and found more damage. When I got to the third sill, I found them: maggoty, pincered, and ant-sized. Termites.

Okay, don't panic, I told myself. *Look, it's taken them six months to eat three window sills. Call the pest-control people tomorrow. Everything's going to be fine.*

This is called wishful thinking. It's a form of denial I've become quite familiar with as a home-rehabber. Always, when faced with catastrophe, my first reaction—as when I saw those

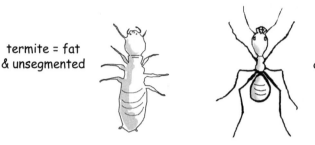

termite = fat
& unsegmented

ant = svelte
& segmented

winged "ants"—is disbelief. I'm thinking horses, not zebras. That's only reasonable, right? The termite expert informed me that a *swarm*—all those gnat-thingies I had dismissed six months ago— was a sign of the termite colony *expanding.* He also pointed out that the termites had tunneled their way up from the crawlspace under the front porch, where it was plenty damp, then through the damp mortar of the brickwork, and then into the main support beam that ran the length of the entire basement. They had eaten through a third of the house's major support joists.

Wait, wait, wait, I stammered. *Termites can eat through mortar?*

No, termites wend their way through the spaces in old mortar. And you can be sure there are plenty of spaces in old mortar. What is more, they feed *all the time,* 24-7, pausing only briefly every twenty-four hours to return to the ground to replenish their moisture. They cannot live without moisture.

The worst part was that I was to blame: I had laid down tarpaper in the crawlspace to force condensation and rain leakage away from the house. The tarpaper kept the soil moist enough for termites, who then tunneled their way through several of the basement joists. I hated myself for having been so stupid. But I'd caught it in time. The construction crew did a good job raising the front of the house (ever so slightly) and installing new joists of treated lumber. Then I got bonded for termites. Every household should, apparently.

20
LEAD HEAVY

IN JANUARY 2002, the start of our third year in the house, we refinanced once again and Jill quit teaching. She didn't like the politics of academe and she didn't like the game we played of acting like strangers in my department. We were having a hard enough time at home. She decided to change careers and go into social work. The change made sense—social work would draw on her expertise and care as a teacher. She applied for graduate school, took two classes to qualify for these programs, worked Saturdays at Traditions, and started a new round of projects in the house. Even though we were strapped for cash, I was pleased that she had more time for the house.

That spring, we drove to North Carolina for my brother's wedding, his second. Dave and his fiancée, Annie, were an unlikely couple. He was an IT manager and she was finishing her Ph.D. in Education. She was quiet and bookish, he was gregarious and fun-loving. An unsympathetic observer might have characterized them as the party boy and the librarian. But she was beautiful and gave him lots to think about. He was adventurous and gave her a new world of friends and fun. Jill worried that it wouldn't last.

"She's got a *Ph.D*," she said. "I love David, but I fear she's going to get bored."

"But Dave's got a Ph.D in *sociability*," I said. "He's a great guy, with a wide circle of friends. He takes her camping!"

Jill rolled her eyes. I had tried to take Jill camping and she did not like it.

I was proud of Dave for giving marriage another try. His first had lasted five years. It hadn't helped that his job at the time took him out to sea for half the year every year. It hadn't helped either that his wife had a small child from her first marriage. Was I just making excuses for him? Mike and Lois had been married for twenty-five years already. And many of my friends had been married for ten years or longer. So marriage works for some people. But I wonder, as essayist Alix Shulman has, "Why are terminated marriages called 'failed,' as though endurance were all? Perhaps a marriage, however brief, ought to be counted a success if it achieves the purpose for which it was undertaken—whether sexual heaven, freedom from parental rule, financial benefit, legitimization of children, companionship, citizenship." Anthropologist Margaret Mead would have agreed with Shulman, since Mead ventured into marriage three times and later asserted that "not one of them was a failure."

Actress Elizabeth Taylor, notorious for her many marriages, once said, "I marry the men I love." Only after my two divorces did I understand what she meant. When I think of all that must happen for love to work—the external and internal elements of attraction, the mutually compatible life-goals, then the resilience to live with the quirks and faults of the other—it seems amazing that any couple lasts. We are not easy mates, most of us. We have quirks, habits, and preferences that cannot be readily accommodated, if at all. One of the sweetest men I know cannot, for the life of him, pick up after himself. To look at him, to talk with him, you'd think he was a treasure. But heaven forbid that you'd have to live with him and his wet towels on the floor, his dirty socks on the kitchen counter, his muddy shoes on the couch. He's not going to change. Pity the woman who thinks he will.

Even though I want the idealized marriage that everyone else wants, I have decided that we ask too much of our marital partners. Where did we get such high-flown expectations, insisting that our spouse be our soul mate, our sexual champion, our confidante, our "better half"? Our predecessors never expected so much of another person. They were okay with compromised companionship. Many of them were even okay with arranged marriages. My generation hooted at the faults that we saw in our parents' stale notion of marriage and we crowed that we'd do better. But statistics don't lie: we have not done better. Not at all. And I don't know that we can say with any certainty that the older generations were less happy than we.

Dave and Annie's wedding took place in a park on a lovely spring afternoon. A hippie preacher presided—a friend of Dave's. Annie and Dave had written their own vows. One of Dave's friends sang, another played guitar. As part of the ceremony, we onlookers were asked to respond in affirmation of the vows Dave and Annie read to each other. I surprised myself by weeping silently as I heard my brother declare his love. I want no more than this from life, I decided: the simple pleasure of seeing people freely express their love, surrounded by their family and friends. In the headlock of our daily workload or the crossfire of our colleagues' petty bickering or the hailstorm of rush hour's incivility, we often forget how little we need to make us happy. Jill and I agreed that our desire to be with family and friends informed much of our motivation for saving the Queen Anne: we would make the house into a great place to gather our loved ones. As I recalled this in light of our first disastrous Christmas, I hoped for another chance to make it right.

That night, at the reception, I danced with my mother—showing off the steps that Jill and I had learned our first month together. Those lessons seemed long ago and I wondered when

Jill and I would get a chance to dance like this again. Dave and Annie looked great, dressed in formal attire. The fancy reception was for the benefit of Annie's conservative, Midwestern parents, who were acting as a couple, but, in fact, were living apart. Her father was paying for the gala. At the dinner table, we sat next to Ruth, one of my mother's long-time friends. She was the one who had helped my mother out of her depression immediately following my father's death. My mother and father were living in North Dakota at the time and my mother was planning to return to North Carolina, but couldn't bring herself to lift a finger. "Ruth came by one morning," my mother recounted, "and said, 'Come on, dear, let's get you packed.' And she stayed with me day after day until it was done and I was ready to go." As my mother told the story, she got weepy and so did Ruth. And then so did I.

I didn't understand what was happening to me. I had never been so sentimental. It seemed that, ever since buying the Queen Anne, I was *feeling* more than I ever had. Was it that I had grasped a new understanding of vulnerability? On our drive back to Baltimore, I felt very close to Jill. I was proud to be her partner. I admired her easy sociability, how kind and generous she was with strangers. At a party, you'd never know she doesn't drink alcohol: she laughs a lot and will be among the first to start singing or dancing, as she was at the reception. Because she is neither competitive nor judgmental, people are drawn to her. This accounted for her success both as a hairdresser and a teacher, and later as a social worker. I was more convinced than ever that she and I would marry. It was just a matter of time, but how much?

* * *

With the exception of the Queen Anne's fat mahogany banister, which runs up all three flights, nearly every piece of originally-varnished woodwork in the house had been painted. And paint was flaking from nearly every one of them. The frat boys had painted latex coats over the old lead paint without priming. The result was that the latex puckered, then popped off in hideous streaks and pustules. Sometimes, Jill and I scraped over this mess with the nozzle of a shop vac; other times we hacked at the flakes with various tools. We had boxes of paint-stripping implements: knives, probes, picks, files, chisels, scrapers. When we considered the math (thirty-three window frames—one-foot deep by six-feet tall—surrounded by six-inch molding on all sides, plus multi-paneled shutters, in addition to all of the doorways and all of the baseboards), paint-stripping seemed an impossible task.

Early on, frustrated by the dirty, mucked-up woodwork, I took a belt sander to some of the broad window sills and I let the machine do its work, filling the room with choking dust. Okay, I was angry and wanted fast results. I realized quickly that this wasn't the best way to proceed. For the record, I would rather do sit-ups, hundreds of them, than strip paint. I was willing to pay somebody else to do it. I brought in a paint expert to examine the first floor bay. As the painter examined window trim and molding and baseboards, he shook his head sadly, it seemed.

"How much would you charge to do this room?" I asked cautiously.

He was a tall, young Latino who was known to do good work in the neighborhood. "It'd be a lot of money," he mused.

"How much?" I pressed.

"I don't know." He stepped back as if to get a better look. "But I can't do it. That's lead paint," he said. "And it's really hard work."

"You don't want to do it?" I asked. The cost was mounting in my mind and I was wondering how much I was willing to pay.

"No, Mr. Tanner. I am sorry. I can't do work like that. It would take a long time."

I stood with him in silence, both of us staring at the painted woodwork. *A long time*, I was thinking. *Everything takes too long.*

Everything is harder than you think. I was half hoping that if we just stood there long enough, the painter would change his mind.

He said, "Sorry I can't help you out, Mr. Tanner."

Okay, fine, it was only a dream anyway. I didn't have money enough to pay an expert like this. But I was curious. I wanted to know what we were up against. So far, the only woodwork we had claimed completely was the oak paneling in the vestibule. On his way out, the painter paused here to stroke the finished panel, which had taken me a week of arduous chemical stripping and scraping and sanding. "Who did this?" he asked. "It's *nice*." I felt myself blush.

The difference between painted woodwork and finished woodwork is the difference between a cloudy and a cloudless sky. Victorian houses like ours were made to show off their wooden refinements. Paint, no matter how pretty, doesn't do them justice.

I started on the living room bay with an expensive infrared heater about the size of a shoe box. It burns the paint in large swaths (about the area of a size ten shoe) but not so hot that the lead is released in the ensuing smoke. This is a long way from the little heat element that Rick had given me the first year. I had, in fact, used his aged heat element so much it burned out finally. I also wore out or broke all of the stripping tools he had given me.

After the initial strip with the infrared heater, I pulled on thick rubber gloves and an elaborate respirator, then used an orange-gel chemical stripper that I slathered onto the trim like jam on toast. Usually within fifteen minutes, it puckers and softens the remaining paint, which demands a lot of prying and scraping.[2] Loops and wads of gummy paint would cling to my jeans and accumulate on the well-papered floor, where inevitably I'd step on them until the bottoms of my shoes were half an inch thick with the mucky paint, which I'd have to scrape off with a knife blade. And

---

2. Some professionals recommend coating your application of stripper with sawdust to hold in the moisture. After letting it sit a while, just wipe off the sawdusty goop.

first floor bay, 2004

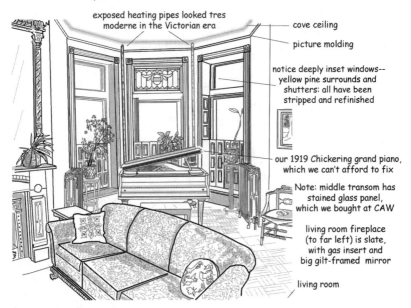

exposed heating pipes looked tres moderne in the Victorian era

cove ceiling

picture molding

notice deeply inset windows-- yellow pine surrounds and shutters: all have been stripped and refinished

our 1919 Chickering grand piano, which we can't afford to fix

Note: middle transom has stained glass panel, which we bought at CAW

living room fireplace (to far left) is slate, with gas insert and big gilt-framed mirror

living room

still, bits and pieces of paint sludge clung to my clothes, which would get so messy I'd have to throw them away.

Then there's scraping. Then a heat gun, which is simply a souped-up blow dryer. Then there's sanding. If you don't get up the smallest bits of paint, those tiny flecks will shine through your finish like a beacon through the night and ruin all of your work. Jill and I learned that we could paint over these little flecks if we mixed a paint color that replicates the final stain of the wood. We did this to good effect.

The entire stripping process takes so long, you can't think about time, you can only trudge on like those hundred-mile marathoners, watching one footfall after the other, never looking to the interminable distance. Jill was really good at it because she has the patience to pick and pick and pick again until every flake and fleck is gone. But she refused to wear a respirator, just as she refused to wear work gloves. Stubborn woman!

Jill discovered a spray-cleaner called Citrus-Clean that is so powerful it strips paint if you let it sit a while. It wasn't nearly as messy as the orange gel. She used it to strip the steep servants' stairs. It took her the better part of a day and a night. The next morning, she couldn't get out of bed. She had a raging headache and felt feverish with the flu. She slept for sixteen hours. That week, she dragged herself through her classes, then fell into bed immediately after dinner. When she slept through the weekend, I got worried. I recalled that our old family friend Mary Jane had been a master paint-stripper and furniture refinisher. Like Jill, she never used gloves or a respirator. After repainting her kitchen a few years back, Mary Jane said she felt run down. One morning she took to her bed and then remained there for months. It turned out she had lung cancer. Nobody blamed her paint-stripping directly, but everyone agreed it could not have helped.

Jill wasn't healthy to begin with. She suffered from chronic headaches, due in part to hypoglycemia. She got colds easily because her mother had been a chain-smoker. Her great fear was that her health would fail as her mother's had. Her mother started having strokes in her early thirties and died of one when she was sixty. One day, as she was driving Jill to a shoe store, her mother collapsed against the steering wheel. The car had just entered the store's parking lot. Ten-year-old Jill grabbed the wheel and steered the car in circles until men from the shoe store ran out to help her, one of them opening the door to grab at the emergency brake.

After Jill spent three days in bed, I suggested she get her blood tested for lead poisoning. I got mine tested too. The results were frightening. My reading was twelve. A normal reading is ten. Jill's reading was twenty. Had she been pregnant she would have lost the baby. Jill took to bed and slept nearly a full week. I'd never seen anyone sleep so much. I fed her soup in bed. I made her cookies. I kept the dogs nearby. I read to her. I tried to ignore my anger at myself for having let this happen. Would we kill ourselves for the dream of a house?

* * *

Lead paint abatement, we learned, is not about stripping paint; it's about *containing* it. You should strip paint only from surfaces that will be abraded by use, like window sashes and door jambs. Abrasion creates dust. Lead dust is insidious because it stays airborne for a long time. The flakes themselves—lying on a window sill, say—aren't dangerous until they're pulverized. Or eaten, which, in the case of small children, is more common than you might think. Baltimore is notorious for its widespread cases of lead poisoning—as many as 1,200 a year—among the poor who occupy its deteriorating, old houses. Children under the age of six are most vulnerable. They absorb fifty percent of the poisons they ingest, whereas adults absorb only ten percent. Adults eventually purge these toxins after the source is removed.

I was surprised to learn that lead paint poisoning was identified by Johns Hopkins University doctors in Baltimore as early as 1914, some years after their diligent investigations of mysterious cases involving children who suffered from fevers, bleeding gums, vomiting, and chronic pain. Unfortunately, since the poisoning was confined to the poor and wasn't contagious, there wasn't much incentive to remedy the problem, particularly among landlords. Not until the 1970s did the federal government outlaw lead paint. Maryland itself did not pass its own legislation until 1996, with the Maryland Reduction of Lead Risk in Housing Act, which requires lead-free certification for all rental properties built before 1950. Though such certification is a laudable goal, Maryland employs only ten inspectors to oversee an estimated 500,000 affected properties.

Lead poisoning is responsible not only for autoimmune disorders but also for a devastating array of brain damage that includes hyperactivity, memory loss, retardation, and unpredictable violence. Some doctors now believe that Ludwig Van Beethoven suffered from lead poisoning, which would account for his chronic ailments and erratic behavior, even his deafness. Chemical analysis of his hair has made this a fairly definitive conclusion. The source of his poisoning was possibly the mineral waters he drank and the spa waters he swam in.

In a house like ours, the easiest abatement would be to replace the windows and doors, discard the shutters, then paint over everything else, followed by frequent inspections to make sure the old paint stayed covered. Jill and I refused to do this. So, wearing my respirator and thick rubber gloves, I took over the paint-stripping and Jill—after three months of rest—moved on to other jobs. The doctor said our blood lead-levels would very likely diminish over time. As my brother Mike was quick to point out: "The body will heal itself if you give it half a chance."

Later that spring, as Jill was growing stronger, we bought an antique bed at a local auction. A 1799 four-poster rope bed made of cherry, it wobbled mightily. I repaired it as best I could. Though it creaked and groaned under our weight, we loved it and believed that, having held up for two centuries, it would hold for us. One morning, I surprised Jill in our new bed with a gift-wrapped book. She unwrapped it with some excitement. Then, seeing that it was a dusty, 1940s textbook on Rhetoric, she gave me a puzzled glance. "Open it," I urged. Inside she found that I had cut a deep square from the pages—making the book into a container just large enough to hold a small jewelry box. Over the cut pages I had scrawled in red marker: "Will you marry me?"

As she opened the box, Jill began to cry. I slipped the antique engagement ring—tiny diamonds set in white gold—onto her finger. "Yes," she said. Then, with uncertainty, she added, "What about the pre-nup you keep talking about?"

"Fuck the pre-nup," I said.

21

THE TOXIC HOUSE

IT SEEMED INEVITABLE that the Queen Anne would have asbestos. I found plenty in the basement. Wholly organic, asbestos is a mineral fiber whose remarkable insulating and fire-retardant properties were discovered in the nineteenth century. In most applications, asbestos is stable if left alone. The tragedy of asbestos resides in the ignorant way people have handled it. Our basement is a good example: the asbestos was mixed with plaster and applied as insulation to the heating pipes, which run the length of the basement. Upon discovering this, I stopped short with fright. How was I going to get rid of ASBESTOS?

Lou, my ever-helpful plumber, said, "It's *nonfriable* asbestos, Ron, it's not gonna kill you. Everybody overreacts when they hear the word *asbestos*. Bag it up and I'll get rid of it for you—I know a guy who has the right disposal."

By the 1970s, everyone learned why *airborne* asbestos is toxic: it will lodge in your lungs and cause chronic scarring, which will very likely turn cancerous. That's why the feds banned its use in 1989. By that time, the public was treating asbestos like a plague. The ironic result of the panic was that everybody was rooting out asbestos wherever it was found, which only created more airborne dangers. Probably half the stuff could have been left and contained right where it was. The asbestos in our basement plaster would have been fine had the plaster held. But now the plaster was crumbling.

Wearing a respirator, old gloves, and clothes I would throw away, I spent a nerve-racking day carefully pulling off and bagging the old asbestos-impregnated plaster insulation, feeling all the while that I was supposed to call the EPA and have a team of HAZMAT-suited experts seal off our house. I learned later that EPA regulations on asbestos abatement do not apply to homeowners, except with regard to disposal. Otherwise, you're free to live with all the asbestos you like, friable or not.

* * *

Jill's illness left her with no tolerance for paint or chemical fumes. Brief exposure would lay her up for a day, fatigued, her head in flaming pain. I cautioned her against the careless use of solvents, cleaners, and paints. Sometimes I'd find her rubbing water stains from table-tops with denatured alcohol—she still wouldn't wear a mask or gloves. "Jill, *please!*" I'd plead. "Protect yourself!" And: "If you die on me, I'll never forgive you." And: "That's just great, Jill, working without protection. Don't come crying to me when you sprout a third eye." Then she'd counter: "What about you with subfloor glue all over your hands? And paint all over your arms?" And caulk, I'd remind her. I applied caulk with my naked fingers.

The irony of our circumstances was that the one place that should have been safe, our hard-won home, wasn't safe at all. Whenever Jill slept for a day, curled among the blankets, she might as well have been drifting out to sea on an oarless raft. I could do nothing to help her. So much for the Cinderella fantasy of a lover's rescue. It was maddening and heartrending. We had nothing to do but proceed carefully.

You can't talk about household toxins without talking about ventilation. No doubt you have seen the small pipes that jut from the roof of a house. Perhaps, too, you have seen chimneys on houses that have no fireplaces. These are not merely ornamental: pipes, chimneys, and ducts are ways to exhaust heat and moisture from a house. Houses have to breathe; otherwise, they become toxic. The concept of venting is as old as human habitation itself. Think of smoke pouring from the top of a teepee. Not until I had the plumbing replaced in the Queen Anne did I learn that all plumbing fixtures have to be vented to the roof because sewer gas—mostly hydrogen sulfide, ammonia, and methane—can kill you. That's why you can't just install a bathroom in any old closet-sized space inside your house: you have to run an exhaust pipe from the sink to the out-of-doors because the sink, don't forget, is a direct line to the sewer below your house. Human waste under every house in every neighborhood is generating millions of cubic feet of toxic gas.[3]

Every chimney that serves a furnace or water heater must be lined. "Lining" a chimney is usually a matter of running an aluminum sleeve—like an accordion conduit—from the roof down to the appliance, in our case, forty-plus feet down. That way, the moist heat exhausted by the gas furnace or water heater can escape from the roof. If not, it would escape into the brick and mortar of the chimney, accelerating its decomposition. Worse, it would leak carbon monoxide into the house.

Called the "silent killer," CO—which is odorless—asphyxiates two hundred or more people a year in American households, due mostly to un-vented space heaters, but also to poorly vented water heaters, ovens, and fireplaces. CO actually replaces the oxygen in your blood because it assimilates more easily: asphyxiation

---

3. Have you noticed that, on a very windy day, the water in your toilet bowl will slosh around as if the entire house were quaking? Your house is not quaking. In fact, it would take a tornado to shake your house enough to make the toilet bowl water slosh. The answer to the mystery of the sloshing toilet water can be found in your ventilation pipe: strong wind blowing over the roof affects the air pressure inside your bathroom ventilation exhaust pipe, causing enough intermittent vacuum to draw the water to and fro.

How the Queen Anne breathes

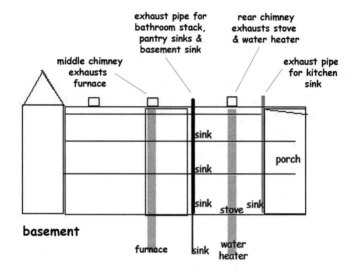

soon follows. Virtually every kind of combustion found in a house creates carbon monoxide. Even the innocuous-seeming wood fire in a sturdy brick fireplace can kill you if the chimney's flue is blocked, preventing the CO from escaping.

Though the dangers of carbon monoxide were only vaguely apprehended by the Victorians, the advantages of ventilation were not. The prevailing theory of disease at the time focused on "bad air," which was believed to be the source of infections—it was just a step away from the germ theory that would revolutionize medicine by 1900. Victorians were fond of sleeping with their windows open, which is why their heating systems—and their radiators especially—were so large.

All Victorian houses were drafty, made more so by their lack of insulation, which in the age of abundant fuel had not yet been invented.

As CO poisoning illustrates, a well-insulated house is problematic. So is insulation itself because the fiberglass variety offgasses formaldehyde. Not at dangerous levels. That is, not at levels that will kill you. . . right away. But at measurable levels nonetheless. Plywood and other lumber off-gasses formaldehyde too. Add to this the off-gassing of chemicals from synthetic carpets, paint and varnish—all of which create that "new house" smell so many of us love. Then there are caulks, glues, and other sealants used in house repair. I myself am very fond of using that spray can of ever-expanding foam to seal up cracks and holes under floors and between joists. As the bright yellow foam snakes from the can nozzle, I can see its off-gas roiling away like heated air from a stove's burner. If you want to give yourself a scare, just read the caution labels on any of these products. Nearly everything in them causes cancer. Highly carcinogenic ketones from cans of spray paint are some of the scariest chemicals. Methyl ethyl ketone is the sweetness you smell in paint. When I spray paint outdoors in the summer or spring, it inevitably attracts the inspection of a curious bee or two. Early on, I spray-painted a chair in our basement—wearing a respirator—and was appalled to discover that, within an hour, the sickeningly sweet odor had pervaded all three upper floors.

* * *

Virtually all paint, sealant, and wood/fiber by-products belong to the class of toxins called Volatile Organic Compounds, which are different from "particulates" like asbestos and lead paint dust. A third class of household toxins contains the "microbes," the most notorious of which are molds. The one thing we didn't have in our house was a mold problem, thankfully. Mind you, we had molds (fungi). Everybody has molds because molds are as ubiquitous as dust particles. Leave your bread out too long and what do you find? Even a covered container of leftovers in the refrigerator will turn surprising colors after a week or so. There's no escaping molds, whose species number over 100,000. The good thing about an old house is that it's fairly difficult to make a lathe and plaster wall moldy because, despite the occasional presence of horse or pig hair, there isn't much to feed the mold. Modern wallboard, on the other hand, is an ideal medium for molds of all kinds because it is covered with untreated paper on both sides and the gypsum in between holds the moisture. If wallboard gets wet and stays damp, it will grow lots of mold—even the dreaded black mold, called *stachybotrys chartarum*. That's why manufacturers have recently started producing a mold-resistant wallboard.

I have been in too many basements that reek of mildew— some so badly they make my clothes reek long after I have left that smelly house. Obviously, the smell of mold or mildew is not something you want to get used to; it is, rather, a warning you should heed. Somewhere, somehow, too much moisture is settling into the building. The most common reaction to mold is allergies. A worse reaction would be asthma. Worse still would be an auto-immune disorder. If a mysterious illness visits Jill or me, mold will be among the primary suspects. Some molds can grow just about anywhere, even on glass, and in temperatures as high as 500°F. Jill and I suspect that we have one of these super-molds living on the rubber lip of our garbage disposal. An orangish slime, it is all but impossible to scrape or scrub off. And no wonder: it thrives in the constant gush of water and dump of leftovers we pour into the disposal. Slime mold is a fungi colony of naked protoplasm. Lacking cell walls, they are gooey. Their entire amoeboid mass is called a plasmodium, and, like an amoeba, the colony undulates *en masse* to move forward. It can live only where there is both abundant moisture and abundant organic matter—which describes the mouth of our garbage disposal perfectly. Generally, it feeds on yeast, bacteria, and decomposing vegetation.

Research tells us that our little plasmodium is called Fungilo Septica, nicknamed, "vomit slime mold" or "dog vomit slime mold." As far as we can tell, it's nontoxic and may even be beneficial to our home's ecosystem. If it did not seem to be indestructible, perhaps we'd be fonder of it. As it is, on occasion Jill will go after it with bleach, knives, and souring pads. After an hour's hard work, she can pretty much obliterate it, an accomplishment that gives her no little satisfaction. Within a week or two, however, the plasmodium has returned, as orange and slimy as ever. I've come to accept its persistent return as a humbling reminder that we are but beggars and borrowers of nature's bounty.

22

THE YOUNG COUPLE

OUR THIRD SUMMER IN THE HOUSE, someone at my college happened to describe to me a young woman she knew who had moved with her husband into a Victorian mansion in downtown Baltimore. The more I heard of this couple's story, the more I realized that they were *my* young couple—the ones who had nearly outbid me for the Queen Anne! I got their number and made the call. Yes, they wanted to get together. Yes, they wanted to see what we'd done to the Queen Anne. And they insisted that we see what they had done to their house. When I told Jill this exciting news, she said, "Count me out."

"Are you kidding?" I said. "You don't want to see their house?"

"It sounds like a competition," she said. "They probably just want to show you how much better they did than us."

"Now, that's an uncharitable thought," I said. "Don't forget, after they lost our house, they sent us the appraisal they'd paid for."

"That was nice," she agreed. "But I don't want to get into a *you-show-me-yours-and-I'll-show-you-mine* game." She shook her head in doubt. Jill has never been competitive. For her, fixing the house wasn't about making something to incite envy. I didn't think it was for me either but, then again, I'm a man and can't help but think of getting bigger and doing better in all things.

border tile in master bath
3 x 6"

The young couple, the Vales, were blond and sunny, his hair nearly as long as hers, both in their late twenties. While Jill was out, I proudly showed them our first floor and described how far we'd come. Which, really, wasn't very far: we had only begun to paint the walls. The wood mantels were too modest for the fireplaces. Ninety percent of the woodwork needed refinishing. When I showed the Vales the master bathroom upstairs, I saw immediately what Jill was talking about: I was feeling competitive and defensive. "This was my Waterloo," I told them. "We ordered the wrong tile for the walls—that was an expensive mistake—and then I couldn't get this partition wall straight and then we put down the wrong tile on the floor. As you can see, it's too white and shiny. But we were pressed for time—those unrealistic 203K deadlines were killing us." I couldn't stop making excuses. Eventually, Jill and I would tear up the master bathroom and do it over again. But now, I felt surrounded by compromises. Though the Vales seemed polite enough, they certainly didn't appear envious. When I got to their house, I understood why.

Less than a mile from the city's financial center, Eutaw Place—where the Vales lived—was once one of Baltimore's grandest thoroughfares, with a wide grassy median down its center and lined on both sides with the mansions of wealthy, mostly Jewish, merchants. Their old synagogue still stands at the entrance to the neighborhood and about a third of the mansions stand too, interspersed with public housing. Nowadays, if you travel one block to either side of Eutaw Place, the neighborhood falls away to razed blocks and boarded up row houses—and some of the city's worst crime.

The Vales' house was a three-story brick mansion surrounded by a six-foot brick wall. As I stepped through the vestibule, the house opened like the nave of a church, a massive staircase zigzagging up one side of the house, with six tall panels of stained glass rising above it. It even had a (nonworking) elevator the size of a phone booth to one side of the stairs. The original hotel-quality kitchen, as befitting a grand house, was still in the basement, which was tiled throughout and featured a servant's dining room, as well as two huge furnaces to service the mansion's various heating zones. None of the woodwork in the house had been painted. None of the huge rooms had been cut up. All of the original marble mantels remained. And everything was in remarkably sound condition, if a little worn and musty.

The house was twice the size of ours. It had a huge walk-in attic on the fourth level, accessible by a narrow staircase; and three small servants' rooms on the third level, next to other rooms that probably would have belonged to the children or been used for storage. There was a large sunroom with leaded glass windows. And there was an ample backyard, but no garage, which meant no safe entry at night.

The Vales were quick to tell me that the neighborhood prostitutes were very protective of them and their new baby. And they assured me that they never felt threatened by the nearby drug traffic or the sirens or even the gunshots, though certainly they were careful. The husband had done impressive work with the furnace installations and the renovation of the master bath—much better than I could have done, I realized with chagrin. But I'd get better, I told myself, it was just a matter of time. The Vales' biggest expense was having the three six-foot-tall stained glass windows made, since the originals had been stolen. All of the brick on the exterior had been re-pointed by the previous owners, so the house was water tight. Re-pointing brick is incredibly time-consuming, pain-staking work. All of the Queen Anne's brick exterior needed it.

I raved about the Vales' house. "You've got a mansion!" I kept saying in disbelief. Privately, I was cataloguing all that would have to be done to make the house the showcase it deserved to be: a new roof—theirs was pitched and slate—attic insulation, refinished floors, repairs to the basement, paint in every room, of course; then new windows or storm windows because these original windows were going to leak badly in cold weather, and I'd want a garage out back—that'd be a major project. Around and round my calculations went.

Our talk was suddenly interrupted by a commotion in the street. Stepping to one of the huge living room windows, we saw—on the sunny sidewalk across the street—a young man chasing an older man and quickly running him down at the end of the block.

"You come back and clean that up!" he yelled, grabbing the older man by the collar and dragging him to the other end of the block. Then, the young man shoved the older toward the side of a building and snapped: "Now do it!"

The older man looked scared. His captor was plenty angry. At last, with half a shrug, the older asked: "Clean it with what?"

"Use your fuckin' shirt. Now do it!"

So the man pulled off his t-shirt, then began to wipe at the dark trickle—obviously a very recent spray of urine—on the brick wall in front of him.

He kept at it until the homeowner said, "I catch you pissing on my house again, I'm gonna kick your sorry ass. Now get outta here!"

T-shirt in hand, the public pisser did as he was told.

When I turned back to the Vales, they were smiling not quite apologetically. They then announced that they were moving.

They had bought their mansion just weeks after losing the Queen Anne and paid only $175,000. They were now being offered twice that by realtors. This was 2002, the market just heating up. That same house is selling for 1.2 million as of this writing. That's Baltimore money. Anywhere else—Boston, New York, D.C.—you'd multiply by three.

"Wait," I said, "you're moving?"

"Yes," they told me. Their original plan had been to buy a house as a kind of time-share with their brother and maybe a couple of friends. They had always planned to take a trip around the world in a sailboat—that's where Mr. Vale spent all of his time, rehabbing an old boat he'd bought.

"So you never planned to stay?" I asked.

No, they said. Never.

How they would have disappointed my neighbors! So Jill and I were the right ones for the Queen Anne. It didn't matter that the Vales were young and pretty and could do better work. That's what I was thinking. I see now that I was profoundly insecure about our stewardship of the Queen Anne. We were such amateurs and it seemed we might still botch the job. But the Vales, in their way, would have botched it too. Now they were going to flip their mansion for a healthy profit, then sail away. I nodded my head as if I understood but, really, I understood only in the abstract. *You'll never, ever, find another house like this,* I wanted to tell them. *A Victorian mansion in original condition?*

For the Vales, the mansion was just a pit stop in their race to other adventures. That's not a bad thing, but I was starting to realize that old house renovation is as varied as the couples who take it on. We and the Vales were the latest wave of the curious, enabled by the growing real estate boom and growing access to antiques and architectural hardware online. The rise of the big-box hardware stores like Lowes and Home Depot gave us an extra push. And then there were television programs like "This Old House" and "Antiques Road Show" that made house rehab and antique reclamation seem as exciting as a lottery. Old houses had become hot property because they gave homeowners a lot of charm and a lot of value (space) for relatively little money. All over Baltimore, decrepit, "marginal" neighborhoods held hope of revival as late pioneers like the Vales moved in.

The true pioneers, like Rick and Charles, came in the 1960s and '70s, when blight and flight plagued then-crumbling rust belt cities like Baltimore, Cleveland, and Detroit, and nobody thought much of tearing down old houses. I remember visiting one such city as a boy and seeing a thoroughfare of grand three-story Victorians that were slated for destruction for a new freeway. I couldn't believe that anyone would tear down such cool, old houses. My brothers and I sneaked into one. Even now, I can picture vividly its yawning gloomy interior, its ceiling-high windows, its great staircase, which wobbled when we stepped onto it. When we turned a corner, we boys edging forward in a nervous huddle, I nearly fainted when I came upon my own reflection in a cobwebbed, door-sized mirror. Maybe the difference between Mr. Vale and me was that, as a child, I spent hours sketching and making cardboard cutouts of the big, old house I hoped to own one day and, ultimately, I was willing to bankrupt myself to buy one when I finally got the chance.

Before I left, wishing them much good luck, the Vales explained that when they'd bid on the Queen Anne, the fraternity's lawyer had not told them there was another offer on the table. Had they known, they would not have made an offer. They didn't learn about us until they arrived—too late—at the bank.

I realized then that the lawyer had simply played me for more money, using the Vales as leverage. That's free market economy.

After I recounted my adventure to Jill, I said, "Don't you wish you'd seen it?"

"Not at all," she said. "They sound like nice people but I can tell you're weirded out."

We were lying in bed, propped on pillows. The dogs were snoring on their beds nearby.

"Well, it was a hell of a house."

"Ours is a hell of a house too."

"I'm not saying it isn't." I glanced at the windows in our bay and wondered when we'd have time to strip the woodwork in our bedroom. "I'm just saying—"

"You see what you're doing?" she said. "You're getting competitive. There will always be something more to yearn after, won't there?"

I turned to her with a sly smile. "Not where you're concerned."

"You're changing the subject."

"It's a better subject," I said.

She pushed me away playfully. "You'll always be house crazy, Ron."

That summer, I started repairing our three-story wood porch: its sagging floor; its archeologically interesting, many-layered crust of paint (it had never been stripped); its sixty-four windows set into sliding frames, each the size of a garage door. Jill discovered a new way to strip cabinet and door hardware: just drop the pieces into a Crock-Pot and boil them overnight. She spent hours picking and scraping door pulls and keyhole escutcheons and hinges and drawer knobs. It was, for her, a kind of meditation.

In July, we carried old Charlie to the vet for the last time. Nearly blind, thoroughly demented—peeing anywhere and everywhere the urge caught him—and unable to eat enough to keep himself going, he was done. More than once, while sitting on the dining room table and watching us eat, Charlie had gotten up stiffly, then walked into a lit candle, his whiskers going up in smoke before we doused him. Unfazed, he seemed completely unaware of what he'd just done.

It was heartbreaking to hand the bony old boy to the vet tech and watch him being taken away, his eyes registering neither alarm nor interest. That was the saddest thing of all; that he had no idea where he was going. He was eighteen.

Outside, in the glare of a too-warm afternoon, as children and parents passed us with their puppies and kittens, Jill and I wept in each other's arms. I feared we were setting a poor example, but we could not stop.

In August, we spent a week at our favorite farm house rental in upstate New York. The second day there, I bent down to tie my shoe and my back went out. It was like I'd been shot at the base of my spine. I lay on the floor for two hours, not sure that I could get to my feet. Jill kneeled beside me and stroked my forehead. "What can I do?"

"Nothing," I groaned. "Just let me die in peace."

She drew nearer, her face over mine, a curtain of her curls shielding me. "Where do you want to be buried?" she joked.

"It came out of nowhere," I said hoarsely. "What the fuck?"

Jill shook her head in disagreement, the curtain of curls swaying. "You don't think you've been under a little stress?" The dogs nosed at our faces. Jill pushed them away.

"I don't know that stress works that way, stores itself up and then strikes like a thunderbolt."

"That's how heart attacks happen," she reminded me. "You've hardly slowed down."

I grimaced as I turned over and tried to rise.

"Easy!" Jill coached.

"Nothing's easy," I joked.

To distract us, I insisted that we visit some historic houses in the Hudson Valley, an hour's drive away. It took me forever to fold myself into the car, and I walked with a ninety-year-old's shuffle and every few minutes I yelped in pain. Jill fretted about me. I explained that because my pain was constant, whether I was lying down or standing up, moving or not, it didn't matter: so, bring on the old houses! We saw some amazing ones, each goading us to return to Baltimore and make ours better.

It would take me six weeks to heal.

23
THE FRENCH DRAIN

Love, I suppose, is a bungee jump from a very high bridge. You must have faith that the cord will hold. That's how I felt as Jill and I began to plan our wedding. Messy dogs, senile cats, termites, broken sewer pipes, pained backs—come what may, we'd see it through. Jill and I decided to hold our wedding in the house. The first floor would accommodate about fifty people. But we'd need a year to get ready. Getting organized meant clearing out the clutter throughout the house—especially the tools and building materials. To do that, we had to finish the basement. The basement floor was the original, no more than a half inch of concrete. Anything in contact with the floor for a week or more would get mildewed. I called around for contractors and hated hearing their estimates. Our plumber, Lou, said he could do the work, but was too busy right now. He recommended one of his apprentices, who'd do the job for a fraction of the price.

Tony was a tall, strapping man with large, capable hands and a complexion as dark as molasses. He stood several inches taller than I and, unlike so many of the subcontractors I'd met, he looked me straight in the eye and called me "Ron," not "Mr. Tanner" or "Mr. Ron." With slightly sleepy eyes, high cheekbones and a square chin, he was gigolo-handsome and he knew it, his confident stride just short of a swagger. The moment she met him,

Jill said, she knew he was bad news, and she worried every day about what Tony would or wouldn't do eventually.

Tony said he could do it all—plumbing, welding, excavation, concrete work. A one-man construction crew. Never mind that he now lived in his mother's tiny house and got by on odd jobs. At forty, though he looked thirty, he was divorced and had two grown children. He had not finished his apprenticeship with Lou and it wasn't clear why Lou wasn't using him now.

After Tony had walked through my basement, explained the work he would do, and we had agreed upon the price—which included materials—we shook hands, his swallowing mine. The plan was that I would be working outside, re-pointing the brick, while he would be working inside. Recent rains had revealed that water was seeping through the seams between our bricks, where the mortar had worn away. So I had to re-mortar ("point up" or "tuck point") the bricks at least to the level of five feet. Meanwhile, Tony would install a French drain in the basement, then finish with a new concrete floor.

A "French drain" is a narrow trench dug just inside the perimeter of the basement walls. A perforated plastic pipe is set into the trench and graded at a slope so that any water getting into the basement goes to the trench and into the pipe, which sluices it to a sump pump, which then pumps the water outside to the street or gutter. Concrete, I learned, is nearly as porous as sand. If your concrete floor meets a wall that's taking in water, the water will travel across your floor like a spill across a paper towel. A French drain breaks the concrete at the wall, causing the moisture to drop into the trench, where the pipe siphons it away. Had I hired a real contractor to do the work, the French drain installation would have cost me four times what Tony was charging.

That first day I made the mistake of driving Tony home, clear across town on the far west side. I further compounded my mistake by picking him up the next morning—because we had supplies to

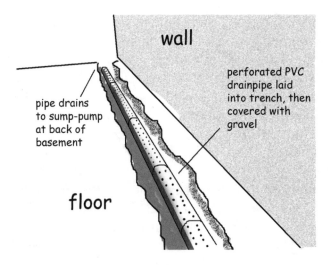

wall

perforated PVC drainpipe laid into trench, then covered with gravel

pipe drains to sump-pump at back of basement

floor

buy. After that, I was Tony's chauffeur, picking him up and dropping him off every day. I didn't have time for this, but then again, I wanted to show goodwill. Also, by picking him up every morning, I would ensure that he got there early and worked a full day.

Tony began work with impressive speed. Using a concrete saw, he cut a path around the perimeter of the basement's interior, concrete dust pluming from the open windows and basement door. Half the time, he worked without a mask. He'd stumble outside for a breather, his t-shirt drenched with sweat, his face and short hair creased with gray dust.

Wearing my most tattered clothes, I was working equally hard outside on the mountainous wall that faces our side street. In most brick walls, the seams are wide enough to accommodate a "striker," a pencil-thin metal tool that helps you slather mortar neatly between bricks. The brick of the Queen Anne, however, was laid with surprisingly narrow joints—too narrow for a striker, at least in my inexperienced hands. So I was working the mortar in with my gloved fingers. By the end of the first day, my fingers were puckered from all the moisture that had collected in my rubber gloves. And my fingertips and joints were aching from all the pressing and wiping.

Halfway through the next day's work, Tony came out to see how I was doing. Such was his confidence that he had already assigned himself the role of supervisor. He said, "How long's that mortar stain been on that brick?"

"Day and a half."

He shook his head in disapproval. "You're gonna have trouble with that."

I had added a sandy-orange color to the mortar to match the original. But it wasn't quite a match. Tony explained that mortar sticks to brick and leaves a tenacious film even after you think you've wiped it off. Sure enough, the staining was so bad that Sue, across the street, phoned to ask why I had started painting the brick of our house. Tony sent me out to buy some muriatic acid. Then, he spent the rest of the afternoon showing me how to scrub the brick. It would take me another day to scrub out that stain—using not only acid but also scouring pads and wet sandpaper.

Okay, I learned: when working with mortar, the cleanup has to be immediate and thorough. That's why I went out and got a power washer. Now I was good to go, pointing the brick, wiping it down as I went, then power washing it, being careful not to shoot into the joints. This was incredibly time-consuming. But I was doing such a good job; passersby stopped their cars to ask me for a card. For a mad moment or two, I contemplated making extra money shoring up people's brick walls.

"I can tuck up the rest of that wall for you after I'm done with the basement," Tony offered later.

"You know masonry?"

"Oh, yeah." As I drove him home that night, he pointed out all he'd done with brick and mortar—on every other block we passed. "I did that block," he said, "and that one, all the way down to the light. And that row over there."

You've done half the damn city? I was tempted to remark.

When I picked up Tony the next morning, he said he'd been up late watching teenagers having sex on the darkened porch across the street from his mother's house.

"You could see clear across the street at night?" I asked.

He turned to me with a knowing look that was almost a wink. "Night vision binoculars, Ron."

Another time he recounted how, a couple years earlier, he had beaten his grown son so badly he put the young man in the hospital. Tony himself went to jail. "I had to teach him a lesson," he said. "He was doin' drugs."

After Tony started digging the drain's trench, he brought in two of his cousins to help him haul out the dirt. The trench was to be lined with gravel. I could hardly believe how much dirt he was wheeling from the basement. But, then, it's a big basement. Tony's cousins were older than he and they arrived in street clothes. They worked for about an hour, wheeling dirt into the backyard, where a big mound was growing. Then, I heard the cousins arguing with Tony in the basement. They were cursing and yelling, but I couldn't make out what they were saying.

Soon, Tony came out to ask me for some cash, explaining that his cousins wanted to be paid up front. I gave him $150 (all I had in the house). Then, money in hand, the cousins left and didn't come back. The next day, they returned. But then, while I was out running an errand, they had another argument. This time, Jill was compelled to go to the ATM and get another $150. She didn't know what else to do to keep the peace. When I returned, the cousins were gone and Jill was upset. "What the hell's going on down there?"

When I asked Tony, he shook his head sadly. "They burned me, Ron."

"You mean they're not coming back?"

"Don't worry. I'll get it done."

"Why would they do this to you?"

He shrugged.

"But aren't they your cousins?"

"That don't mean they won't fuck me up."

The next day, he worked like a dog, digging his trench, then wheeling dirt into the yard. Shirtless, dripping sweat, dirty from head to toe, he looked defeated by the day's end.

"Look at all that dirt!" I exclaimed. It was a mound five feet high and ten feet across.

"You got to order a Dumpster, Ron."

The original plan was that Tony and his cousins were going to truck it out in a pickup.

I looked at Tony leaning wearily against his shovel, sweat dripping from his face.

"All right," I said. "I'll have one dropped first thing tomorrow."

By noon the next day, Tony hadn't filled a third of the Dumpster, which the Dumpster company was going to pick up at 4:00 sharp. So I grabbed a shovel and started helping. We worked without stopping. Still, when the driver arrived, we hadn't filled the container to the "full" line. I hopped up to the window of the cab and handed the driver $35. "Just give us twenty minutes more," I said. He took the money.

Then, he backed the cab to the Dumpster to get himself ready. Briefly, he tested the load. He found that he couldn't lift it. "What you got in that dirt?" he complained.

"We're not even up to the fill line," I said.

"I can't move it," he called.

"Well, we can't unload it either—I paid for a full twenty-yard haul."

"I got to call in." He radioed his dispatcher.

Tony and I watched. We were drenched and panting from the work.

After the driver hung up his radio, he leaned out the window: "They're calling me back to the yard."

"You're gonna leave the container?" I asked. "Blocking my garage?"

The driver let his eyebrows rise in the equivalent of a shrug. "Got to go!" Then he drove off, taking my $35 with him.

Tony turned to me with a grin. "Isn't that the shits?"

He took the bus home that night. When I awoke the next morning, with an aching back, the Dumpster was gone. There was still a lot of dirt left, so Tony and I decided to haul it to the city Dumpster in Jill's little Honda. We filled the back of that mini-SUV to the brim. Then, very slowly, I drove it to the dump, Tony in the passenger seat. When we arrived, the Dump Master sent us to the back of the line. One of the waiting contractors looked under Jill's car and said with a smirk, "You're gonna bust your axel, bud."

He was right, the axel had bent like a u-shaped straw. It was all but touching the asphalt. I'd had no idea we'd put in that much weight. After we shoveled out all the dirt, the axel seemed to recover but, even now, I wonder if someday soon it will snap, having been overstressed by a half ton of dirt that day.

It took two days for Tony to prep the floor for concrete. His plan was to lay down about four inches over a web of rebar and mesh, which would keep the new concrete from cracking. Before Tony's prep, I had insisted on power washing the floor to make sure the new concrete would adhere. That chore took me most of a day, Tony sweeping up behind me.

The morning the concrete truck arrived, Tony brought in another man, Bryant, a little guy about forty who had worked with Tony on other jobs. I had managed to clear the street for the truck's arrival. We would run the chute through the basement windows into wheelbarrows, then roll the stuff where we needed it. It was going to be hot work. August in Baltimore is as bad as the Amazon.

By this time, I had been toiling alongside Tony for nearly a week, my work outside long forgotten. Already, Tony was over budget. I could tell it was wearing on him because he was working with much less enthusiasm. And much less boasting. I feared he had already burned himself out. But the worst was over: we only had to pour the concrete, then Tony would smooth the surface. And Jill and I would have our basement back.

The concrete truck arrived on time, backed onto the curb at the front of the house, then we maneuvered the chute into the front basement window. I felt like Mr. Construction as I halted traffic on our busy street and directed that behemoth truck over the sidewalk. When the first dump of concrete hit the floor, Tony yelled for the driver to stop the run. The concrete wasn't the right kind: the stone in the mix was too big, made for pouring walls, not walks. We wouldn't be able to rake the stuff out, much less smooth it.

"It's what you ordered," the driver said.

"I wouldn't have ordered stone that big," I said.

He shrugged. "Then you better call the dispatcher."

The dispatcher said that's what I ordered. I said I wouldn't have ordered stone that big because I had made clear that I needed concrete for a floor, not a wall. Secretly, I wondered if I had made the mistake. As Jill knew too well, I wasn't good with details.

The dispatcher and I went back and forth until he agreed to send another truck tomorrow morning with a smaller stone in the mix.

So we tried it again the next day.

Nothing's tougher to work with than concrete. Slogging through it is like trudging through thick mud. And you've got to spread it fast because it dries fast. Once it begins to set up, there's no changing what you've got.

pouring concrete,   circa 1897

As the chute sluiced concrete through the basement window, each of us, in turn, held our wheelbarrow steady until it was brimming, then we wheeled it away, fighting to keep the barrow from capsizing. Pretty soon we were ankle deep in concrete, pushing and pulling it with our shovel blades or raking it with wide scrapers. Within an hour, the concrete truck was gone and we had a basement full of wet mix. Drenched with sweat, arms aching, we bullied it for hours.

To keep themselves going, Bryant and Tony were drinking beers. I didn't want to be uptight, so I let them. It was tough work. And soon we'd be done. But, by seven that night, I knew we were in trouble. The floor wasn't leveling out. In fact, it looked like waves on the bay in a high wind. Tony had bought a "float," a wide flat blade used to smooth out wet concrete. He was using it now to make feeble passes at the stiffening mixture. It occurred to me that we were missing something—one of those propellered machines that rides over the top of the concrete to smooth it. Then I knew: Tony's big talk had gotten the better of him. He didn't know how to finish the job.

I went upstairs to collect myself. As I stripped off my concrete-saturated clothes, dropping them onto sheets of newspaper Jill had laid across the kitchen floor, she looked at me with deep concern.

"What's wrong?" she said. "What's happened?"

"I think we're fucked," I said.

"But you said you got the right concrete this time."

"Jill, it's such a mess down there, I can't even talk about it now. It's just too depressing."

"Oh, god," she groaned. "Is our basement ruined?"

"Looks that way."

An hour later, after I had steeled myself for a return, nothing had improved downstairs. And now Tony and Bryant were both drunk and exhausted.

Tony assured me that we'd make it right tomorrow. Had I not been so exhausted myself—and hoping that a miracle would yet occur—I would have said: *Make it right? The concrete's hardening even as we speak! How are we ever going to make it right?*

24

THE MAN ON THE SCOOTER

WHEN I PICKED UP Tony the next morning, he was wearing new jeans and a fresh shirt—and he was carrying a gym bag.

I asked him what was up.

He said he needed some money and a ride to the bus station.

"Bus station?" I blurted.

"I got to go see my girlfriend," he said.

"What about my basement?"

"I'll be back," he promised.

"When, Tony? This work needs doing now!"

"Two days—Friday," he promised, "it's gonna be cool. But right now I've got to see my girlfriend."

"I didn't know you had a girlfriend."

"Of course I got a girlfriend. She's in Jersey."

"Is she hurt?'

"It's a *situation*," he said. "She's upset and wants me there NOW. I can't put her off."

"But you've got work to do!"

"Don't matter to her. Can't talk sense to her on the phone when she's like this. Got to be there face to face."

On and on he went, offering a story that made so little sense it just might have been true. Never mind that I hadn't heard about his girlfriend or his girlfriend problem until now.

By this point, I was in a quiet, dizzying panic. Our basement floor was ruined. I didn't even know where to begin. Would I have to call in a real contractor to pour more concrete and finish it out? I had no money left for that.

When I dropped Tony off at the bus station, after picking up Bryant—who was as confused as I—Tony took what cash I could offer, then he sauntered off to the bus.

"What the hell is that about?" I asked Bryant, who was in the back seat.

"I don't know," he said.

Twenty minutes later, when Bryant and I surveyed the basement, it could not have looked worse. The floor appeared pebbled. Some places it rose, some places it dipped. The basement was suitable now for storing coal or sand maybe, but nothing else.

Bryant massaged his goatee as he shook his head in puzzlement. I was hoping he'd come up with a solution, but he admitted that he had never worked with concrete.

I knew of topcoat or finishing concrete so I suggested we try that. Bryant was game as long as I kept him working. Specialty concrete like that is very expensive, more than twice the cost of regular concrete. I bought seven bags, wondering if that would be enough for 1400 square feet of basement.

Topcoat concrete mixes to the consistency of pudding and smooths out just as easily. Working on his hands and knees with a trowel, Bryant began to experiment with the stuff. Always a cheap cigar in his mouth, he was a steady worker. It took him most of the day to get a feel for the material, as I continued mixing batches for him. By the day's end, he hadn't even gotten out of the basement's front bay. But he had managed to smooth the floor in that small area, at least. At this point we weren't going to worry about how level it was. One nightmare at a time, please.

When I drove him home, Bryant talked a little about his life and asked some about mine. I told Bryant that I teach young people how to write. He nodded his approval. It would be another week before I'd understand that Bryant didn't know how to read or write. He said he was trying to get to a place in his life where "things settled down." He had a wife who was trouble, he said, and two small children. His biggest frustration lately had been the men—drug dealers—loitering on the steps of his house. He couldn't get them to move.

He lived in the worst part of West Baltimore, on a block of half-abandoned row houses, in a neighborhood that looked bombed and besieged. Every cliché that applies to inner-city life applied to his block. I drove down the dirt alley behind his house to let him off, his chained mutt yapping a greeting. Most of the windows on the backside of his place were dark; a couple were boarded up. The weedy lot behind his house showed traces of houses that had long been razed.

Bryant was soft-spoken, almost gentle in his manner and quick to laugh. As I got to know him, I kept waiting for him to reveal some bitterness or anger but he never did. When he described how someone was always trying to steal his motor scooter, he sounded only disappointed. He loved his motor scooter, a little Vespa, which was laid up with a flat. When he described it to me in detail, he revealed that he couldn't drive a car because he wasn't able to "make sense" of the test.

Three days into our mind-numbing work—Bryant troweling and smoothing the pudding-like topcoat, wiping ever-widening circles until the surface was reasonably level—he asked me if I could buy him a tire for his Vespa. So I stopped work and took him on a field trip to a big motorbike store out near the beltway. I'm not sure how far the compass of Bryant's life extended. It seemed clear that it didn't extend this far. In fact, I don't know that he had ever been in a big motorcycle store. He was elated at the sight of the big Kawasakis, Yamahas, and Suzukis. "Oh, man, look at that!" he exclaimed.

His joy made me joyful.

When we got to the counter, the clerk was obviously not pleased to see my companion. Though both of us were wearing our work clothes, Bryant—with his messy hair and his dirty hands and his now-awkward smile—was clearly the outsider.

As he tried to explain what he needed, I realized that we had made a mistake.

"What size tire?" the clerk asked impatiently.

"Goes to a Vespa," Bryant said. "Something like that." He pointed to the motorbike displayed atop a nearby counter.

"Sixteen inch tire? Fifteen inch?" The clerk could hardly hide his disdain, which pissed me off.

"Something like that," Bryant said, nodding as if this would make things clearer.

I asked the clerk, "How many tires would we be choosing from?"

"At least four sizes," he answered.

I turned to Bryant. "Let's come back when we know exactly the size we need."

"Okay," he agreed.

The clerk almost rolled his eyes in disgust.

I wanted to bark at the clerk: *Who are you to sneer at this man?*

The next day, Bryant brought me the flat from his Vespa. While he continued working, I drove ten miles to the other side of the beltway to another motorcycle shop—it seemed all of them were way the hell out there. But when I got to the store, with tire in hand, I discovered that I had forgotten my wallet. This is so typical of me, always moving too fast. I hated that I had to return to tell Bryant that I didn't get the tire. But he accepted it calmly, too used to disappointment apparently.

While I was on the errand, Rick—on one of his daily patrols— had almost called the police as Bryant was leaving through the backyard gate for lunch. But Bryant, at a glance, interpreted the situation immediately and called to Rick that it was all right, he was working for Mr. Ron, helping fix the basement.

On the way home that night Bryant told me his wife was in a bad state right now. She would not get off her drug, he explained, and he didn't want his kids to see that. He had "knocked her around," but it didn't seem to help. He said he didn't know what he could do.

I never knew how to answer such admissions except with an expression of dismay or sympathy—or, in the case of wife-beating, silence.

As I let him out, I promised I'd get him the scooter tire tomorrow. Which I did. Then Bryant had his wheels back. He arrived the next day on his white Vespa, chaining it to the tree on the sidewalk, just outside the basement. He wore a white helmet and was smoking his usual cigar as he swung off the scooter, grinning.

By this point, Bryant was working on his own in the basement while I continued working on the wall outside. We rarely mentioned Tony. When I went in to check on Bryant one day during our second week of work, he was nearly in tears. He said, "I just can't do this anymore, my knees are killing me." So I promised to pay him more to do whatever he could and I would help him finish the work. Which we did in two days.

The basement looked almost normal. Only if you knew concrete would you be able to tell that some things down there were screwy. The floor is not level at all, but it's mostly smooth—remarkably so, considering how it looked when we started.

I kept Bryant on for another week as he helped me frame out a utility room in the basement. Then, I was out of money and out of work for him.

When he drove off on his scooter, offering me a wave, I believed—or hoped—that I could give Bryant more work in the near future. But this never happened, in part because it'd be another year before I'd have the money to hire anyone again.

In part too because Bryant had no phone and, short of driving back to his bombed-out neighborhood and shouting for him from the backyard—as I had done a few times but was afraid to do now—I didn't know how to reach him.

* * *

The basement done, we could at last make good use of its considerable space. I built workbenches and shelves for our many tools, storage areas for brushes and paints (we had twenty gallons or more), sorting areas for architectural bits and pieces, stacking areas for bins of Christmas ornaments and dishes. It took us weeks to move everything down. Then, finally, the upstairs was clear and every room could now accommodate better uses.

Jill knew it was my fantasy to fill the house with guests, to host big dinners with friends, to have five couples sleep over in our five empty bedrooms, to make breakfast with the crowd, then lounge around on the first floor, which is flooded with morning light. My desire for this grew from fond memories of the crowds at my grandmother's house. My mother had nine siblings, which made Sunday dinners at grandma's a big event: aunts, uncles, and countless cousins sitting at a variety of tables that spanned the length of two rooms.

"Nobody's staying here for the wedding," Jill announced.

"No?"

"We're going to be a little distracted, don't you think?"

"Maybe you're right about that," I agreed.

"I've got an idea: let's get our friends to help out—instead of giving us gifts. Les could help us move the furniture and Tim could make his killer au gratin potatoes, Sue could do her Swedish meatballs. . ."

On and on we went. It would be both a celebration of love and of the rehab.

"You know," I mused, "we should test out the house beforehand to make sure it's ready."

"It'll be ready," Jill insisted. "We've got time."

"No, I mean *really* ready."

She eyed me warily. "What are you thinking?"

"We should invite my family for Christmas again."

"Oh, no!" she groaned.

"This time we'll do it right!" I promised.

"Why do you want to torture me?"

"We'll have the fireplaces blazing and the windows caulked.
And a really good tree. It'll be great."

She shook her head in grave doubt. "I don't know where you
get your optimism."

It wasn't simply optimism, it was an attempt to make things
right. She must have seen that I needed a second chance.

"It'll be great," I said again. "Really."

Jill sighed. "This will make you happy?"

I nodded yes.

"Okay." She smiled and rolled her eyes. "Round two: Christmas
with the Tanner family."

I kissed her.

25

TRIMMING SAILS

A WEEK AFTER BRYANT'S DEPARTURE, Tony phoned to say he wanted to get paid. I told him I had paid him all I could—well over the $2000 we'd agreed upon. It didn't seem to matter to him that he had abandoned the job, which I had to pay Bryant to finish. I said it at least three times: "You left the job, Tony. Bryant and I had to finish it without you. There's no more money left." He tried to get indignant, as if I had cheated him, but, really, there was nothing to argue about. At last, he said he had to come by to pick up his tools. I said that would be fine.

When I got off the phone, Jill was staring at me as if my hair were on fire.

"You're letting him come over?"

"He's got to get his tools," I explained.

"Ron, he's going to hurt you!"

"He's not going to hurt me."

"We should call the police—they should be here when he arrives!"

"Tony's not going to hurt me," I insisted.

She reminded me what he'd told me about beating his son senseless. I told her that was different.

"He thinks you owe him money!"

The more she talked, the more I began to worry.

When Tony arrived, I saw that his cousin had driven him—the same guy who had yelled at him a few weeks earlier. Quiet and brooding, Tony didn't seem inclined to argue, much less beat me senseless. He looked exhausted.

I don't like to leave anybody with bad feelings, but in this case I was wholly at a loss for words. I didn't want to be patronizing, but I didn't want to be conciliatory either. I was sure that Tony would try to take advantage of any concession on my part. I watched him load his things into the trunk of his cousin's car. Standing to one side, like Tony's father, his cousin nodded politely to me.

Tony asked where the big pry bar was. I said I didn't know. Tony said he'd left it outside—he'd borrowed it from Lou. Well, it was gone, I said. We often had things like that stolen from the backyard. A pry bar like that wasn't cheap. For all I knew, Tony had spent all of his money and lost his girlfriend, in addition to having blown this job and gotten on Lou's bad side.

When Tony left, I wished him good luck. He nodded glumly and was gone.

As I walked up the porch, I saw that Jill was watching. She opened the kitchen door for me. "I had the phone off the hook and ready to dial," she said.

"Horses, not zebras," I said.

"I'm amazed you can still toss out that tired expression after everything that's gone wrong," she said. "What would you have done if Bryant hadn't been around to help you fix that mess?"

"I would've found someone else—or done it myself."

She nodded as if to say, *Of course.* Then she pursed her lips and gave me a kiss.

* * *

The other big chore that needed doing before the wedding was restoration of our staircase balusters. We needed seventy-four of them. Estimates for having these made ran as high as $60 apiece.

Old staircase balusters are easy to come by but, apparently, no two staircases in this town are alike, not even in neighboring houses. We looked everywhere for something comparable, but could find nothing. Briefly, we considered putting in a variety of vintage balusters to create a motley, funky look. But we quickly scratched this idea because, increasingly, we saw the value of doing everything right and bringing the house back to its original condition.

Never having replaced balusters, I assumed they were all the same size. Jill left the job to me because she was busy teaching herself how to grain-paint, which would allow her to restore our faux mahogany pocket doors. When I was ready to take a sample of the original baluster to the wood-turner, however, she insisted on double-checking.

"How did the measurements come out?" she asked.

"What is there to measure?" I said. "They're all the same."

"Tell me you're joking."

"All we need is a single size. Then I'll cut the bases to fit the different runs."

"What about the tops?"

"I'll cut those too."

"So you're going to make all the tops and all the bases the same measurement?"

"Then cut them to size."

"Ron!"

"What's the problem?"

She was overthinking it, I was sure. But, what the hell, she could measure the balusters herself if that would make her happy. I handed the job over to her. She spent more than an hour measuring and making notations. Then, she showed me the results: there were seven different baluster sizes.

"Wow," I said sheepishly, "I guess I had it all wrong."

Jill stared at me in disbelief. "Why do you act as if you know what you're doing when half the time you don't?"

"It's my father's legacy," I said. "The confident man wins the day."

"What would you have won if I had let you walk out that door with your original measurement?"

"Oh, let me see," I joked, "a few thousand dollars worth of wrath?"

"You bear watching," she concluded. "I think I've learned that lesson."

"I'd put it another way," I said. "I need backup."

"As in 'behind every good man there's a woman'?"

"Well," I said, "you're hardly behind me."

"I'm not exactly ahead of you either," she said. "I don't want to second-guess you at every turn."

"It's only the sharp turns that need your scrutiny," I said.

"The fast turns," she added.

"Yeah, I need to slow down."

"Are you saying you're learning that?" she asked hopefully.

"Learning it isn't the same thing as living it," I said. "But, yeah, I'm getting comfortable with the idea that I might not always be right."

"Wow," she joked. "If you keep talking like that, I might get religious."

There will always be friction between Jill and me. We make jokes about it, but it's there nonetheless—large differences in the way we approach the world. By this time, it was clear that neither of us was going to change much. But we discovered that if we took a little more time to communicate, we got along better and the results, in every case, were mutually satisfying. I know this sounds obvious—when a couple confers and consults with each other, they will increase their chances of success—but we had been so rushed, distracted, and stressed out our first three years together, communication had been very hard to come by. Two things helped: we started leaving each other notes every day. Some

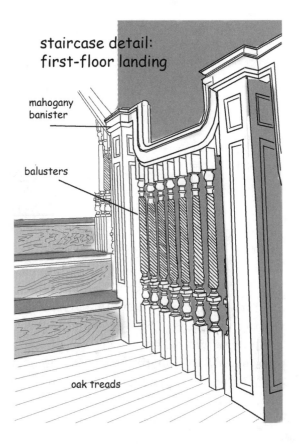

staircase detail:
first-floor landing

mahogany
banister

balusters

oak treads

were announcements of schedule changes, our days and nights seldom in sync; some were love notes (always helpful to remind our
partners that we're thinking of them); some were doodles—we
enjoy drawing cartoons of each other and/or the pets; and others
were jokes. Jill is fond of trumping me in a debate by scrawling
down one of my empty assertions and sticking it to the fridge: "It's
not as though the world is flat, Jill! Is the world flat?" Or she'll
tack a note onto one of my experimental dinners, too much of it
left over in the fridge: "Ron: should we donate this to Science?"
This helped us lighten up.

a fridge doodle of harriet

Just
Love
me!

The other thing we did was stop yelling for/at each other when we were in different rooms. The Queen Anne's big rooms and high ceilings swallow voices easily. As a result, we too often found ourselves shouting, "*What?*" angrily in response to a repeated call from the other, who never seemed to hear. Both of us were touchy about issues of listening and being heard. So, without discussing it, we developed the habit of calling each other's name playfully as we walk through the house, no matter what we are doing. I call, "Jilly," she calls, "Ronny," and that way we know where we are. It has a surprisingly calming effect. I know, it is such a simple thing. It works because it creates balance: you call my name, I call your name; eventually we'll meet up and figure out what the other needs.

* * *

Although preparations for our wedding was a great excuse to get things done—and go on a "rehab rampage," as Jill called it—the prospect of my family's visit at Christmas motivated me even more.

I would not get it wrong this time. I made sure our first floor fireplaces were ready. I rebuilt the hearths that summer, then replaced the modest wooden mantels with slate mantels. Rick and Charles had given us a slate mantel as a housewarming gift. It was in nine pieces. It had never occurred to me that mantels came in pieces, but it only makes sense. For the longest time I stared at those nine stone-heavy mantel sections and wondered how I would put them together. After phoning a stonemason, who said he could do the job for $1500, I determined to do it myself. The story of my rehab life.

After I put the thing together, we liked the look of slate so much we decided to find another mantel like it. Slate is a fitting match for the Queen Anne because it's fancier than wood but not too fancy, like marble. I had Lou run new gas lines to the hearths. All of our shallow fireplaces (except an odd one on the second floor) were designed for gas, not wood. Wood, I learned, was the poor man's fuel: cheap, but dirty and inconvenient. Most households used coke or coal, heaped on small grates. Gas was cleaner and more manageable, but more expensive. For gas, however, you needed some kind of small stove. Made of tin, copper, or brass, these things are easy enough to find nowadays and come in countless varieties. They could be as ornate as an Ottoman harem screen or as stripped down as a Bauhaus sculpture. But good luck getting any of them to work. For starters, these things aren't up to code. And, really, there's no market for the repair of antique gasworks. Jill knew somebody who could do the job.

Jake Gallopean said he had "worked in gas" for twenty years. We had already been to his house to look at his antiques. He was expert at stripping furniture, which probably explained his bad health. A small, bent man, with a large nose and pale, pockmarked face, he couldn't stand straight and loped as if one leg were shorter than the other. Jill knew lots of guys like Jake. They were jacks-of-all-trades: speculating in antiques and refurbishing them, cleaning out basements and attics in the hope of finding a treasure, haunting cheap auctions, holding yard sales, renting space in consignment shops, sometimes selling at online auctions, and sometimes selling from the trunks of their battered cars. The last time we called Jake, his phone had been disconnected. Like others of his kind, you could never tell how long he'd be available. But, eventually, he'd turn up again.

When Jake appeared at our front door, he was wearing black jeans, a black silver-trimmed cowboy shirt, a turquoise-studded belt, a black leather vest, and a large, broad-brimmed black cowboy hat, a pheasant feather protruding jauntily from the diamondback band. It looked like he was doing well, I observed. His nod was the equivalent of a shrug.

Following his instructions, I had bought an assortment of gas stove parts, which now lay like an array of surgeon's tools beside the gas insert in the living room fireplace. As Jake loped over to the fireplace, he kept his gaze fixed on the insert. "Will it work?" I asked eagerly. Made of tempered steel and copper, the insert looked like a pile of logs neatly framed by an ornate surround, which would fit precisely the hearth opening. Jill had found it at an antiques mall.

"Yeah, sure, it'll work," Jake said. He set his hat on a nearby couch, then he stretched himself out on the floor to examine the insert, trying the lever, inspecting the jets, fingering the valves. Fireplace inserts are the simplest gas stoves: they have an intake valve for the gas line; a lever to control the flow of gas; and a series of jets—little holes—from which the flaming gas escapes. My worry was that the jets would malfunction or the whole thing would leak. Or blow up.

"What you got to worry about," Jake explained, "is how they burn. Most people like an orange flame, but orange means you're burning too much oxygen. It won't give enough heat. And it might make more carbon monoxide than you can get rid of."

"Yes, exactly," I said, "I don't want to kill myself."

Detail:
fireplace
insert

asbestos/clay
logs = gas jets

surround tiles

faux marbled
mantel

grill conceals
gas pipes

Jake made the insert burn a deep blue flame. Secretly, I was disappointed because I wanted that orange wood-burning flame, but Jake assured me that this was the *official* flame. Nobody a hundred years ago would have questioned it. He said he'd have to come back to finish the other one in the dining room. That one Jill and I had brought back from upstate New York: an Art Nouveau-style stove about the size of a washtub, it had two mica-windowed doors that opened onto a bed of glowing lava rocks. It was unique and way cool, we thought.

Jake didn't seem impressed one way or the other. I was hoping that he'd notice my neat brick and mortar work. These fireplaces were ready for action.

"You repair these fireboxes?" he asked, glancing around finally.

I nodded eagerly.

I realized that I wanted the approval of guys like Jake more than anybody's.

When I saw him off at the door, he said he'd get back to me in a couple of days. Knowing what I did of nonlicensed workers, I was pretty sure a "couple of days" could mean a couple of weeks or even months. So I offered Jake a bonus if he could finish our hookup by the end of the week. He said he could do that. Then he loped away, leaving me feeling like a lucky man.

Two weeks before Christmas, Jill and I wrapped our big banister in pine bows, then draped more over the gilt mirrors above the first floor fireplaces and across the archway between the living room and music room. At last, we were beginning to see what a Victorian Christmas would have looked like in the Queen Anne. We bought a ten-foot tree for the front bay and now, thanks to our friend Scott, we had loads of vintage ornaments to hang. Unlike our first Christmas, we had carpets on the floors—well-worn Orientals—and comfortable furniture. The walls, painted at last, glowed warmly: dark sunshine in the living room, topaz in the dining room, mustard in the hallways. And the fireplaces blazed.

26
DECK THE HALLS

THE WEEK OF HER ARRIVAL, my mother sent a spiral ham—because you can't have Christmas without one. I bought extra carrots for Michael's daily juicing. And whiskey for Mom, just in case. The windows and floors gleamed. The house smelled of pine. Wreaths hung on the front doors. Jill and I had already forgotten how raw the house must have appeared that first Christmas, three years before. But we knew this was a significant change. We had even installed a cute powder room on the first floor, inside the former larder closet: no more long treks upstairs for relief.

This time, when my mother entered the house, she said, "Oh, Ronald, oh, Jill, this is *lovely*. Really, this is lovely."

"Need to use the bathroom?" I asked. "It's just over here."

"I've got to take some pictures," she said, waving one hand in excitement. "Come here, stand in front of the tree. Jill, stand in front of the tree with Ronald. That tree is so big! How'd you get it inside? I hope you had somebody help you—you could've hurt yourself."

Dave brought Annie, who immediately became best friends with Jill. Mike still enjoyed talking about raw foods and health but he was surprisingly low-key about it. Maybe Lois had cautioned him. Or he had simply gained some perspective. Mrs. King didn't make this trip, so there was no scuppernong wine.

view: living room to
music room & dining room

Nobody would go near Harriet, despite her insistent company. Jill and I encouraged their caution at every turn. We'd made a private wager: I predicted that Harriet would bite at least one brother. Jill predicted that both would be bitten.

Though it wasn't as cold this Christmas as the first, we kept the gas fireplaces burning. The potbellied stove in the dining room was downright infernal, lava stones glowing orange behind its mica windows.

In two cars, we caravanned around town, driving by the famous 34th street block of overloaded, kitschy decorations, then through historic Roland Park, which had been Baltimore's exclusive country retreat a hundred years ago.[4] Late in the day, we caught the last tour of the Hampton mansion, a national historic site that Jill and I hadn't known about until Lois mentioned it. The mansion, just seven miles from our house, was once the largest in the nation. Booker T. Washington was born as a slave there.

---

4. For information about Hampden's famous Christmas street, go to
http://www.christmasstreet.com

When the guide began our tour, my mother announced, "These two have an old house downtown, you know."

"But it's not a mansion," I added.

"They've done *so much* work on it," she continued. "Poor dears!"

"Really?" the guide said politely. Our party—seven of us— were the only ones on the tour.

"You wouldn't *believe* what they've been through," my mother said.

"It's just a row house," I said.

"It's *historic*," my mother persisted. "They earned a *historic* credit for it."

"Oh, sure," the guide said. "A tax credit. Congratulations."

"I wish you could see pictures of it," my mother said.

"Maybe next time," the guide offered.

"Ronald, you should invite this nice man to visit you—he'd like to see what you've done."

I smiled politely.

The guide returned the smile. Then, he showed us a couple of rooms that were not on the tour. We were very appreciative.

That night at dinner, we toasted to a prosperous new year, then Mike toasted to our engagement.

"Oh, this is wonderful!" my mother said. "Isn't this wonderful?"

"It's about time." Dave winked at Jill.

"Just following your good example," I said, raising my glass.

Annie hugged Jill. We toasted some more.

I described our plan. We'd have to coordinate calendars to find a date that was suitable for everyone.

After we cleared the dishes, I insisted that we play UNO. My mother, who loves to play Bridge, found this children's game delightful. The object of the game is to unload penalty cards on the person next to you until you have no cards left. Mike, who was always the family's practical joker, could hardly suppress an evil grin every time he sprang a stunning penalty on his neighbor. My mother yelped every time it happened to her. I loved to hear her laugh. Jill said, "Ruby, you've got to get meaner at this game."

"Then I'll need another drink!" she said.

Later we moved to the living room and played Balderdash, the bluffing dictionary game. I was proud of my family: my brothers had always had a good sense of humor. I couldn't remember when we'd laughed this much, except as children.

By the time Jill and I got to bed, we were buzzed and exhausted.

"It couldn't have gone better, don't you think?" I said.

"I must admit," she said, "it was painless."

"It was better than painless."

"Okay, it was fun. I really like my new sister-in-law. And Lois is so solid, I'd trust her with my life."

"Did you notice, at dinner, how my mother had to take off her sweater?"

Jill chuckled. "You sat her right in front of the fireplace, what'd you expect?"

"It was great!"

"I'm glad you're happy."

"This is what I wanted the house to be," I said, picturing every person in his or her room, doors—front and back—secured, the dogs snoring nearby. "It's a ship safely put out to sea."

"Okay, captain, can we sleep now? Tomorrow's a long one."

"Yes, my first mate."

"Your *only* mate. And don't forget it."

She kissed me goodnight.

In the early morning, as light began to leak through the shutters, Jill made one of her usual vigorous turns, the bed creaked and swayed, then something snapped and we went down.

"What was that?" she asked groggily.

I was already on the floor. "We've capsized, my love."

"What?"

"The bed fell."

She sat up partly. The front end of my side had hit the floor. She regarded the steep angle with half-shut eyes. "Can you fix it?"

I shrugged. "Probably. But you'll have to get out first."

"You think?"

It took an hour. I found some steel bands to secure the pegs where the posts attached to the frame. Now, if the main pin on any corner came loose, the bands could keep the bed from collapsing. "Not pretty," I said, "but practical."

"Welcome to our world," Jill remarked. "I guess it's time for coffee."

At breakfast, I did not announce that our bed had collapsed. Though it would have been good for a laugh, I just didn't want to get into it.

Sue and John, our friends from across the street, joined us for Christmas dinner. Sue, a Southerner, all but adopted my mother on the spot. We visited Rick and Charles, where my mother took a lot of pictures. Already, she was in the habit of sending them greeting cards six times a year.

"Have you seen what Ron and Jill have done to their house?" my mother exclaimed.

"Certainly we have," Rick answered. "I've been watching every step of the way."

"And laughing much of the time," I added.

Rick laughed now. "He can be quite funny."

"Especially when I'm burning something up or using the wrong tool," I said.

"But we're proud of him and Jill," Rick continued. "They've done wonderful work."

"The whole neighborhood's proud of them," Charles added.

"I saw the place from the beginning," Rick said. "I know what they've been through!"

"We saw it too," my mother said. "That first Christmas."

"What you saw was *nothing*," I said, suddenly feeling defensive. "Nothing compared to the way it was at the beginning."

With a subtle look, Jill signaled for me to go easy.

"You poor dears," my mother said. She lay a hand on my cheek. "What you've been through. You've almost killed yourself working on that house."

I sighed. It seemed there was no middle ground for Mom. Either our lives were pitiful or miraculous.

"You're going to stop now, aren't you?" she continued.

"Actually, we've only just started," I said. "There's plenty more to do. Look around you at our inspiration."

Rick grinned and wagged a finger at me. "It took us twenty years!"

"What can I get everybody to drink?" Charles asked. "Another bourbon, Ruby?"

When we returned to the Queen Anne, I was proud to see our big tree lighting up the first-floor bay, making the house look as grand as it must have been a hundred years ago.

By the time we took everyone to the airport the next day, some of us were hung over and all of us were weary, but not, this time, from trying to stay warm all night or listening to the caterwauling of a demented cat. Annie said she'd never had so enjoyable a family Christmas. Everyone agreed it had been most pleasant—and not too cold.

27
THE HOUSE AS HABITAT

"I HATE THESE ANTS!" Jill shouted from the kitchen. It was spring and the ants had come out in force, ever marching across our countertops.

They aren't big ants but they are persistent—and they've been with us from the start. I'd first seen them when I was cleaning out the old mortar between the bricks on the outside of the house. Called the "pavement ant," the *tetramorium caepitium* is hardly larger than two grains of coarse pepper. Apparently, they live deep in the sandy mortar of our brick walls. Nut brown and slow-moving, they visit us indoors come early spring, then retreat in the coldest months, though warmer weather will bring them out even in winter. They seem to have no special preferences, as happy with a spot of grease as with a drop of honey. When Jill tires of their company—especially after they have discovered the sugar bowl—she goes after them with a bright green kitchen cleanser that kills them instantly in their tiny tracks, even though she knows as well as I that we will never rid ourselves of these insistent guests and should worry more about the toxic cleanser she sprays across our countertops.

My father, an amateur naturalist, took us boys camping every summer. After he died, I inherited most of his camp gear, including his camp pullover. The first day I wore it, somebody—at a gas station I'd stopped at—asked me if I was going hunting. It hadn't occurred to me that his old pullover looked camouflaged, though I guess it did. He never took us hunting. Not that he ever spoke against it; he simply wasn't a hunter. For us, the fun was in watching wildlife—always from a respectful distance. The first time I saw a garter snake eating a frog, my father told me to let it be, *it was just doing what snakes do.* As a result of such lessons, I find myself telling Jill that the ants are just doing what ants do. It's nothing personal.

It seems personal, though. For the life of him, Jill's father can't fathom why wild creatures, large or small, would want to come anywhere near his house. He is so obsessed with gopher abatement; he spends hours standing in his yard with a pitchfork in hand, waiting for the tell-tale mound of movement. Then, he strikes, stabbing the ground.

"I never see blood on the tines," he observes, "so I can't be sure if I got them."

"The dirt clears the blood when you pull out the pitchfork," his wife assures him. "Sure, you got them!"

This is a man who, when a snapping turtle wandered into his yard one day, beat the thing back with the flat of a shovel.

His need to thwart all wild things explains why he and his wife keep their windows shut throughout the year. *We never open our windows,* they will proudly tell you. When Jill and I visit, however, I do the unthinkable: I open a window. It's so stifling in their house, the chemical sweetness of plug-ins wafting from every other wall socket and dusty mold-rich effluvia rising from the thick pile of synthetic wall-to-wall carpeting, I feel myself choking as I lie on my single bed—an arm's-length from Jill in her single. It takes a while to strong-arm one of the windows, which pops open at last like the hatch of the Orbiter. There is no screen, of course, because *we never open our windows!*

The next night at dinner, Jill's father sees a tiny wasp-thing curiously parading across the dinner table. He promptly squashes it with one thumb, asking, "Where'd that come from?" *Because we never open the windows!* Flying ants, lacewings, beetles, lady bugs, fireflies, and moths of every variety have found their way in—the house now hosting a winged menagerie. This will confound Jill's father and keep him busy for hours pursuing the interlopers with a rolled up newspaper.

By contrast, if a wayward spider wandered into our house when I was a child, my father would instruct us to gather it up and deposit it outdoors. Not even my mother was quick to kill an intruder; and she's the one who, when pregnant with her first son, screamed at the sight of a marauding tarantula in our grandmother's garage, at which point Nana rushed out with a broom and killed the confused thing.

Like canaries in a coal mine, the lowliest creatures in our house are the harbingers of our home's good or ill health. We may not like their company, but their presence is a good sign (in most cases). And surely they're no less attractive than the company we host on our own bodies—everything from tentacled, microscopic mites in our eyelashes to vast colonies of bacteria in our intestines. Fear-mongering pesticide manufacturers and pest control companies would have us think that every living thing in the house—other than us, our plants, and our pets—is either a nuisance or a health hazard. Warns one pest control ad, "If bugs aren't already in your new home, they're waiting to get in." This chicken-little assertion sounds suspiciously xenophobic. Attempting to thwart the little creatures that would share our houses is like attempting to change the course of a river. As Thoreau observed after building his home "where a woodchuck had formerly dug his," every "house is still but a sort of porch at the entrance of a burrow."

A Florida couple of our acquaintance, having moved into a new neighborhood adjacent to Little Manatee State Park, reported a strange visitation one morning: they heard scratching at their front door. When they opened it, they found a turtle as big as a dinner plate waiting to pass through. Apparently, their house was in the path of the turtle's route, which might have been there for centuries. The homeowners picked up the turtle and carried it to the pond on the other side of their house. Maybe they will observe this courtesy everyday until the turtle finds an alternate route.

Just the other day, I was running electrical cable in one of the many dark corners of our large basement, where I was compelled to bypass a leggy, teardrop-sized spider in his nest. I had leeway, after all; he did not. Spiders are the humblest cohabitants of our old house. One variety prevails—the cellar spider, or *pholcid*, which looks something like a daddy longleg. Unlike the daddy longleg, who is known as the "harvester" or "harvestman" because he roams for his prey, the cellar spider stays put and builds a messy little web no wider than a teacup. Though they are numerous in our basement, they can be found throughout the house, discreetly hanging in a nook or cranny. Male and female either nest next to each other or share the same web, a fitting arrangement for a domestic couple.

A third lowly cohabitant of our old house is the ugliest, and, without question, speediest: the thoroughly misunderstood *scutigera coleoptrata* or household centipede. Up to three inches in length, these are black-striped grayish speedsters with twenty-eight legs and two elegantly flowing antennae. I am very sorry to say that I have stamped on a number of these, thinking they were like silverfish, which eat into books, papers, and clothing. But they are nothing like silverfish. They are, in fact, related to crayfish, sea monkeys (brine shrimp), krill, horseshoe crabs, and trilobites— all of which are members of the phylum arthropoda, the most successful of all phyla, comprising three-fourths of all living *and* fossil organism. Theirs is an amazing family.

Fond of darkness, the household centipede darts out from under a baseboard or loosened brick whenever I'm doing repairs; then, like a current of electricity, he's gone. Despite their speed,

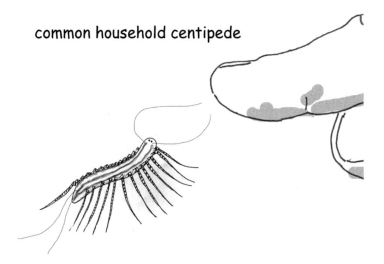

common household centipede

you—or better, an agile cat, like our bug-crazed Tess—can catch and kill one, but to what end? There must be thousands of them in our old house.[5] Generally, they stay on their side of the wall, as we stay on ours. Like spiders, they are pincered predators, chasing after cockroaches, fly larvae, and silverfish, among other wastrels. A word of warning: if cornered and fingered by you or me, the household centipede may be impelled to bite. The resulting injury would be akin to a honey bee sting. I myself have cornered the *scutigera coleoptrata* on several occasions and stared straight into his black compound eyes, which provide surprisingly good sight— the best among the centipedes. I can say, without hesitation, that I sensed in that stare a benign intelligence, which is why, well before I knew this creature's value, I often let him go.

---

5. Their courtship is notable, for the male does a little dance for his mate (attracted by pheromones); then, like a fastidious gentlemen, he spins a silk purse into which he deposits his sperm. The female takes the purse to fertilize her eggs. After birth, the little *scutigera coleoptrata* stay with the mother for about two weeks for protection.

* * *

Most of us have forgotten that middle- and upper-class families did not get rid of fleas, lice, bedbugs and other inconvenient co-habitants until the late nineteenth century. We can't begin to fathom—by today's standards—how befouled and infested were the homes of George Washington, Ben Franklin, John Adams, and all the rest of our revered forefathers and mothers. Consider this from an 1837 nature book for children: "Every boy has seen the little white maggots which are found in cheese, and which are the cleanest and most elegantly formed of all the class of insects, while in grub-state; *nor need any one be afraid to eat them, for they are perfectly harmless.*" Obviously, our level of tolerance changes over time. My mother was fond of recounting how, when my father was aboard ship in the Navy, he had to eat bread infested with mites. Appalled and fascinated, we three boys often begged to hear the story repeated. When we asked Dad, *How could you eat that?*, he simply shrugged and replied: "It was all we had."

My father's generation—as adults—was the first to enjoy the benefits of super toxins like DDT and Malathion. So effective was the reign of poison (approx. 1945–1975) that the Baby Boom generation—at least among the middle-class and higher—was the first to live a fairly pest-free existence. There are now generations of Americans who have never been bitten by a bedbug or seen a single louse, which is quite extraordinary when you consider that every civilization before us knew these creatures intimately. The result—for us—is that wildlife seems wilder than ever, and now, most Americans know of bugs and beasts only by hear-say, sometimes through such quaint farm-life expressions as "sleep tight, don't let the bed bugs bite." This explains why the presence of a possum hissing at Jill's father from his front yard dogwood some years ago seemed as outlandish to him as a visit from an extraterrestrial. And he speaks of the event pretty much that way.

* * *

Shortly after installing a fan over our kitchen stove, which vents into the house's third and rearmost chimney, Jill and I were alarmed to hear a creature trapped one morning above the fan housing. The animal thrashed, seeming to hurl itself from one side to the other inside the exhaust conduit, which was as big around as a volleyball. This is how animals kill themselves, panicking when trapped.

"Is it a rat?" Jill asked in alarm. Our neighborhood is notoriously rat-infested.

"It's a bird," I said with more confidence than I felt.

Quickly, I removed the fan housing, slipped on a leather work glove, then gingerly reached up through the opening until I was elbow deep into the exhaust pipe. Suddenly, the thrashing ceased. Then I felt the animal in my gloved hand and knew it was indeed a bird.

A soot-gray chimney swift, to be exact, tucked neatly into my palm, where I held it firmly. Forever in flight, swifts never perch, settling only when they reenter their chimney roost, where they cling to its roughened wall. No doubt this one had gripped a loose piece of mortar and fallen. Quickly again—afraid that my captive would have heart failure—I took it to the porch door, where I released it, the swift arrowing away at a steep angle. I felt electrified, as if I'd just shot a thunderbolt from my palm.

I am convinced that if each of us could release a bird to its flight everyday, there would be less crime and hate, and, perhaps, fewer wars.

Every time I'm on the roof in the spring, I take time to watch the swifts. If you pause long enough to listen beyond the wind, you'll hear them—their chittering—before you see them. The sky is aswirl with swifts. Roosting in the many crumbling brick chimneys of our old neighborhood, they spend their days wheeling and soaring at stunning heights.

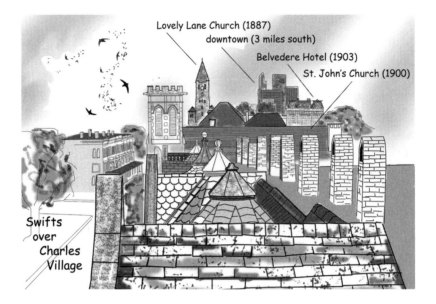

Lovely Lane Church (1887)
downtown (3 miles south)
Belvedere Hotel (1903)
St. John's Church (1900)

Swifts
over
Charles
Village

When I opened up the living room's fireplace, I found decades of debris, most of it soot and sand from the chimney's wear, but also a few desiccated swift carcasses. I decided that I could not have swifts living in the chimneys—for their sake. When I went to the roof to screen the first of our four chimneys, I saw, to my dismay, two swifts roosting deep inside, their black bullet-like bodies affixed to the masonry. So, returning to the kitchen, I inserted the nozzle of a shop vac up the chimney and let it blow. The swifts shot away and then, hastily, I was able to screen the chimney from the rooftop.

A number of conservation groups advocate the construction of "swift towers" to replace the rapidly disappearing, or increasingly sealed, chimneys. Chimney swifts are thoroughly helpful, eating one-third their weight in mosquitoes, flies, termites and other insects everyday. What is more, they need no special habitat, only the sky above your house, where they dive and soar at tremendous heights. In dark, whirlpool flocks, they arrive here in March, nest in May, building twiggy hammocks—only one nest per chimney—then, in November, they migrate to the Amazon Basin.

* * *

As I began to button up our old house, especially after screening the chimneys, I wondered how far I would go to shut everything out. Was I becoming like Jill's father? I worried most about the bats. One or more were in the attic when we bought the house. I suspected their presence long before I saw them. Shortly after Jill moved in, I awoke abruptly one night, convinced that we were not alone. Wary, vaguely scared—and envious of Jill's sound sleep—I lay still and listened, my eyes open to the dark. Short of an axe murderer having sneaked into the house, what could be the worst case? This is what I ask myself in the light of day. In the dark of night, however, I am not so reasonable.

Lying there, waiting, I must have seen it—its dark darting form—several times before I admitted that, yes, it was a bat. After the initial spill of chill bumps (A *bat!*), I hunched out of bed and skittered to the bay, where I opened three big windows. Returning to bed, I waited for the bat's exit. He/she flitted into the room from the hallway, then returned to the hallway, then swooped again into the room, back and forth. All the while I was murmuring, *C'mon, find the window, you're almost there, c'mon. . .*

At last, it sailed out the window, then I was able to shut them all, wondering, *How did it get in?*

Our visitor was probably a *pipistrellus subflavus,* or eastern pipistrelle, known to be a loner. Or the little brown bat, *myotis lucifugus.*

A small bat can eat as many as 1,200 mosquitoes an hour. This is a comforting thought nowadays since mosquito-borne West Nile virus has made inroads to temperate zones like Baltimore. What is more, bats themselves are not susceptible to the virus. Some insects can hear a bat's approach from a hundred feet away.

This means that the mere presence of bats sends some of the peskiest bugs packing. In warmer climes, bats help pollinate and spread the seed of many food-bearing plants, including bananas, avocados, dates, figs, peaches, mangoes, cloves, and cashews. A few of these are pollinated by bats alone. Because bats eat so many insects, however, they are highly susceptible to insecticides, which they pass on to their young. This is why, among other reasons, they are endangered. Sadly, many people still associate bats with rabies, even though ninety-nine percent of rabies cases worldwide are caused by dog bites. Rabies among bats is largely limited to one kind, the silver-haired bat, which does not live in buildings of any kind.

Our bat kept visiting, showing up in the early morning hours, rousing my atavistic radar, which woke me with a start and the firm conviction that *we are not alone*. We could not go on like this, of course. After the fourth visit, I finally, reluctantly made my way to the attic so that I could seal it up while the bat was away on its nightly flight. It was easy to see where he/she was getting in: at the attic's front there was one opening large enough for a cat. I closed the opening, satisfied that our house was secure at last. But, then, once the bat's visits ceased, I felt a vague loss: I worried about the thing, especially if it was a loner. Obviously, I couldn't live with the bat. He wasn't a pet. But couldn't I accommodate him somehow?

* * *

In cleaning up our house that spring before our wedding, I felt increasingly bad about destroying the habitats I've just described. When I announced to Jill that I was going to undo some of my damage and welcome back some of the animals I was thwarting, she was all for it. First, I opened up one unused chimney for the swifts. Then, Jill and I agreed to let the spiders be—we have cobwebs in many corners. Whenever we saw a centipede sprint past,

we cheered it on. The ants, however, remain an object of debate. As for the bats, of all the animals I have catalogued, they seemed most vulnerable. With their quiet flight and modest retreat, they are thoroughly self-effacing. Even the way they huddle together for sleep in the humblest recesses—some under loose tree bark—make them seem deserving of sanctuary. So I decided to build them two houses on the roof.

When my neighbor Dan asked, "What's that thing on your roof?" I told him flat out.

A minister, Dan's not prone to judge others. In this instance, however, he offered me a puzzled look.

"It's no joke," I assured him.

"A bat house, did you say?"

As I explained all the good that bats do, he just stared at me, apparently waiting for the punch line. "Really, Dan. Bats are great!"

Convinced that I was serious, he smiled and shook his head in wonder. "My, my," he said.

My father would have understood, and, in fact, might have suggested we keep watch—from a discreet distance, of course. With binoculars from the kitchen window, he and I used to watch birds at the feeder I had erected in our backyard. He went so far as to set up his telephoto camera on a tripod, so that we could get some great close-ups. Leaning together near the camera, his head nearly touching mine, his familiar scent of cigarettes and spicy cologne suddenly strong in my nose, this was as close as we got towards the end of his too-short life. The camera stayed up for months.

He would have helped me build a bat house, I am sure. A bat house isn't particularly large but it is of a particular design. It must be made of untreated lumber to spare the bats exposure to chemicals, for instance, and is best mounted on a brick building like ours. I've erected mine over the chimney at the middle of our roof—which puts them nearly fifty feet above the street. It may take a year or two for the bats to find or accept my house, I've learned. You have to be patient. I never imagined I'd be wishing for the return of something I'd been so eager to be rid of. But, then, I never imagined a house might be an ark, a haven for so many creatures, and that we homeowners could be stewards of their safe passage, each of us waiting on our roofs for the sound of wingbeats and a sign of hope.

28
BELLS ARE RINGING

JILL DECIDED WE NEEDED A GRAND PIANO for our wedding. We didn't have money for a grand piano, but that didn't stop Jill from dreaming. She'd been teaching herself to play piano on an aged upright she'd gotten nearly for free. So it's not as though the piano would be only for decoration. "This house deserves a grand," she declared. I liked the idea—I could invite my musician friends over to play it.

"You can have this piano for two hundred," Sal, our junk-dealer friend in Pennsylvania, said. We were standing in his glorious, gloomy Victorian living room. Like all square grands we'd seen so far, his was an antique ruin. "It needs work," he added. "I don't know how much." I was almost tempted to take it. The dark mahogany case looked great, like a massive, lion-legged coffin. Two hundred seemed a bargain. But something held me back. Maybe I'd seen too many projects go wrong by this point and wasn't willing to take on one more that was obviously far gone.

Sal was downsizing because he and his partner were breaking up. "I didn't think it'd get this ugly," he said sadly. "We were so in love."

I wanted to commiserate, to share the tattered fund of wisdom I had wrested from my own failures. "Sometimes," I began authoritatively. But then I remembered what Jill said about my always stepping out too quickly, pretending I have the answers when I don't.

Squinting through his cigarette smoke, Sal looked at me hopefully. I didn't know what to tell him. What, exactly, did I believe about love now that I was in love again?

Above all, I wanted to believe that love lasts. But sometimes it doesn't. When I was in my twenties, I made friends with an older guy (age thirty-five) who had been married three times already. I judged him harshly for that because I was raised to believe that those who divorce aren't willing to work. You'll recall my mother's mantra: "Marriage is hard work!" Hers is a simplistic view, I have discovered. A lasting partnership takes more than hard work. Sometimes, those who divorce have worked themselves to exhaustion. Sad to say, love *doesn't* conquer all. Divorce isn't exactly about love or, rather, the loss of love, I've decided; it's about how hard it is to live with another person.

I'll say that again: we often divorce because we can't live with the other person, no matter how much we may love him or her. Jill and I pushed and pulled for several years trying to win a tug-of-war of wills. I want the dogs leashed. She wants the dogs untethered. Who wins this fight? At one point, I'm ashamed to say, after I found yet another pile of dog poop on the living room carpet, I bagged it up and set it next to Jill's coffee maker. We didn't speak to each other for a week. It got to the point where either we were going to give each other a break or we were going to break apart.

I was sure that Sal would rebound from his breakup. Most of us do, thankfully. When we saw him the next time, he had moved into a small ranch house and bought himself a new Audi coupe to assuage his pain. That was a start.

Jill and I gave up on square grand pianos because her research revealed that they were notoriously ill-made and impossible to restore. Ever persistent, however, Jill set her heart on acquiring a Chickering grand. They were very respectable pianos, whose production started in 1823 and ceased in 1983. Jill located a 1919 model for $800. When fully restored, they're worth $35,000. But this one—like everything else we've bought—needed restoration. We were wise enough to call in a piano technician to inspect the instrument before we bought it. He said for a few thousand we could have it playing fine. We thought we might be able to scrape together that much. After we got the piano home, we sought a second opinion. The second tech said the soundboard was ruined and restoration would cost more. A lot more. It was clear at this point that, even if we had the money, we wouldn't get the piano fixed in time for the wedding.

Next, Jill decided she needed a vintage wedding gown. These are hard to come by, especially since most people a hundred years ago were Munchkin-size—or so it seems whenever I pick through vintage clothing. Eventually, we found ourselves at a sprawling multi-estate auction in Philadelphia, where somebody was selling an impressive array of aristocratic Victorian and Edwardian clothes. While Jill searched through rack after rack of gowns, I wandered to another part of the warehouse to poke through the leavings of somebody else's estate: grocery boxes of moldy books, dusty tools, worn kitchenware, cheap glassware, vinyl record albums of the geezer variety (Lawrence Welk, Mario Lanza, the Lennon Sisters), a box of index-carded recipes, plastic alarm clocks and so on—the aggregate of everything you can imagine a retired couple of modest income might have in their two-bedroom bungalow. I found it depressing. It made me wonder at all the junk I have accumulated and how one day somebody will be looking through *my* boxes.

We Americans own way too much junk, in part because we inhabit a country big enough to hold it all. My frugal parents were scavengers who often brought home odd finds. After one of her rounds of Saturday morning flea-marketing with her best friend Mary Jane, Mom presented us boys with a box of antique baseball mitts. Though they were useless—flat, unpadded, and ill-shaped compared to new mitts—we thought them too interesting to discard. Dad's shop in our basement was crowded with salvage: hammers and levels, soldering irons and drills, electrical meters and pressure gauges, and jars and jars of diodes and transistors, which were as colorful as penny candy. He was especially fond of Army-Navy surplus stores, dusty warehouses that smelled tartly of old canvas and were packed with used G.I. boots, knapsacks, half-track treads, walkie-talkies, tortoise-sized canteens, and other curiosities. He would drive a long way to get to these stores, found always in the seediest parts of distant towns, just as my mother would drive a long way to get to a flea market or auction. She took me to my first flea market when I was eight. I couldn't believe people were selling such cool stuff for so little—old board games and dusty toy soldiers that you'd never find in the stores anymore. About once a month she'd take us boys to see the "newspaper man," a bedraggled fellow who owned a decrepit, poorly lit shop crowded, from floor to ceiling, with old newspapers, magazines, and comic books. Used comics were three for a dime. My brothers and I carried home armsful.

In short, I learned that used stuff is good stuff because it's not made anymore, or not made the same way anymore. Early on, my brother Mike collected old coins, Dave collected old stamps, and I collected old toys. Nana, Dad's mother, who lived with us, often brought home miniatures she called "trinkets," penny and antique Cracker Jack toys—brass-plated curios we couldn't get in our plastic-packed gumball machines. I loved these. Some of this old stuff, like antique pocket knives, made for extravagant trading with schoolmates.

The antique furniture of my grandparents and aged relatives had always fascinated me: claw-feet as large as lion's paws, settee-backs reminiscent of dragon's wings, bureaus as big as Golems. Every other piece seemed big enough to swallow a child whole,

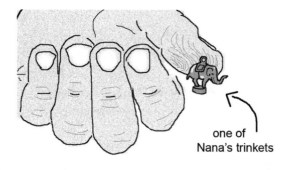

one of
Nana's trinkets

each drawer a deep and odorous maw, redolent of potpourri, stale linens, and aged oak, walnut, pine, or maple. My interest in these things was almost archeological. The homestead of Mom's mother offered half a dozen decrepit outbuildings, crowded with rusted tools that looked medieval—and old jars and tins, as well as piles of nuts and bolts and ancient-looking nails. There was a massive grindstone that Grandpa used to operate by pumping a wooden pedal. There was the tractor shed, with its rusted John Deere, stinking of oil and decaying rubber. There was the empty pigpen, the abandoned chicken house, and the mule stall—all still sweetly pungent from a mash of corncobs, straw and manure, which made the ghosts of those absent animals nearly palpable. And there was the long neglected outhouse, which we never entered except on a dare.[6]

In short, my childhood was steeped in the past. I collect old things now, not to preserve that past, but to contain it; to keep it from overwhelming me; to curate just enough for a taste of what I've missed and those I miss. That's why Jill and I have promised each other that we will not turn our house into a museum. We hold back. And we try to follow the Rule of Scott, our friend who is an antiques expert: for everything you bring into the house,

---

6. Grandpa had often retreated here to get some relief from us grandchildren (during a weekend visit there might be as many as fifteen of us). Years later, we came to understand that this had been his drinking hideout.

something else must go. Still, we have a lot of stuff because we have a large house. I tell myself that when I'm near the end of my days, I'll unload all of my collectibles and tools and curios and half-finished projects; I'll strip down as if preparing for life in a monastery. But, because I live in a land of excess, it is just as likely that I'll die surrounded by all of my possessions, as indulgent in the end as a Pharaoh in his tomb.

Jill got lucky and won her bid for a hundred-year-old wedding gown. Made of lace over silk, it had a small train and half sleeves—and no stains. Judy, a craft-savvy friend, helped her with the fitting. Judy was also able to make new outfits, from crepe, for the bisque Cupie dolls that had adorned my parents' wedding cake. Many years ago, my mother gave these to me. I had forgotten I had them—wrapped in tissue paper among my many collectibles.

* * *

It took a while to pick a date for the wedding because we had a lot of schedules to coordinate. We thought we were being careful, but then, after sending out the invitations, we discovered that our wedding fell on the same day as several college graduations in town and, worse, the same day as Baltimore's famed Preakness race at Pimlico, about three miles from us. The city would be packed. Most hotels were booked already. Sue and John, our friends across the street, whose house is pretty much a mirror image of ours, offered to put up most of my family. Jill's would be sent to outlying hotels.

With Les, the Traditions moving expert, directing furniture removal to our garage, we cleared out the entire first floor of the house, with the exception of our recently-acquired grand piano, which we pushed into the front bay. The result was an open space, from the front bay to the living room fireplace, as large as a cozy meeting hall. We rented four eight-foot tables for food and fifty folding chairs. One friend got us discounts on wine. Twelve others

my parents' cupie doll cake topper,
which Jill & I used for our wedding

signed up to bring their specialty dishes. Two others offered to bring the flowers. Others volunteered to set up chairs and lay out cutlery and plates. For months, Jill had been collecting white plates from every thrift store and junk shop in the area. She had discovered a style of vintage plate that was classy but common and inexpensive. When she was making her final inventory, sitting on the dining room floor surrounded by plates and silverware, I said, "This is the woman I love, thoroughly resourceful."

"And cheap," she added.

Traffic was so bad the weekend of our wedding that Dave, Annie, and Billie Jean, our cousin, were stalled on I-95 for four hours between DC and Baltimore, normally a forty-minute drive.

When they arrived, Billie Jean said, "I don't know why my good luck didn't rub off on David!"

Billie Jean is the same age as my brother Mike. The luckiest person we know, she seems to win every time she gambles or enters a contest. In love, however, she has been impulsive like me and now has three marriages behind her.

The night before the ceremony, my family and Jill's ate at our favorite Indian restaurant. Mike was delighted by the choice because there were plenty of vegetarian dishes to choose from. He and Lois announced that they had just bought a new house. A new *big* house: 3,500 square feet. For twenty years, they had lived in a seven-hundred square foot duplex: two cramped bedrooms, a living room, and a kitchen. For twenty years, they had been socking away their money for a comfortable retirement. They never expressed an interest in getting a bigger or better house. This made them exceptional, even odd, among their peers because the hallmark of our generation is that we refuse to wait for our rewards. Jill and I epitomize that model. I doubt that we'll pay off our mortgage before we die. This may be an affront to the ideal our parents lived by, but is it such a bad thing? Time will tell. It is possible that Mike, having exceeded my father's age at last, reconsidered his too-frugal, too-cautious way of life.

"Christmas at *our* house this year," Lois announced. She raised her wine glass.

Mike smiled proudly, nodding *yes!*

Dave raised his glass. "I'm there!"

"I can't wait," I added.

We toasted to their new house.

Later, after we were home again, Jill said, "They're not talking to each other, did you see?"

Her gown—which had taken her two hours to press—was hanging on the back of the closet door. My tux was laid out across the nearby fainting couch. Though we were excited about the wedding, tomorrow's ceremony didn't seem an occasion for worry. As we undressed for bed, I was grateful we didn't have guests to fret over—and grateful I was getting in the habit of listening to Jill.

"Who isn't talking?" I turned to her. "Mike and Lois?"

"*Dave and Annie*—didn't you notice?"

"It was a lousy drive," I reminded her. "They were exhausted."

"Didn't you hear Dave say, 'I'm there!' when we were talking about going to Mike and Lois's for Christmas?"

"Oh, come on."

"No, I was *watching*."

I felt my heart somersault. Jill has a good eye—I couldn't ignore her observation. "They can't be on the skids already," I moaned. "It hasn't even been two years!"

"I'm sorry, Ron. I think they're done."

"Oh, god, don't tell me that!" I clapped my hands over my face, then fell back onto the bed, which creaked and swayed.

Jill lay beside me and began stroking my forehead as if I had a fever. "I know, I'm heartbroken about it."

"I want my brother to be happy!"

"They really weren't cut out for each other, you have to admit."

I groaned again and closed my eyes. "He's just like me, isn't he? He did the same thing on his second try!"

"It looks that way," she said sadly. "I really love Annie but she's got that goodbye look written all over her pretty face."

"Maybe they can pull it out," I said. "Maybe they'll get counseling."

"Maybe," she said, smiling a smile I'd seen many times. *Dreamer*, it said.

The next morning, a May Saturday—sun pouring through the windows—our first floor looked better than ever, the parquet gleaming, fresh flowers arrayed along the mantels and window sills. When our friends arrived at the appointed hour, Nicholas shook his head in wonderment at all we'd done. "I didn't think it was possible," he said. "But then I didn't know you were a madman." Many of our friends had seen the Queen Anne from the start. They traded stories about the most memorable sights:

There was the room filled with garbage—do you remember that?

How about all the rats in the backyard?

I liked the eyeball graffiti!

They still have an eyeball left in one closet—I think they're going to keep it.

Jill's room had a Confederate flag painted on one wall.

Did Ron tell you about the bucket of shit?

The kitchen had no ceiling.

None of these fireplace mantels was here.

And the staircase—half the spindles were knocked out.

With baseball bats!

Over here, there's a bullet hole in the sidelight, did you notice?

Rick seemed to take as much pride in the Queen Anne's transformation as Jill and I: here was proof, after all, that hard work and good deeds (his own) could make a difference.

To stand among my friends and family, in our bright and splendid house, which had once seemed so dark and impossible a challenge, made me speechless with gratitude and wonder. At last, everyone quiet, with a string quartet playing from the speakers I had installed high in the walls and a friend presiding as justice of the peace, Jill and I made our commitment public—almost exactly four years after we'd first met. Jill began, "I love Ron dearly. He's accepted me fully and has never judged me harshly, even though I can be a little crazy sometimes. He's shown a lot of patience, especially with my old and crabby animals—I can't tell you how many times Harriet's bit him." Everyone laughed. They had met Harriet.

After Jill read her statement, I read mine:

Jill, the first night we went out, I felt immediately comfortable with you because you were so comfortable with yourself. You laughed so freely, you were so sharp-witted, and so happy to meet my friends. Your most distinctive attribute that night—your laughter—remains central to who you are and why I love you. So much of the world incites your laughter and you invite others to laugh with you. And you're not afraid to laugh at yourself. You are not afraid also to tell me what you think and even to tell me when I am wrong. You respect me enough to offer me that honesty. I love that about you. I love also your compassion and warmth, how generous you are with friends, how kind you are to strangers, and how much good you seek for others. I love how enterprising you are, how determined, how inspired you can be. At every turn, you delight me with your schemes, your plans, your designs, your inventions. Here, I have to tell the bottle-opener story. . . That's you in a nutshell. You are open to the possibilities and many times—as with the house—you will not say no. When we walked into this house, I said, "I don't know." You said, "Yes, this is it." I love that so much about you says *yes*. You are so thoroughly capable and so deeply caring that I feel with you a trust and a faith that in my adult life I have never felt with another person. I am excited about our life together. We have so many adventures before us, so many flea markets to scour, so many books to share, so many pets to housebreak. My funny, passionate, arty Jill: you are the love of my life.

When we kissed as husband and wife, I wanted to fall into everyone's arms as if falling into a warm pool.

After a very good buffet, we cleared the floor for dancing. My mother took a lot of pictures. I'd been watching Dave and Annie all night and I feared the worst: as Jill had observed, they weren't talking to each other. Then they left as early as the old folks. Our families would return in the morning for breakfast, so I'd have time to make more observations. I reassured myself with the thought that anything broken could be fixed if only given sufficient time and attention.

After the older crowd was gone, I put on some CDs I'd mixed, then the rest of us danced late into the night, including cousin Billie Jean, who whooped as she twirled and stomped. Jill and I had got to show off our swing dancing steps just as we had at Dave's wedding. So now, as one favorite song after another shook the walls of our old house, I took Jill's hands in mine. Like the solid old couple we aspire to be one day, it seemed we knew exactly what to do.

EPILOGUE

WHEN JILL AND I RETURNED from our honeymoon in Maine, we found Harriet had gotten sick. "Don't you ever leave me with a sick dog!" the owner of the kennel complained. "Your old girl is not doing well." Harriet's health had been tenuous for years. Several times, we had taken her to the vet to remove her recurring subcutaneous tumors. We suspected Harriet was crabby in great part because she was often in pain.

In Harriet's last years, not even Jill had been safe from the old dog's wrath. Still, if Jill sat on the lowest step of the servant's stairs in the early morning—when Harriet was in her best humor—Harriet would waddle over, lean her head into Jill's knees, then allow Jill to pat her rump (and only her rump), signaling her pleasure with a slow wag of her graying tail. Harriet liked showers too, and would grumble her enjoyment as Jill soaped her all over—the only time Harriet would allow that much contact. And, yes, there was sledding. Harriet loved sledding. For the most part, though, she kept to herself, getting up only at the prospect of food.

After we got her home from the kennel, Harriet was especially lethargic. Soon, she stopped eating, then retreated to the backyard. She refused to come inside. For days, she lay in the ivy behind the rose bushes. Finally, Jill and I decided it was time, so Jill gathered up Harriet in both arms, then we drove to the vet, talking quietly to her all the way. All fight gone from the old dog, Harriet accepted Jill's embrace without complaint. Jill said it was as if Harriet were young again, friendly and happy to be held. At fourteen, Harriet lived far longer than she should have. Still, we were in mourning for weeks.

* * *

Jill is finishing her Ph.D in social work. She's been counseling battered women and the homeless. None of us understands why the work doesn't depress her. But she's always been an advocate of the underdog. Sometimes, I think that's why she was drawn to me and this old house. We have been rehabbing the Queen Anne for ten years. Every year, I go project crazy for a couple of months and undertake major work that throws the house into chaos. Jill is fairly tolerant of it. Whenever I'm planning something—and it seems I'm always planning something—I confer with her, we debate the pros and cons, check the calendar, then arrive at a compromise. Inevitably, nothing goes according to plan. Almost always, I set a deadline at the most inconvenient but compelling time—before my family arrives for a week's visit, before the neighborhood's annual holiday house tour, before school starts in the fall, and recently before a visit from *This Old House* magazine.[7]

I do get the job done, but at what price? Jill reminds me.

One morning, not long ago, we found a package on our front doorstep. It contained two of our missing door knobs and door plates. The note said, "I took this from the house when I lived there years ago. Thought you could use them." A gift from a former fraternity brother. It still angers people when they learn how the Queen Anne suffered at the hands of these thoughtless young men. It took me years to forgive them. In the end, I realized that a grudge is pointless. The young men made a mistake. They have grown up. As evidenced by the anonymous gift, some of them

---

7. For more about our THIS OLD HOUSE visit, go to http://houselove.org.

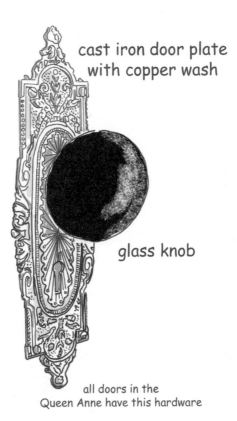

cast iron door plate
with copper wash

glass knob

all doors in the
Queen Anne have this hardware

regret what they did. What more can we ask or demand after all this time?

In good weather, Jill spends a lot of time in our backyard, where she tends the flower beds, which she designed, and watches the fish and frogs in our raised pond, which I built a few years ago. The goldfish—which cost $1.29 each—have grown remarkably large. There are snails too. Our tadpoles turned into bullfrogs that threatened to eat everything in sight and, in fact, ate the other frogs, including a group of little leopard frogs that were living in the flowerbed. So we drew down the pond, gathered up

back yard: rat free

new wall

fountain & raised pond

all of the frogs, dropped them into a bucket, then released them into a nearby lake. Then, we got green frogs and more leopards. They're a civilized bunch. Our yard remains rat-free, thanks to a new brick wall we had built where there had been only a wood fence. Eventually, we will pave the yard with brick to create a courtyard. Right now it's pea gravel, which the dogs love to dig at. We can't keep them out of the flower beds either.

Our new dog, Frieda, is another basset hound. When Jill read about her, she simply wanted to look her over, she said. So, the next thing I knew, we were driving to the basset hound rescue society in Pennsylvania. I've learned to abandon all expectations whenever Jill gets in her got-to-have-it mode. Frieda was living in a foster home with seven cats, three dogs, and four exotic birds. She was so pretty and so friendly, it seemed we could not say no. We soon learned that Frieda will eat anything: apples, banana peels, carrots, you name it. And she wants to eat all the time. She also likes to gallop through the house, especially if you're angry at her for having snatched sausage from the kitchen counter. When you catch her, she's as docile as can be, rolling over in surrender. Sloppy and giddy and always into trouble, she will forever be a puppy, apparently. She turns six this year. P.J. loves her. They jaw each other in play. And they sleep together.

Jill and I have come to a tenuous agreement about the dogs. They are her responsibility. She's in charge of cleaning up after the incorrigible pair. And the third floor, where I work, is off limits to both. As a result, I am much calmer about sharing the house with them. Whenever I hear Jill downstairs, shouting at yet another dog catastrophe—"Oh, Frieda, what have you done!"—I must admit I gloat a little, privately.

The lead levels in Jill's blood are down to a reasonable reading of ten. But she has to be careful. Paint or solvent fumes can still send her to bed for a day. I worry about her. She worries about me. I pull my back out about once a year. We joke that if the house kills us, at least we'll die happy. Generally, we don't use chemicals in the house if we can help it. Jill still strips paint, though, using a heat gun. She has learned to do all kinds of cool stuff, like faux paint wood grain and repair stained glass. We've (safely) stripped almost all of the woodwork, upgraded many of the chandeliers, restored the porch exterior and the garage, planted trees in the backyard. And I've built cabinets I never thought I could build, including a Victorian library on our third floor. Rick and Charles gave us all of their vintage molding and trim—piles of it, which I've used in many ways throughout the house and have dispensed to neighbors for their houses. Dan, the retired minister down the street, gave us glass-paned doors for our butler's pantry, which we finished recently. The skeptic who told us we'd never bring the house back to its original glory, has reconsidered. "It looks mighty fine," he's told us. "Mighty fine."

When Jill and I work on our front yard, we meet passersby who are curious to know more about the Animal House we brought back from the brink. It seems that everyone who moves to our neighborhood hears about us eventually. Often when we meet newcomers, they say, "Oh, we know who *you* are" or "Oh, *you're* the ones!" This still tickles me. It was inevitable that our house would involve us deeply in the neighborhood. I now serve on the civic association's board and maintain its website. Jill and I have invited the neighborhood to our house for various occasions, including a celebration of the community's annual house tour, which I chair every year. The only thing missing from these festivities is Rick and Charles.

The year after our wedding, at the height of the real estate boom, Rick and Charles sold their gorgeous house for top dollar, then moved to an historic town on the Illinois side of the Mississippi, where they bought a mansion for next to nothing. They are both from the Midwest and felt it was time to be closer to family. Their new house is grand and needed very little restoration. They've sent us long letters and lots of photos. Their absence was a huge loss for our block. Even now, when I survey the sidewalk from any window of our house, I long to see Rick on his rounds.

If Rick and Charles could leave their stunning Baltimore row house behind, I decided that any of us could. So I don't discount the possibility that one day Jill and I may tire of our Queen Anne and try for something different, maybe an Arts and Crafts cottage—or even a houseboat. But right now, we're still in the big house frame of mind and, in fact, have our eye on a mansion up the block. Not that we'd ever be able to afford it. It does look ideal, though. Despite Jill's resistance to house envy, she concedes that the mansion in question would be a challenge. We've talked at length about all we would change if the place was ours.

Just the other day, as we sat at the intersection lights in front of the mansion, Jill said, "What were they thinking when they put in that massive barbecue?"

"Looks like they were dreaming of the suburbs," I said.

Jill clucked her tongue. "I fear they've made all kinds of bad decisions inside too."

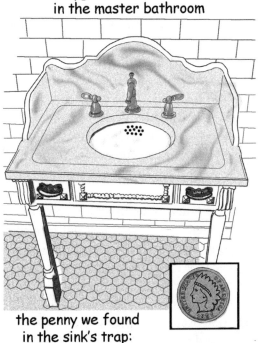

A recent upgrade: 1880's barber's sink
in the master bathroom

the penny we found
in the sink's trap:

"I bet we could undo every one of them," I said. "You know it's rumored they're going to move in a few years."

"Save your money, honey!"

We haven't saved our money, of course. It's all in the house. Jill and I were lucky enough to leverage out of our second mortgages because we bought the house cheap and upped its value through our own labor. Two historic rehab credits helped too. But since the real estate bust, it's not likely we'll be going anywhere anytime soon, if ever.

Just as I hoped, our old house has centered me. As I have learned a lot about repairing things, I have learned that I can partner with my dead father and celebrate his competence instead of fearing that I'll never live up to his example. Knowing what I can do with my hands, knowing how much I can learn if I take the time to learn it, knowing how hard I can work if I keep my temper even and my head clear—this sustains me in a world that sometimes seems designed to strip us of our abilities. Our house has allowed me to do things my father never did, and so now I have something to share with him. Dad would have loved this adventure; it would have given us lots to talk about; it would have made him proud.

Maybe it's unnecessary to say, or just too corny, but here it is: our house has become an expression of the love Jill and I have built. And just as I dreamed, it has allowed us to create a special place for friends and family. As one friend puts it, "Your house has become THE party house." It's an ironic observation, given that the Queen Anne once hosted the most notorious fraternity parties in the city. Gathering friends, taking care of them, creating a comfortable space for talk and laughter—life doesn't get better than that. Because we delight in feeding those we love, Jill and I have become good cooks, trying out new dishes and refining old favorites in our now-well-equipped kitchen. Because the Queen Anne can accommodate many guests, we have become adept at hosting large gatherings. We have enjoyed sit-down dinners for twenty to celebrate Easter and other occasions. Since fixing up the backyard, we have started having garden parties in the spring and fall. Sometimes, we have a winter theme party, like the time we served nothing but pies—apple pie, chicken pot pie, blackberry pie, peach pie, spinach pie, etc. Some nights, we eat a simple meal with friends on our porch, which overlooks our lovely backyard and its goldfish pond. Our annual holiday party brings as many as seventy people into the house. Perhaps the Queen Anne is at her best then, holding so many people in her embrace.

Sometimes, there's entertainment, as when a friend played her dulcimer and sang Irish love songs or the evening a professional pianist played a Gershwin concert on our new old grand piano (an auction find, by the way). During a recent visit by my family, we asked a jazz band to perform to celebrate Mom's eighty-third birthday. At Halloween, not long ago, we gathered our entire family in the living room to watch *Arsenic and Old Lace* projected onto a queen-sized bed sheet I draped from the ceiling. In so many ways, in its large spaces and small, the Queen Anne allows us to bring friends and family closer and show our love for them, and this has deepened our connections and made us more humane, happier people. In the best of all possible worlds, isn't that what a house is supposed to do?

My family has decided that they like spending Christmas at our house and it seems we're making it a biannual event— with one modification: we celebrate in early November or late October. That way my mother doesn't have to endure "that awful Baltimore winter."

My brother Dave and Annie, his wife of only three years, divorced amicably. It seemed they were both relieved to get out of the marriage. Jill and I still don't understand it. We moped about it for a year. Dave insists that he's happier now. We tried to stay in touch with Annie but, after her parents died abruptly, one following the other, she returned to Kansas to tend the family business. Whenever Annie's name comes up, Jill and I exchange a regretful glance. It seems there's so much we'll never know about love. I'm working hard *not* to second guess what others do. If there's one thing I understand from my own setbacks and challenges— including work on our old house—it's that nobody on the outside can fully understand what you're going through on the inside.

OTHER BOOKS BY RON TANNER:

Kiss Me, Stranger

A Bed of Nails